Genoa Area by Area

Il Centro Storico
Pages 52–69

Le Strade Nuove
Pages 70–83

Further Afield
Pages 84–93

EMILIA
ROMAGNA

Torriglia

Pegli

Genoa

Nervi

Rapallo

RIVIERA DI
LEVANTE

TUSCANY

Sestri Levante

The Riviera di Levante
Pages 108–133

Levanto

La Spezia

Sarzana

EYEWITNESS TRAVEL

THE ITALIAN
RIVIERA

DK

LONDON, NEW YORK,
MELBOURNE, MUNICH AND DELHI
www.dk.com

Produced By Fabio Ratti Editoria Srl, Milan, Italy

Project Editor Emanuela Damiani
Editors Emanuela Damiani, Giovanna Morselli
Designers Silvana Ghioni, Alberto Ipsilanti, Modi Artistici

Contributors
Fabrizio Ardito, Sonia Cavicchioli,
Maurizia De Martin, Gianluigi Lanza

Photographer
Lucio Rossi

Illustrators
Andrea Barison, Gianluca Fiorani

Cartography
Roberto Capra, Luca Signorelli

Dorling Kindersley Limited
Publishing Managers Fay Franklin, Kate Poole
Senior Editor Marisa Renzullo
Translator Fiona Wild
Editor Emily Hatchwell
Consultant Leonie Loudon
Production Linda Dare

Printed and bound by
South China Printing Co. Ltd., China

First published in Great Britain in 2005
by Dorling Kindersley Limited
80 Strand, London WC2R 0RL

14 15 16 17 10 9 8 7 6 5 4 3 2 1

Reprinted with revisions 2008, 2011, 2014

Copyright © Mondadori Electra SpA 2003.
Published under exclusive licence by Dorling Kindersley Limited.
English text copyright © Dorling Kindersley Limited 2005, 2014.
A Penguin Random House Company.

Front cover main image: Riomaggiore, Cinque Terre

◀ Pastel coloured houses in the village of Manarola, Cinque Terre

Contents

How to Use
this Guide **6**

Ecce Homo by Antonello da Messina,
Palazzo Spinola, Genoa

Introducing the
Italian Riviera

The Ligurian Gothic church of Sant'Andrea
in Levanto

The delightful scene at Paraggi, near Portofino

The port of San Remo, a popular resort town in the Italian Riviera

Prized Ligurian olive oil

Genoa's revamped Porto Antico

HOW TO USE THIS GUIDE

The detailed information and tips given in this guide will help you to get the most out of your visit to the Italian Riviera. *Introducing the Italian Riviera* maps the region of Liguria and sets it in its historical and cultural context. The section *Genoa Area by Area* describes the main sights in the regional capital. *The Italian Riviera Area by Area* describes the sights and resorts east and west of Genoa along the Riviera di Levante and the Riviera di Ponente respectively, using maps, photographs and illustrations. Restaurant and hotel recommendations can be found in the section *Travellers' Needs*, together with information about shopping, outdoor activities and entertainment. The *Survival Guide* has tips on everything from transport to making a phone call.

Genoa Area by Area

The centre of Genoa has been divided into two sightseeing areas, each with its own chapter. Further Afield describes areas outside the city centre. All the sights are numbered and plotted on an Area Map. Detailed information for each sight is presented in numerical order, making it easy to locate.

All pages relating to Genoa have red thumb tabs.

Sights at a Glance lists the chapter's sights by category: Churches, Museums and Galleries, Historic Buildings, Streets and Piazzas.

A locator map shows where you are in relation to other areas of the city centre.

1 Area Map
All the sights are numbered and located on a map.

2 Street-by-Street Map
This gives a bird's eye view of the heart of each sightseeing area.

Stars indicate the sights that no visitor should miss.

A suggested route for a walk covers the more interesting streets in the area.

3 Genoa's major sights
Museums and galleries have colour-coded floor plans to help you locate the most interesting exhibits.

1 Introduction
The landscape, history and character of each region is described here, showing how the area has developed over the centuries and what it offers to the visitor today.

The Italian Riviera Area by Area
The Italian Riviera has been divided into two areas, each of which has a separate chapter. The most interesting sights to visit are highlighted on a *Regional Map*.

Each area can be quickly identified by its colour coding.

2 Regional Map
This shows the road network and gives an illustrated overview of the whole region. All the sights are numbered and there are also useful tips on getting around the area.

Visitors' Checklist box provides all the practical information that you will need.

3 The top sights are given
two or more pages. Historic buildings are dissected to reveal their interiors.

Bullet numbers refer to each sight's position on the area map and its place in the chapter.

4 Detailed information
All the important towns and other places to visit are described individually. They are listed in order, following the numbering on the Regional Map. Within each town or city, you will find detailed information on important buildings and other sights.

INTRODUCING THE ITALIAN RIVIERA

DISCOVERING ITALIAN RIVIERA

The following tours have been designed to capture the highlights of Genoa, the Riviera di Ponente, to the west, and the Riviera di Levante to the east. The first itinerary outlined here is a two-day tour of Liguria's fascinating capital, Genoa. Next, there is a seven-day tour, which includes visiting Genoa. This itinerary can be extended to ten days. Finally, there

is a 14-day tour of the wonderfully scenic Ligurian coast and its hinterland. Both stretches of the Riviera are well connected by train, the A10 and A12 motorways and the slower SS1 road, which stretches to the coast from Balzi Rossi in the west and as far as Sestri Levante in the east. Choose a tour based on the time you have available or just be inspired.

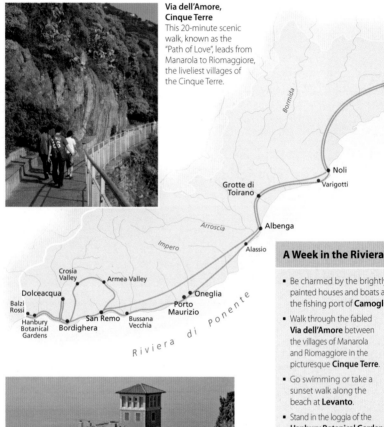

Via dell'Amore, Cinque Terre
This 20-minute scenic walk, known as the "Path of Love", leads from Manarola to Riomaggiore, the liveliest villages of the Cinque Terre.

A Week in the Riviera

- Be charmed by the brightly painted houses and boats at the fishing port of **Camogli**.

- Walk through the fabled **Via dell'Amore** between the villages of Manarola and Riomaggiore in the picturesque **Cinque Terre**.

- Go swimming or take a sunset walk along the beach at **Levanto**.

- Stand in the loggia of the **Hanbury Botanical Gardens** and soak up the pretty view of the sea.

- Admire the collection of paintings, ivories and enamels at the **Museo Amedeo Lia** in **La Spezia**.

- Stroll the seafront boulevard and try your hand at the **Casino** at **San Remo**.

Hanbury Botanical Garden, Riviera di Ponente
Around 11 km (7 miles) west of San Remo, close to the French border lies the famed Hanbury Botanical Garden, where exotic plants grow in the grounds of a charming 14th-century palazzo.

◄ Boats docked at the port in Genoa

Two Weeks in the Riviera

- Watch the world go by from a waterside bar at the lovely sheltered cove of **Portofino**.

- Gaze at the dazzling sea view from the headland church of **San Pietro** at beautiful **Portovenere**.

- Take a boat ride to the beachside Benedictine abbey at **San Fruttuoso**.

- Enter the fanciful underworld of stalagmites, stalactites and crystals in the **Grotte di Toirano**.

- From the charming square in central **Albenga**, take in the Roman **Baptistry** and medieval **Cathedral of San Michele**.

- Tour the ancient and unspoilt villages of the **Armea** and **Crosia Valleys** in the hinterland of **San Remo**.

- Follow in the steps of the French Impressionist painter, Claude Monet, in the pretty medieval village of **Dolceacqua**.

0 kilometres 20
0 miles 20

Pentema
Torriglia
Lago di Brugneto

Genoa

Lavagna

Camogli
Rapallo
San Fruttuoso
Portofino

*Ligurian
Sea*

Sestri Levante

Riviera di Levante

Vara

Levanto
Monterosso
Vernazza
Corniglia
Manarola
Riomaggiore

Cinque Terre

La Spezia
Sarzana
Portovenere

Key

— A Week in the Riviera
— Two Weeks in the Riviera

Portofino, Riviera di Levante
Nestled in a protected inlet, surrounded by lush cypress- and olive-clad slopes is the beautiful Ligurian town of Portofino.

Two Days in Genoa

Genoa is a rewarding city to explore. Both the modern port area and the historic centre on the steep slopes above can be covered on foot.

- **Arriving** Genoa's Cristoforo Colombo Airport is 6 km (4 miles) west of the city and a 25 minute bus ride to the town centre.

The pedestrianized Via Garibaldi, a UNESCO World Heritage Site, Genoa

Day 1
Morning Start the day at **Via Garibaldi** (*p74*) to explore all the marvellous palazzi (*all closed Mon*). Devote at least three hours to see the collection of paintings, including portraits by Van Dyck and Dürer, and the splendid decoration of the **Palazzo Rosso** (*pp76–9*). Be sure to see the Genoese and Flemish masters in the **Galleria di Palazzo Bianco** (*p75*) and the magnificent court-yard of the **Palazzo Doria Tursi** (*p75*). Admire the richly decorated, marble interiors of the church of **San Siro** (*p80*). Pause for coffee and pastries at **Café Klainguti** (*p188*) in Piazza Soziglia, a favourite haunt of the composer Verdi.

Afternoon Head towards the sea to see the lavish 18th-century rooms of the **Palazzo Reale** (*closed Mon, p81*), and to learn about the history of maritime Genoa at the **Galata Museo del Mare** (*closed Mon, p82*). On your way, explore the warren of

The sriking structure of Il Bigo, inspired by the masts of a ship, Genoa

caruggi (alleyways) and browse the authentic little shops. Take the train from Genoa to **Nervi** (*p93*). Finish the day with a sunset stroll along the 2-km (1-mile) long Passeggiata Anita Garibaldi followed by a quiet dinner.

Day 2
Morning Spend the morning at **Porto Antico** (*pp64–5*). Take the lift at **Il Bigo** (*p64*) to enjoy panoramic views, then move on to the interesting **Aquarium** (*pp66–7*) to see hummingbirds, penguins, tactile and shark tanks. Don't miss the butterflies and chameleons of the **Biosfera** (*p65*). If you have kids in tow, head for the **La Città dei Bambini** (*closed Mon, p65*). For lunch try foccacia, for which the city is famous, and then return to the city centre.

Afternoon From **Piazza Matteoti** (*pp54–5*) view the sculptures in the **Museo di Sant'Agostino** (*p61*), walk past the **Porta Soprana** (*p60*) and the **Casa di Colombo** (*p60*), the supposed birthplace of Christopher Columbus, to Piazza De Ferrari, home of the renowned **Teatro Carlo Felice** (*p59*). See the extravagantly Baroque interior of the church of **Il del Gesù** (*p58*) and stop for refreshments in the **Palazzo Ducale** (*p58*). If time allows, browse the shops and exhibitions on display here. The striped cathedral of **San Lorenzo** (*pp56–7*) has plenty of architectural appeal as well as sacred treasures in its atmospheric **Museo del Tesoro** (*p57*). End the day with an evening performance at the Teatro Carlo Felice (*book ahead*).

A Week in the Riviera

- **Airports** Arrive and depart from Genoa Airport.

- **Transport** There are good train and bus connections, but for the extended ten-day tour you will need a car. Use the train for the Cinque Terre.

- **Booking ahead** Keep in mind to book ahead for the Casella train (*p92*) and reserve accommodation in the Cinque Terre in advance.

Day 1
Pick a day from the city itinerary.

Day 2
Camogli and Rapallo to Sestri Levante
Stroll through the alleyways of the typical, tall houses at **Camogli** (*pp112–13*). Then, continue on to **Rapallo** (*p113*) where you can board a boat, which will take around 30 minutes to **Portofino** (*p115*), a favourite of the jet-setters. Next, take to the water again to reach the delightful Benedictine abbey of **San Fruttuoso** (*p114*). Return to Rapallo by boat and continue on to the lively resort of **Sestri Levante** (*p120*) for the night.

> **To extend your trip…**
> Take the **Casella** train (*p92*) and enjoy the lovely mountain scenery. Spend the night in **Camogli** (*pp112–13*).

Day 3
Sestri Levante and Levanto

For the best view of the two bays at **Sestri Levante** (p120) – the sandy Baia delle Favole, loved by Hans Christian Andersen, and the more intimate Baia del Silenzio – make for the 1920s Grand Hotel dei Castelli. Afterwards, spend some time on the beach or continue on to another excellent beach at **Levanto** (p121). End the day exploring the Ligurian Gothic church Sant' Andrea, with white marble and green serpentine stripes.

Boats moored at the idyllic resort of Sestri Levante

Day 4
Cinque Terre to La Spezia

Board the train at Levanto to head for the five villages of the **Cinque Terre** (pp122–3) – Monterosso, Vernazza, Corniglia, Manarola and Riomaggiore. It is possible to explore all five villages by rail. Be sure to walk the 2-km (1-mile) Via dell'Amore ("Path of Love") between Manarola and Riomaggiore. There are plenty of restaurants with a view here. Try the local *schiacchetrá* wine at any of these restaurants. Return to Levanto if you are travelling by car, or continue on to **La Spezia** (pp128–9).

> **To extend your trip...**
> Walk or cycle the **Strada dei Sanctuari** (p123) high above the terraces of olives and vines, with spectacular views of the coast.

Day 5
La Spezia and Portovenere to Noli

Experience bustling city life at **La Spezia** (pp128–9). Explore its little gem of a museum, the **Museo Amedeo Lia** (p128), which is full of paintings, miniatures and enamels. Next, stop at the important naval museum, the **Museo Tecnico Navale** (p128). From here a narrow, winding road leads to the beauty spot of **Portovenere** (p124). Walk to the striped church of San Pietro on the headland for lovely views, which the poets Byron and Shelley enjoyed. Head back to the motorway, bypass Genoa, and spend the night in the medieval town of **Noli** (p145). There are train connections here too.

Day 6
Grotte di Toirano and Albenga to San Remo

Start the day early in **Noli** (p145) with a visit to the lovely

Church of San Pietro at Portovenere, Riviera di Levante

Romanesque church of San Paragorio before moving on to the **Grotte di Toirano** (pp150–51). Take time out to appreciate the caverns of stalagmites, stalactites and crystal formations here. Next, continue on to the historic city of **Albenga** (pp152–3) where the prime sights are Piazza dei Leoni, the Roman **Baptistry** (p155) and the **Cathedral of San Michele** (p154) with its fine bell tower. Stop at **San Remo** (p168) for the night; you may wish to try your luck at the **Casino** (p168).

> **To extend your trip...**
> Tour the ancient villages of the **Armea** and **Crosia Valleys** (pp164–5).

Day 7
Dolceacqua, Hanbury Botanical Gardens or Balzi Rossi

Wander through the old town (La Pigna) and see the waterfront at **San Remo** (p168). The **Casinò Municipale** (p168) is a wonderful example of the many Art Nouveau villas here. At your next stop, **Dolceacqua** (pp170–71), follow in the footsteps of Monet who famously painted the Ponte Vecchio. Try the local *Rossese* wine here. Opt to finish the tour with a visit to either the beautiful **Hanbury Botanical Gardens** (pp174–5) or the nine caves and museum at the prehistoric site of **Balzi Rossi** (closed Mon, p173), just next to the French border, before returning to Genoa.

Colourful Riomaggiore, one of the pretty villages of the Cinque Terre

Picturesque harbour at Portofino, with its colourful houses

Two Weeks in the Riviera

- **Airports** Arrive and depart from Genoa airport.
- **Transport** A car is needed for this tour. The distance from Genoa to Balzi Rossi in the west is 169 km (105 miles) and from Genoa to La Spezia in the east is 113 km (70 miles).
- **Booking ahead** Remember to book ahead for accommodation in the Cinque Terre.

Day 1 and 2
Genoa
See the two-day city itinerary on p12.

Day 3
Torriglia, Pentema and Lago di Brugneto to Camogli
Before taking the road to the coast, take time out for a trip inland to the pretty Antola mountains. After spending time in **Torriglia** *(p112)*, drive to the sleepy stone village of **Pentema** *(p112)*, where time has stood still. Next, head to the peaceful environs of **Lago del Brugneto** *(p112)*. Enjoy a picnic by the lake before returning through the chestnut woods to **Camogli** *(pp112–13)* for the night.

Day 4
Camogli, Portofino and San Fruttuoso to Rapallo
After an early morning walk round the harbour at Camogli

(pp112–13), head inland to the resort of **Rapallo** *(p113)*. Be sure to leave your car here. A boat ride from here takes around 30 minutes to reach idyllic Portofino *(pp115)*. Stop for a waterfront lunch, then continue by boat round the headland to the abbey of San Fruttuoso *(p114)* before returning to spend the night at Rapallo.

Day 5
Rapallo, Sestri Levante and Levanto
Promenade the palm-fringed Lungomare Vittorio Veneto at Rapallo *(p113)* past the Castello, then visit the Museo del Merletto *(closed Mon, p113)* for lovely examples of historic lace. Have lunch in Sestri Levante *(p120)*. Afterwards, take a stroll in the park at the Grand Hotel Castelli. Spend time on the fine sandy beach or at the charming harbour. Alternatively, end the day with a trip to Levanto *(p121)*, which is an ideal place for surfing, windsurfing and canoeing.

Day 6 and 7
Cinque Terre
Take the train from Levanto

for the Cinque Terre *(pp122–3)*. All five villages of Monterosso, Vernazza, Corniglia, Manarola and Riomaggiore are connected by rail and are easily walkable pathways. There are plenty of good seafood restaurants in Riomaggiore. On your second day, opt to walk or cycle on the Strada dei Santuari *(p123)* from where colourful houses clinging to the cliff can be seen. Stay both nights in the Cinque Terre or choose to drive from Levanto to La Spezia *(pp128–9)* for the second night.

Day 8
La Spezia
Look up **La Spezia's** *(pp128–9)* maritime past in the **Museo Tecnico Navale** *(p128)*. Next, marvel at the exquisite collection of paintings, miniatures and ivories in the attractive **Museo Amedeo Lia** *(closed Mon, p128)*. Drive the narrow road carefully, or opt to take a bus to **Portovenere** *(p124)*. Walk past the pink- and yellow-hued houses here to the church of **San Pietro** *(p124)* for a breathtaking view. Portovenere is a picturesque spot to stop for the night.

The futuristic-looking Biosphere in the old habor, Genoa

The bridge leading into the medieval village of Dolceacqua

Day 9
Sarzana to Noli
Head inland for the town of **Sarzana** *(pp132–3)* and soak up its sophisticated atmosphere. Visit the Cathedral and see the imposing round towers of the citadella. Famous for its antique market, shopping is an enticing option here. Next, head west on the motorway towards Genoa for the Riviera di Ponente and the town of **Noli** *(p145)*, which still retains some of its medieval towers. Spend the evening visiting the fine Romanesque church of **San Paragorio** *(p145)*.

Day 10
Varigotti and Grotte do Toirano to Albenga
Drive a few miles down the coast to **Varigotti** *(p148)* for a morning dip. See the ancient houses of fishermen, before pressing on to the **Grotte di Toirano** *(pp150–51)* a remarkable karst cave system full of magical stalagmite, stalactite and crystal formations mirrored in pools. Continue on to **Albenga** *(pp152–5)* for the night.

Day 11
Albenga and Alassio
Spend the morning in the city of **Albenga** *(pp152–5)* admiring the medieval houses lining the long Via Bernardo Ricci and **Piazza dei Leoni** *(p153)*, as well as the 5th-century **Baptistry** *(p155)*. The sandy beach at **Alassio** *(p156)*, will beckon, but leave some time for the Art Nouveau villas and the famous names cast in tiles in the **Muretto** *(p156)* opposite **Caffè Roma** *(p156)*. Take a stroll on the beach in the evening.

Day 12
Imperia and Bussana Vecchia to San Remo
Imperia is split into two parts, the newer **Oneglia** *(pp158–9)* and the older **Porto Maurizio** *(pp160–61)*. In the latter, learn all about life aboard a ship at the **Museo Navale Internazionale del Ponente Ligure** *(p160)*, while in Oneglia find out about the history of olives in the **Museo dell'Olivo** *(p159)*. Watch the fishermen bring in their

The intriguing artist colony of Bussana Vecchia, San Remo

afternoon catch here before setting off for dolphin and whale watching. Call in at the artists' colony of **Bussana Vecchia** *(p168)* en route to your night's stop at **San Remo** *(p168)* where you can enjoy the night life.

Day 13
San Remo and the Armea and Crosia Valleys to Bordighera
Make an early start to see the **Cathedral of San Siro** *(p168)*, and the **Russian Orthodox Church** *(p168)* in San Remo, before going inland to the green hills. Pass the **Armea** and **Crosia Valleys** *(pp164–5)*, which are a drive of 50 km (31 miles), and admire the Alpine views. Spend the evening back on the coast in **Bordighera** *(p169)*.

Day 14
Dolceacqua and Hanbury Botanical Gardens or Balzi Rossi
Be enchanted by the Ponte Vecchio and Castello dei Doria at your next stop, **Dolceacqua** *(pp170–71)*. The last afternoon of the tour can either be spent wandering through the exotic plants at the **Hanbury Botanical Gardens** *(pp174–5)* or exploring the interesting caves and museum of **Balzi Rossi** *(closed Mon, p173)*. Return to Genoa.

Putting the Italian Riviera on the Map

Liguria covers 5,418 sq km (2,090 sq miles) and is the second smallest region in Italy. Administratively, it is divided into four provinces: from west to east, these are Imperia, Savona, Genoa and La Spezia. Squeezed between the Mediterranean and the peaks of the Maritime Alps and the Apennines, Liguria's population is concentrated largely along the stunning coastal strip of the Riviera di Levante and the Riviera di Ponente, known collectively as the Italian Riviera – a term commonly used to describe the regio of Liguria as a whole.

SWITZERLAND

Altdorf

San Bernardino

Locarno

Chiave

Colico

Verbania

Como

Lecco

Aosta

VALLE D'AOSTA

Biella

Bergamo

Monza

Ivrea

Milano (Milan)

Novara

LOMBARDIA

Lodi

Grenoble

Modane

Susa

PIEMONTE

Pavia

Torino (Turin)

Asti

Piacenza

Briançon

Carmagnola

Alessandria

Tortona

Gap

Alba

Marsaglia

Barcelonnette

Argentera

Cuneo

LIGURIA

FRANCE

Mondovi

Carcare

Genova (Genoa)

Pontremoli

Digne-les-Bains

Calizzano

Savona

Entrevaux

Tende

Albenga

La Spezia

Escragnolles

Nice

Imperia

Monaco

Sanremo

Cannes

Antibes

Fréjus

Toulon

Ligurian Sea

Isola di Gorgona

Barcelona, Tangier, Tunis

Centuri

Isola d' Elba

Key

- ▬ Motorway
- ▬ Major road
- ─ Railway line
- ▬ International border
- --- Ferry route

Bastia

Calvi

L'Ile-Rousse

Porto

Corte

Corsica

Ajaccio

Ghisonaccia

0 kilometres   75

0 miles   75

Solenzara

Sardinia, Sicily

A PORTRAIT OF THE ITALIAN RIVIERA

The blue water of one of the loveliest stretches of sea in Italy laps the coast, with its rocks, maquis and pastel-coloured villages proud of their maritime tradition. Just behind, hills tbat are often silver with olive trees rise steeply to the Apennines, which separate Liguria from the other regions of northern Italy.

Bound to the north by alpine Piedmont, to the south by rolling Tuscany and to the east by the plains of the Po Valley, liguria is a world apart: no other Italian region has such a generous climate or mountainous landscape, nor one where the sea and the mountains are in such close proximity (in Liguria you are never more than 35 km/22 miles from the Mediterranean). This is a region that was always more easily reached by sea than by land.

The characteristics of Liguria derive from the geology that has shaped it. The margins of the region are clear: the mass of the Alps, partly handed over to France after World War II, lead as far as the threshold of the Colle di Cadibona, which marks the point where the long chain of

the Apennines begins, running first east-and then southwards. To the south of these mountains is the narrow strip of land where, over the course of millennia, the Ligurian civilization developed: the people were naturally more inclined to turn to the sea and the large islands of the Mediterranean than towards the peaks behind.

It would be wrong, however, to assume, when pausing to admire the waters of Portofino, Genoa or Camogli, that a Liguria of the hinterland does not exist. Reached along steep roads, en route to the mountain passes that were once crucial staging posts on any journey northwards, are fascinating towns such as Dolceacqua, beloved of Monet; Triora, known as the

The spectacular rocky coast of the Cinque Terre, plunging into the sea

◀ View of the church of San Pietro with a fantastic location overlooking the sea, Portovenere

The picturesque seaside town of Camogli, one of the most attractive resorts along the Ligurian coast

And the inhabitants of one valley would almost certainly be suspicious of the inhabitants of a neighbouring one. Such complex relationships are still part of everyday life in Liguria. To further complicate matters, there has been a steady exodus of people from the mountains towards the coast. While agriculture in the interior is in decline, tourism on the coast is booming.

Demographically, Liguria is in deep water. It has the lowest birth rate in Italy, making it the lowest in Europe, and an unusually aged population: 25 per cent of Ligurians are over 65 years old; one reason for this is the influx of retirees, attracted by Liguria's warm climate.

village of witches; or the villages of the Val di Vara. These places are just as Ligurian as the gentrified ports of the jet set.

The People

The temperament of the Ligurian people can be said to vary according to the character of the coast, being generally more open and sunny on the beach-rich Riviera di Ponente and more terse and taciturn along the rockier Riviera di Levante. The writer Guido Piovene noted in his *Viaggio in Italia*, published in the 1960s, that "The greatest diversity can be observed going from Genoa to the west. Here, the air of Provence breathes on a Liguria that is closed, laconic… and lacking imagination, creating a loquacious, colourful Liguria of storytellers, a halfway link between the Genoese and the Marseillais".

There is also a third Liguria, that of the mountainous region behind the coast. Traditionally, the people of the mountains mistrusted not just the coastal folk but the people living in the valleys.

Retirees immersed in playing *bocce*, the local version of the French *boules* (game played with metal balls)

Tourism

The tourism industry started in the Italian Riviera in the 19th century, and it is now the dominant industry. The main attraction is, of course, the coast, with its 300 km (186 miles) of sandy or pebbly beaches, cliffs and small islands. Many of the towns and even the old fishing villages, from San Remo to Portovenere, are now devoted to tourism. While in the most famous seaside resorts you will find grand hotels built for the visiting aristocrats of the 19th century, many of the old fishing villages have a harbour rather than a beach and

A typical *gozzo*, fishing dinghy

Fishermen, here on the beach at Spotorno, pulling nets in at dawn

are riddled with the characteristic *carruggi* (the narrow alleys found in every medieval *centro storico* in Liguria), which rise and fall between tall, pastel-coloured houses.

Genoa, the Ligurian capital regally positioned at the centre of the region, is not easy to get to know. There is an abrupt change between the open spaces of the port and the narrow alleys of the town. The former has been the subject of a major but gradual regeneration, which has seen the creation of, among other things, the futuristic Aquarium, considered one of the finest in Europe. However, a Mediterranean soul can still be found in the streets of Genoa's historic centre, still redolent of those distant centuries when the galleys of "Genoa The Proud" were familiar in all the ports of the Levante. When you have had your fill of the wealth, ostentation or over-development of the coast, then you should head into Liguria's interior, which is attracting growing numbers of visitors. They come looking for an unspoilt land of woods, rivers, lakes and peaks, where towns show another aspect of the history and people of Liguria.

Ligurian olives, used for some of Italy's finest oils

The Cuisine

Getting to know the Italian Riviera also involves trying the local food and wine, which is offered in most local restaurants. Liguria's olive oil can compete with Italy's best, the fish and seafood are superb, and there are all sorts of other traditional foods, including delicious snacks, known as *stuzzichini*.

The food is just one facet of a region which, even to the most ardent fans of the sea, should not be regarded as merely a seaside resort.

Charming view of Apricale, in the hinterland behind the provincial capital of Imperia

The Landscape of Liguria

For most visitors to Liguria, the region means only one thing – the beaches, luxuriant vegetation and rocky slopes of the Riviera. Behind the coast, on the fertile plains and in the valleys, agriculture takes over – in particular, the age-old cultivation of olives and a burgeoning modern horticultural industry. Step further back and you're in the mountains, with their isolated villages and silent forests (Liguria is the most forested region in Italy). In winter, snow whitens the peaks just a short distance from the Mediterranean.

The rocky coast of Portovenere

The Coast

Liguria's coastline would measure 440 km (274 miles) if a line were traced following the shore into every inlet and cove. To the west, the beaches are wider and the coastline gentler, while to the east, the landscape is characterized by cliffs and mountains reaching down to the shore, making beaches a rarity. The Ligurian Sea is the richest area for cetaceans (whales and dolphins) in the Mediterranean.

The Coastal Plains

Although the plains occupy just one per cent of the region, they have always performed an important function. The climate is temperate and favourable for agriculture, and the soil very fertile. As a result, the plains are crammed with cultivated fields, as well as industries that cannot be located in rockier areas. This is the most densely populated part of Liguria: despite large areas of natural landscape, the plains have an average population of more than 300 inhabitants per square kilometre.

Dolphins can be seen in the Ligurian Sea, especially in the sea off the coast of the Cinque Terre, as well as sperm whales and the occasional marine turtle. It is not unusual to see groups of these friendly creatures following the wash behind ferry boats, emerging from the water and performing somersaults.

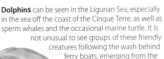

Mimosa, originally from southwestern Australia, brightens up many parks and gardens with its bright yellow flowers in spring.

The palm tree ("la palma" in Italian) was imported from North Africa and is now so common on the Riviera that it has given its name to a stretch of the Riviera di Ponente.

Glasshouses are a common feature of the plains. The cultivation of vegetables, fruit and flowers is one of Liguria's prime economic resources.

Wildlife in Liguria

Seagulls, never far away

Roe deer, found in the hills

The natural habitats of Liguria are very varied and the animal species that live there are equally diverse. In addition to the rich marine life, including whales in the waters extending southwards towards Corsica, there are many species of seabird (cormorants, shearwaters, gannets and terns). The hills are home to small mammals such as the fox, marten, badger and wild boar. In some areas roe deer and fallow deer have been reintroduced. At higher altitudes, in a gradual recolonization of the Apennine mountains, wolves have returned.

The Hills

Thirty per cent of Liguria consists of hill slopes, where the economy is based on the cultivation of olives (producing high-quality olive oil), ornamental plants, flowers and vines. In places where nothing is grown, the natural shrubby vegetation of the Mediterranean (known as maquis or macchia) dominates, followed, at higher altitudes, by pine woods and woods of chestnut and oak.

The Mountains

The Maritime Alps, to the west, and the Apennines, to the east, account for the largest chunk of Ligurian territory: as much as 69 per cent of the region is over 1,000m (3,281 ft) high. The proximity of the mountains to the Mediterranean has resulted in some botanically fascinating close juxtapositions of alpine and coastal plant and flower species. At the highest altitudes, conifers such as Scotch pine, silver fir, Norway spruce and larch predominate.

Olives are cultivated on hill terraces, often overlooking the sea, as in the area of the Cinque Terre. The best-quality olive variety is the taggiasca, which yields a fine extra virgin olive oil.

Edelweiss, a lovely alpine flower, is found at higher altitudes. Look out for it during the flowering period, from July to August.

The fox, like other small mammals, is a constant presence in hillside woods. They can also be seen in inhabited areas, searching for food.

The wolf has been gradually moving up through the Apennines and has recently appeared in the Parco Naturale Regionale dell'Aveto, close to the border with Emilia-Romagna.

Parks and Nature Reserves

The wildest and most unspoilt natural areas of Liguria are found, not surprisingly, in the hinterland. Here, a crisis in upland agriculture has seen the abandonment of mountain villages, with many vineyards and olive groves left to lie fallow; plants and wildlife are the main beneficiaries of such depopulation. Liguria's protected areas make up around 12 per cent of the region's land area and include six national parks, as well as nature reserves, mostly in the mountains. Each has a different character, from the Alpine valleys on the border with Piedmont, to the hills close to Tuscany. On the coast, after decades of tourist development, a series of marine and coastal reserves aims to conserve the last remaining unspoilt fragments of the Ligurian coast.

The Parco del Finalese *(p148)*, above Finale Ligure, has fascinating karst formations.

The Alta Via dei Monti Liguri

The Alta Via dei Monti Liguri, offering stunning walks and views

Created around a series of mule tracks which criss-cross the region and traverse more than one regional park, the Alta Via dei Monti Liguri is a protected trail which extends the length of Liguria *(see p201)*. It can be explored either on foot or, for the more energetic, by bike.

Isola Gallinara *(see p155)* and Isola Bergeggi *(see pp144–5)*, already regional nature reserves, are set to become marine reserves.

Piana Crixia

Beigua

Flume Bormida

Varazze

Savona

Finalese

Finale Ligure

Alpi Liguri

Albenga

Isola Gallinara

Imperia

Ventimiglia

0 kilometres 20

0 miles 20

Key

- National Park
- Regional Nature Reserve
- Other protected area
- Marine reserve
- — Alta Via dei Monti Liguri

The Parco del Monte Beigua *(see pp138–9)* is a park of high mountains. Its territory includes Monte Beigua and a series of other peaks which are only 6 km (4 miles) from the coast and yet exceed 1,000 m (3,280 ft) in height. Towards the border with Piedmont, the vegetation is typically alpine, while lower down, pines and larches give way to chestnut forest and then to Mediterranean maquis.

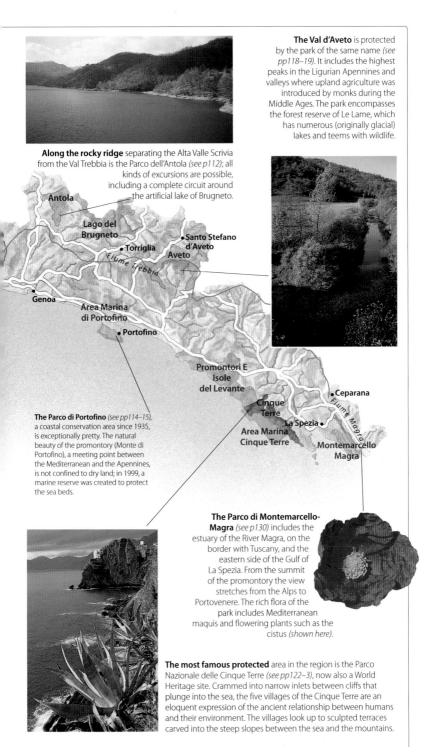

The Val d'Aveto is protected by the park of the same name *(see pp118–19)*. It includes the highest peaks in the Ligurian Apennines and valleys where upland agriculture was introduced by monks during the Middle Ages. The park encompasses the forest reserve of Le Lame, which has numerous (originally glacial) lakes and teems with wildlife.

Along the rocky ridge separating the Alta Valle Scrivia from the Val Trebbia is the Parco dell'Antola *(see p112)*; all kinds of excursions are possible, including a complete circuit around the artificial lake of Brugneto.

Antola

Lago del Brugneto

Torriglia

Santo Stefano d'Aveto

Aveto

Fiume Trebbia

Genoa

Area Marina di Portofino

Portofino

Promontori E Isole del Levante

Ceparana

Cinque Terre

La Spezia

Area Marina Cinque Terre

Fiume Magra

Montemarcello Magra

The Parco di Portofino *(see pp114–15)*, a coastal conservation area since 1935, is exceptionally pretty. The natural beauty of the promontory (Monte di Portofino), a meeting point between the Mediterranean and the Apennines, is not confined to dry land; in 1999, a marine reserve was created to protect the sea beds.

The Parco di Montemarcello-Magra *(see p130)* includes the estuary of the River Magra, on the border with Tuscany, and the eastern side of the Gulf of La Spezia. From the summit of the promontory the view stretches from the Alps to Portovenere. The rich flora of the park includes Mediterranean maquis and flowering plants such as the cistus *(shown here)*.

The most famous protected area in the region is the Parco Nazionale delle Cinque Terre *(see pp122–3)*, now also a World Heritage site. Crammed into narrow inlets between cliffs that plunge into the sea, the five villages of the Cinque Terre are an eloquent expression of the ancient relationship between humans and their environment. The villages look up to sculpted terraces carved into the steep slopes between the sea and the mountains.

The Italian Riviera Coastline

The density of the population along the Italian Riviera's coast is due largely to the fact that, unlike the marshy shores of Tuscany, Liguria's often rocky shores are eminently habitable and, historically, easy to defend. The beaches are more often pebbly than sandy, with pebbles at San Remo and Rapallo, for example, but sugar-fine sand at Alassio and Lerici. Many beaches show a Blue Flag and have gorgeous, limpid waters.

The shores around Savona are generally low-lying. From Albissola, Celle Ligure and Varazze, pebbly and sandy beaches alternate as far as Arenzano, at the western edge of the sprawling city of Genoa.

Key

━ Motorway
━ Major road
━ Minor road
─ River

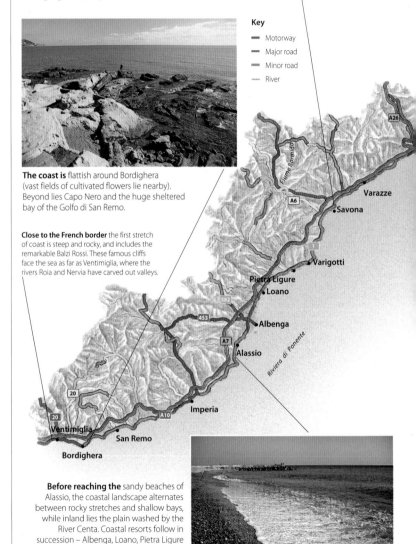

The coast is flattish around Bordighera (vast fields of cultivated flowers lie nearby). Beyond lies Capo Nero and the huge sheltered bay of the Golfo di San Remo.

Close to the French border the first stretch of coast is steep and rocky, and includes the remarkable Balzi Rossi. These famous cliffs face the sea as far as Ventimiglia, where the rivers Roia and Nervia have carved out valleys.

Fiume Bormida

A26

Varazze

A6

•Savona

•Varigotti

Pietra Ligure
•Loano

S82

•Albenga

453

A7

•Alassio

Riviera di Ponente

20

Imperia

20

A10

Ventimiglia

San Remo

Bordighera

Before reaching the sandy beaches of Alassio, the coastal landscape alternates between rocky stretches and shallow bays, while inland lies the plain washed by the River Centa. Coastal resorts follow in succession – Albenga, Loano, Pietra Ligure and Borgio Verezzi – as far as the cliffs of Finale and Capo Noli.

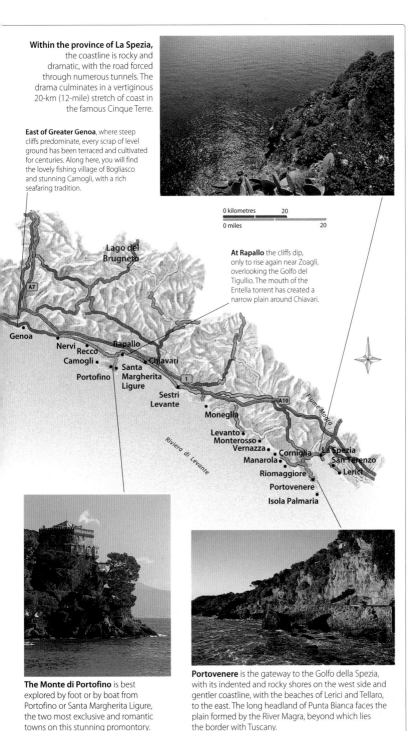

Within the province of La Spezia, the coastline is rocky and dramatic, with the road forced through numerous tunnels. The drama culminates in a vertiginous 20-km (12-mile) stretch of coast in the famous Cinque Terre.

East of Greater Genoa, where steep cliffs predominate, every scrap of level ground has been terraced and cultivated for centuries. Along here, you will find the lovely fishing village of Bogliasco and stunning Camogli, with a rich seafaring tradition.

0 kilometres 20
0 miles 20

At Rapallo the cliffs dip, only to rise again near Zoagli, overlooking the Golfo del Tigullio. The mouth of the Entella torrent has created a narrow plain around Chiavari.

Lago del Brugneto

A7

Genoa

Nervi
Recco
Camogli
Rapallo
Chiavari
Santa Margherita Ligure
Portofino
Sestri Levante
Moneglia
Levanto
Monterosso
Vernazza
Corniglia
Manarola
Riomaggiore
Portovenere
Isola Palmaria
La Spezia
San Terenzo
Lerici

1

A10

Fiume Magra

Riviera di Levante

The Monte di Portofino is best explored by foot or by boat from Portofino or Santa Margherita Ligure, the two most exclusive and romantic towns on this stunning promontory.

Portovenere is the gateway to the Golfo della Spezia, with its indented and rocky shores on the west side and gentler coastline, with the beaches of Lerici and Tellaro, to the east. The long headland of Punta Bianca faces the plain formed by the River Magra, beyond which lies the border with Tuscany.

Art in Liguria

Since the time of the Romans, Liguria has always been an important region, even a rich one from time to time, but it has never really been at the centre of events, whether political, cultural or artistic. Of crucial significance artistically, however, was Liguria's role as a major crossroads between the European mainland and the Mediterranean (and, beyond, the rest of the world). This meant not only that works of art from foreign parts passed through Liguria, but that foreign artists (including from other Italian states) visited and even stayed on to work.

Antiquity

The earliest evidence of artistic expression in Liguria include Palaeolithic carvings linked to famous sites such as Balzi Rossi *(see p173)*.

Surprisingly few traces of the Romans survive in Liguria. Much of their energy was spent gaining control of the area (only Genoa gave in willingly). The city of Luni *(see p131)*, founded in 177 BC, has some examples of Roman sculpture, but these are best described as well-made crafts rather than works of great artistic merit.

Crucifixion (1138), Sarzana cathedral

Middle Ages

Liguria in the Middle Ages, which consisted of walled towns linked to one another by sea rather than by land, was of greater interest architecturally than artistically.

The first important examples of figurative art from this era emerged from the Lunigiana (the area around Luni, an important port until the 12th century), which was culturally close to Tuscany. One such example is the *Crucifixion* (1138) now in the cathedral of Sarzana *(see p132)*. The work of a Tuscan called Maestro Guglielmo, this is probably the only work of significance from the 12th century in Liguria. In fact, in the 13th and 15th centuries,

it was generally easier to find Tuscan artists rather than local ones working in Liguria.

In terms of sculpture, one of the period's most significant works was the funerary monument (1313–14) of Margaret of Brabant, now in Genoa's Museo di Sant'Agostino *(see p61)*. It was commissioned by emperor Henry VII from the Tuscan Giovanni Pisano. The same museum has the remains of a 14th-century statue of Simone Boccanegra, the first doge of Genoa.

Political and territorial upheavals increasingly opened up Ligurian cities to the influence (and presence) of artists from Lombardy and Flanders: the *Crucifixion* (15th century) by the Pavia artist Donato de' Bardi, now in Savona's Pinacoteca Civica

Funerary monument of Margaret of Brabant

(see p140), was one of the first "Nordic" works to find favour.

Trade with Flanders and Burgundy brought a series of painters (David, Provost, Van Cleve) to Genoa; their religious works are now found throughout the region.

Equestrian portrait of Gio Carlo Doria by Rubens

The Renaissance and Baroque Periods

In the 16th century, an era in which Genoa's top families became rich through their dealings in international finance, new artistic genres reached Liguria, including the art of fresco-painting.

Among Liguria's best-known fresco painters was Luca Cambiaso, born in Moneglia in 1527 and active mainly in Genoa. His works can be seen in the Cappella Lercari in Genoa's San Lorenzo cathedral *(see pp56–7)*, and also in the Santuario della Madonna delle Grazie, not far from Chiavari *(see p118)*.

In the 17th century Genoa was a rich city, in terms of both commercial banking and art, and several of the city's fine private art collections were begun in this period: the city's newly wealthy families needed a large number of paintings to fill their vast palaces. The work available in the city attracted artists from all over Italy, as well

Annunciation by Paolo di Giovanni Fei (14th century)

as from abroad. In general, most of the works commissioned or bought by Genoa's noble patrons were not by Liguria's home-grown artists.

It was around this time that works by Flemish artists started to reach Liguria, evidence of the cultural and commercial influence that the Low Countries had on Ligurian merchants. The Palazzo Spinola di Pellicceria gallery in Genoa *(see p68)* houses several international master-pieces dating from this period, such as the *Ecce Homo* by Antonello da Messina and *Equestrian portrait of Gio Carlo Doria* (1606) by Peter Paul Rubens. The latter arrived in Genoa in the early 17th

century, and fell in love with the city. He became a major influence in the development of Genoese Baroque. Another influence at this time was Antony Van Dyck, some of whose works are on display in Genoa's Palazzo Rosso gallery *(see pp72–9)*. Among other fine Renaissance works on show in the same gallery are *Judith and Holofernes* (c.1550–80) by Veronese, *San Sebastiano* (1615) by Guido Reni and *The Cook* (c.1620s) by Bernardo Strozzi. There are also some fine portraits by Dürer, Pisanello and Paris Bordone.

The Pinacoteca Civica in Savona *(see p140)* has interesting works of art from the same era, including works by Donato De' Bardi and Taddeo di Bartolo.

La Spezia's Museo Amedeo Lia *(see p128)*, affectionately known as the "Louvre of Liguria", houses various Renaissance works of considerable value. Among these are the *Portrait of a Gentleman* (1510) by Titian and an *Annunciation* by Paolo di Giovanni Fei (14th century), as well as works by some of the great artists of the 16th century – including Raphael and Veronese. Liguria's greatest fresco painters, both active in the 17th century, were Gregorio De Ferrari and Domenico Piola, rivals whose work can be seen side by side in Genoa's Palazzo Rosso.

Anton Maria Marigliano (1664–1739), from Genoa was

a pupil of Domenico Piola, but made his name as a sculptor of wood. His fine crucifixes can be found in churches all over Liguria.

Portrait of the *Contessa de Byland* by Boldini (1901)

Present Day

The 19th and 20th centuries in Liguria have been more remarkable for the developments in architecture than in art. Modern art in Liguria lacks a strong regional identity.

Among the most significant collections of modern art in Liguria are the Villa Croce in Genoa *(see p61)* and two collections in Nervi *(see p93)*. These are the Raccolta Frugoni in Villa Grimaldi, and the Raccolta d'Arte Moderna. The latter's vast collection of drawings, sculptures, paintings and engravings dates from the 19th and 20th centuries. The core of the collection consists of the art owned by Prince Oddone di Savoia, which was donated to the community in 1866. The museum's collection is largely regional with some works by national and international artists.

The Sandro Pertini Collection, in the Pinacoteca Civica in Savona *(see p140)*, is devoted to modern art, mostly Italian. There are paintings by Morandi, De Chirico, Rosai, Guttuso and Birolli, and sculptures by Henry Moore and Joan Miró.

Fresco by Cambiaso, Santuario della Madonna delle Grazie, Chiavari

Architecture in Liguria

The truly creative expressions in Liguria's past lie less with art, or sculpture, than in the people's exceptional capacity to adapt their buildings to the contours of an often harsh and difficult landscape. Perched above the sea and hemmed in by the Apennines, the cities of the Italian Riviera developed in a totally individual way. In Genoa, in particular, the defining characteristic of the city was as a meeting point between the port – the hub of commercial traffic – and the city streets.

Coloured marble on the façade of San Lorenzo, Genoa

Ancient Architecture

The first examples of individual buildings were Bronze Age settlements which, although they bore similarities to other megalithic structures of the same period, introduced a new element: a fortification capable of defending people and their work. In the Roman era various cities were built or expanded, among them Luni, Genua (Genoa) and Albingaunum (Albenga), which were all given typical Roman features, such as bridges, aqueducts, amphitheatres, and trading quays in the ports. The most impressive amphitheatre in Liguria can be seen among the ruins of ancient Luni, at the foot of the Apuan Alps (a source of white marble much in demand in ancient Rome). The remnants of a Roman road also survive between Albenga and Alassio.

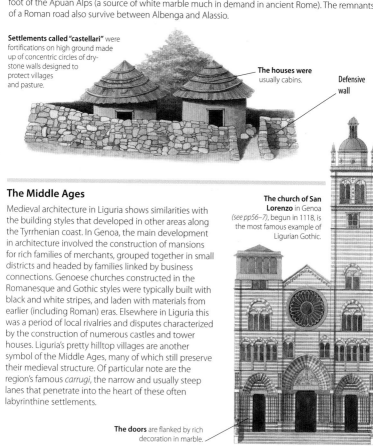

Settlements called "castellari" were fortifications on high ground made up of concentric circles of dry-stone walls designed to protect villages and pasture.

The houses were usually cabins.

Defensive wall

The Middle Ages

Medieval architecture in Liguria shows similarities with the building styles that developed in other areas along the Tyrrhenian coast. In Genoa, the main development in architecture involved the construction of mansions for rich families of merchants, grouped together in small districts and headed by families linked by business connections. Genoese churches constructed in the Romanesque and Gothic styles were typically built with black and white stripes, and laden with materials from earlier (including Roman) eras. Elsewhere in Liguria this was a period of local rivalries and disputes characterized by the construction of numerous castles and tower houses. Liguria's pretty hilltop villages are another symbol of the Middle Ages, many of which still preserve their medieval structure. Of particular note are the region's famous *carrugi*, the narrow and usually steep lanes that penetrate into the heart of these often labyrinthine settlements.

The church of San Lorenzo in Genoa (see pp56–7), begun in 1118, is the most famous example of Ligurian Gothic.

The doors are flanked by rich decoration in marble.

Renaissance Palazzi

In Genoa, the 16th and 17th centuries were a boom period – referred to as the "Genoese Century" – during which a handful of powerful families financed the construction of numerous grand palaces. A figure of particular importance in Genoese Renaissance history was Andrea Doria (1468–1560), admiral and patron of the arts, who built the magnificent Palazzzo Doria Pamphilj *(see pp82–3)*. The laying of Via Garibaldi, or "La Strada Nuova", in the mid 16th century, was a great example of civic town planning. The palazzi along this monumental street, including Palazzo Doria Tursi, symbolized the power of the great Genoese families. Other impressive schemes included the construction of the Molo Nuovo (new quay) and of the famous Lanterna (lighthouse), both in the port. Such was the reputation of Genoa's architects that they exported their palazzo designs and materials to Spain, France and northern Europe.

Palazzo Doria Tursi
(see p75), begun in 1565, is now Genoa's Town Hall. It is three times the size of the other palazzi on Via Garibaldi.

Decorations in white marble and pink stone

The side loggias were added in 1597.

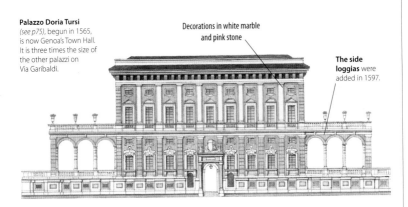

The Architecture of Today

After decades of crisis, years during which Genoa's historic centre was abandoned to its own devices, the city has rediscovered pride in itself and a capacity to undertake grand projects. The 500th anniversary of the discovery of America by Columbus (1992) provided the impetus to revamp the port area, which had long been blighted by the presence of the coastal motorway; and Genoa's role as European City of Culture in 2004 has prompted renovation and building work elsewhere. One of the aims of the restoration of the port area was to link it, finally, to the narrow alleys of old Genoa.

The colossal structure of Il Bigo *(see p64)*, designed by local boy Renzo Piano, echoes the cranes of Genoa's mercantile past, while the sphere is a glasshouse containing palms and vast ferns. The Aquarium was built in 1992 for the Columbus celebrations.

Glass panels

Structure in aluminium

The "arms" support a panoramic lift.

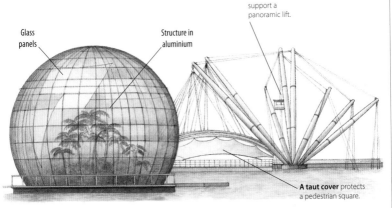

A taut cover protects a pedestrian square.

THE ITALIAN RIVIERA THROUGH THE YEAR

The pleasant and mild typically Mediterranean climate, the intense contrasts of light and colour, the romantic coastline and the equally fascinating interior have made Liguria a desirable destination for tourists since the mid-19th century. The clear blue sea, the beaches and the stunning and lush coastal scenery are consistent attractions all year round, but there are also numerous special events which can add extra local colour to any trip. These events include many religious and gastronomic festivals and also historical re-enactments and regattas, the latter a colourful reminder of the importance of the seafaring tradition to this part of Italy.

The mid-May fish festival at Camogli

Spring

Mild temperatures and pure air characterize spring in Liguria, which welcomes visitors with colour and unforgettablescents. The profusion of colourful flowers contrasts with the blue of the sea and the snow-capped peaks of the Ligurian Alps.

March

Rassegna dell'Olio d'Oliva, Balestrino. This village north of Albenga is proud of its 17 different types of olive. During the festival the public can taste different types of oil and olives as well as other traditional foods.

Fiera di San Giuseppe, La Spezia *(19 Mar)*. This immensely popular festival is held in honour of the town's patron saint, San Giuseppe. It offers more than 800 street stalls and vendors and abundant entertainment for all the family.

Milano–San Remo *(first Sat after 19 Mar)*. A classic, long-distance cycle race.

Festa di Primavera *(all month)*. Music, art and flower shows along the Riviera dei Fiori, to celebrate the advent of spring.

A cyclist celebrating his victory in the Milano–San Remo race

April

Good Friday processions, Good Friday (Venerdí Santo) has a fervent following, especially on the Riviera di Ponente. It is celebrated with processions in which local confraternities file past, with *casse* (carved wooden sculptures) portraying scenes from the Passion. The processions in Savona and Genoa are particularly popular, but similar events take place in the Ligurian hinterland, too.

Settimana Santa, Ceriana. Processions of confraternities and representations of the Descent from the Cross *(Calata della Croce)*, with religious songs.

May

Sagra del Pesce (fish festival), Camogli *(second Sun in May)*. A gigantic frying pan is used to fry a huge quantity of fish, which both locals and visitors are then invited to eat: a lovely gesture done in the hope that the seas will be equally generous to the fishermen.

Festa della Focaccia con il Formaggio, Recco *(fourth Sun)*. A bustling festival held to celebrate the famous cheese focaccia of Recco, a small but gastronomic town just north of Camogli. Abundant tastings on offer.

Summer

The high season for tourists, summer is hot and sunny along the coast while it is fresher and wetter in the hilly interior.

Average daily hours of sunshine

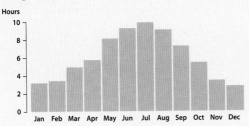

Sunshine
In both spring and summer the long days of sunshine, which are never excessively hot, are perfect for swimming and sailing. The light and colours of autumn, meanwhile, are delightful, while a clear winter's day means that the white peaks of the Alps are visible in the distance.

June

Infiorata *(first week of Jun)*. To celebrate Corpus Domini (Corpus Christi), many towns strew carpets of flowers along processional routes; the best take place in Sassello, Imperia, Diano Marina and Pietra Ligure. There is also a *Battaglia di Fiori* (battle of flowers) in Ventimiglia.

Regata delle Antiche Repubbliche Marinare, Genoa *(early Jun, every four years)*. A regatta in which teams from the cities of the four ancient maritime republics (Genoa, Pisa, Amalfi and Venice) compete in old sailing ships; there are processions, too. Genoa is the host every four years. In 2013, the regatta was held in Pisa.

Festa di San Giovanni, Genoa *(24 Jun)*. Celebrations in honour of St John. Also in Laigueglia, where 5,000 lit candles are placed on the water, and Triora.

Festa e Palio di San Pietro, Genoa *(29 Jun)*. A race with traditional boats, as well as illuminations.

Palio marinaro del Tigullio *(Jun/Jul)*. Regattas in resorts along the Tigullio coast, including Chiavari, Rapallo and Lavagna.

Girl in historical costume

July

Raduno delle Fiat 500, Garlenda *(early Jul)*. Participants come in their Fiat 500s from all over Europe.

Cristo degli Abissi, San Fruttuoso di Camogli *(end Jul)*. Nocturnal mass and torchlit procession of divers to the massive statue of Christ on the sea bed.

Sagra delle Rose and Sagra delle Pesche, Pogli d'Ortovero *(end Jul)*. A lovely celebration of the roses and peaches grown in this area near Albenga. This event gives visitors the chance to try local specialities.

The Muretto of Alassio, during a beauty competition

August

Stella Maris, Camogli *(first Sun)*. A festival of the sea, with a procession of boats to the Punta della Chiappa, with thousands of little wax candles bobbing on the waves.

Torta dei Fieschi, Lavagna *(14 Aug)*. The re-enactment of the lavish 13th-century wedding between Opizzo Fieschi and Bianca de' Bianchi, with a historical procession and the cutting of an enormous cake.

Castelli di Sabbia, Alassio *(mid-Aug)*. National competition for the best sandcastle on the beach.

Processione dell'Assunta, Nervi *(15 Aug)*. Evening procession, with a blessing of the sea and a firework display.

Festa della Madonna Bianca, Portovenere *(17 Aug)*. At 9pm torchlights are lit during a procession to the headland of San Pietro.

Miss Muretto, Alassio *(end Aug/ early Sep)*. The prettiest girl is elected and given the title dedicated to the town's famous "Muretto" (wall) of celebrities.

An enormous carpet of flowers, part of an Infiorata

Average monthly rainfall

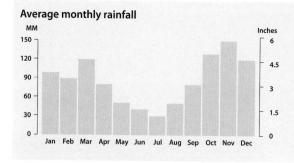

Rainfall
Liguria's weather is characterized by a fair amount of rainfall, especially during the autumn, when violent storms may occur and sometimes rivers may flood. The Riviera di Ponente is generally drier and sunnier than the Riviera di Levante.

Yachts at their moorings in Imperia

honour of the grape *(uva)*, including a costumed procession, a challenge in dialect and a series of contests between grape harvesters.
Sagra della Lumaca, Molini di Triora *(last week)*. Enormous frying pans full of snails *(lumache)* are cooked following an ancient recipe once used by the village's noble families, who would present them as the pièce de resistance at sumptuous banquets, because of their supposed magical powers.

Autumn

Autumn, with its warm colours and still balmy and sunny days, is the ideal season for visiting Liguria. Towns and villages are less crowded, and it is easier to find accommodation; in short, you can get to know the area's sights, towns, culture and gastronomy in greater peace.

September
Regata Storica dei Rioni, Noli *(first or second Sun)*. The four districts of the town challenge each other to a rowing race; processions in historical costume, too.
Sagra del Fuoco, Recco *(7–8 Sep)*. Festival in honour of the patron saint, Nostra Signora del Suffragio.
Anchovy Festival, Monterosso Al Mare *(second week)*. People come from all over Italy to celebrate the village's specialty. There are tastings, music and fireworks.

Sagra del Pigato, Salea di Albenga *(early Sep)*. A festival in honour of Pigato wine, with exhibitions, food pavilions, dancing and sporting events.
Festa della Madonna della Villa, Ceriana *(early Sep)*. Solemn candle-lit processions and a music festival of folk music in the village square, with choirs singing traditional songs.
Commemorazione della Battaglia Napoleonica, Loano. Exhibitions, ceremonies and parades in historical costume are staged in order to commemorate the Battle of Loano, in 1795, in which the French revolutionary army succeeded in routing the Austrian army.
Sagra dell'Uva, Varazze. A traditional festival with tastings and the sale of local wines. A similar festival is held at Vezzano Ligure *(see below)*.
Sagra dell'Uva, Vezzano Ligure *(mid-Sep)*. A festival in

Bottle of Pigato white wine

October
Salone Internazionale della Nautica, Genoa *(first and second week)*. This is the largest nautical fair to be held anywhere in the Mediterranean, with yachts, motorboats, inflatables and associated nautical paraphernalia.
Sagra della Farinata, Voltri *(late Oct)*. Tastings of local, mostly Genoese, gastronomic specialities, including Liguria's famous baked chick-pea snack *(farinata)*.

A motor launch on display at Genoa's nautical fair

Average monthly temperature

°C | °F
(bar chart showing average monthly temperatures for Jan, Feb, Mar, Apr, May, Jun, Jul, Aug, Sep, Oct, Nov, Dec)

Temperature
The coastal strip, exposed to the south, experiences sea breezes which refresh the hottest and sunniest summers and temper the winter temperatures; the latter are never too severe, even in the interior. Autumn and spring offer warm and clear days.

Bonfires lit in the streets during the Festa dei Furgari at Taggia

November
Olioliva, Imperia (late Nov). Held in the area where *taggiasca* olives are grown. Visits to olive presses *(frantoi)* are arranged, and a produce market is held at Oneglia. Restaurants offer special menus.

Winter
Although it can be windy, winter in the Italian Riviera often provides days with full sun, making it a good time to explore the region's medieval towns and villages.

December
Natale Subacqueo, Tellaro (24 Dec). The village is illuminated with 1,000 torchlights, and at midnight divers emerge with the statue of Baby Jesus, which is welcomed with fireworks.
"U Confogu" (Confuoco), Pietra Ligure and Savona (Sun before Christmas). Traditional ceremony with a costumed procession and the lighting of a propitiatory bundle of laurel: auspices for the coming year are divined from the resulting flames.

January
Festa di Capodanno (New Year), Genoa. The city's *carrugi* and the Porto Antico are thronged with people.

February
Festa dei Furgari, Taggia *(early Feb)*. Dedicated to San Benedetto. *Furgari* (bamboo canes filled with gunpowder) are set alight, while banquets go on all through the night.
Fiera di Sant'Agata, Genoa *(5 Feb)*. Stalls sell knick-knacks and sweetmeats, on the Sunday closest to 5 Feb. (Also in San Fruttuoso.) **Carnevale**, Loano. Allegorical carriages and people in fancy dress parade through the town.
Sagra della Mimosa, Pieve Ligure. Floral carriages and costumed processions.
Festival della Canzone Italiana, San Remo (last week Feb). Annual pop-music festival with international guests.

Public Holidays

New Year's Day (1 Jan)

Epiphany (6 Jan)

Easter Sunday

Easter Monday

Anniversario della Liberazione (25 Apr)

Labour Day (1 May)

Festa della Repubblica (2 Jun)

Ferragosto (15 Aug)

All Saints (1 Nov)

Immaculate Conception (8 Dec)

Christmas (25 Dec)

Boxing Day (26 Dec)

Mimosa in flower, brightening the gardens of the hinterland

THE HISTORY OF THE ITALIAN RIVIERA

The history of Liguria is linked inextricably with the sea. The coastal climate encouraged early settlement and the Romans built the first ports. Most importantly, from the start of the second millennium, the Republic of Genoa became a major seapower whose tentacles reached all over the Mediterranean and beyond.

The climate and geography of Liguria were highly favourable to humans in the far distant past. The coast was suitable for settlements and navigation on the open sea, while travel to what is now the Côte d'Azur and France was made easy by the low coastal hills. As a result, the population of this part of the Mediterranean was very scattered. Proof of this comes from the numerous traces of tombs and hearths found in the caves and on the hills of the region, forming an almost uninterrupted line from Liguria to Provence.

The first Ligurians appeared during the Bronze Age. In an era of migration and battles to occupy the best positions, the Ligurians fortified their settlements with walls to defend villages, pasture and access to the sea. They were mentioned for the first time (under the name of Ligyes) in the 7th century BC by Greek sources, who described how the land controlled by the ancient Ligurians extended far beyond the current boundaries of the region, as far as the limits of Catalonia and the Cévennes. While clashes and power struggles were taking place both in the lowlands and in the mountains to the north, new arrivals turned up on the Ligurian coast: the Greeks and the Etruscans who were, at the time, in total control of the Mediterranean and its markets. The Greeks were by then firmly installed in Marseille, and sought space to settle in the Ligurian valleys. The Etruscans had founded ports and trading cities along the Tuscan coast.

A series of settlements was established during this period, including proper villages at Genoa, Chiavari and Ameglia. Traces of necropoli in which the ashes of the deceased were buried have been discovered.

The onset of the Roman era was marked by the arrival of Roman legions in around 218 BC; this represented a much more significant change for the region than the disruptions caused by previous populations of travellers and merchants. For Rome, Liguria represented a fundamental transit point for expansion into nearby Gaul.

240,000 BC First burial in the cave at Balzi Rossi	**80,000–60,000 BC** Presence of Neanderthal man in Ligurian sites		**12,340 BC** Date of hand and foot prints found in the Grotta di Toirano	**218 BC** The Romans establish their first base in Liguria	
300,000 BC	**100,000 BC**	**50,000 BC**	**10,000 BC**	**1,000 BC**	**100 BC**
Finds in the Balzi Rossi museum		**36,000–10,000 BC** Era of *Homo sapiens sapiens*	*Footprints in the Grotta di Toirano*	**First millennium BC** Golden age of the Ligurians and contact with the Greeks and Phoenicians	

◀ Detail from the frescoes by Perin del Vaga in the Loggia degli Eroi, Palazzo Doria Pamphilj, Genoa

Prehistoric Liguria

The long rocky coast, with steep, vertical cliffs facing the sea, made Liguria a particularly attractive destination for our ancient ancestors. The rise and fall of the sea level, over the course of millennia, has brought about the emergence and disappearance of hundreds of caves which have been inhabited by man since the prehistoric era. As well as offering coastal shelter, food and fishing possibilities, Liguria also provided a series of staging posts between the coast and the hinterland and the plains of the Po valley. At the end of the prehistoric era, man regularly made use of the remote Monte Bego and the Vallée des Merveilles, just across the border into France. In the western Riviera, in the meantime, a new urban and military set-up had emerged: the settlements known as *castellari,* which protected villages and pastures from invasion by peoples approaching from the sea, intent on expanding their dominion in the hinterland.

Monte Bego
In the area around Monte Bego, a sacred mountain, and in the Vallée des Merveilles, prehistoric man has left over 100,000 rock carvings of religious significance on rocks smoothed and etched by the passing of ancient glaciers.

The Triplice Sepoltura (Triple Grave)
Found in the Barma Grande at Balzi Rossi, this provides important evidence of human presence in the area. Accompanying the skeletons of one adult, a boy and a girl was a rich collection of funerary objects.

Pieve di Teco

Triora

Imperia

Taggia

San Remo

Ventimiglia

The caves of the Balzi Rossi form part of a reddish, calcareous wall jutting out over the sea. There are 12 caves in all.

Craftmanship in Liguria

The first crafts to be discovered in the region date back 35,000 years, to the late Paleolothic period. Treasures from the Balzi Rossi caves (now in the museum) include a unique Przewalskii Horse incised on a wall of the Grotta del Caviglione 20,000 years ago, and 15 soapstone Venus figurines, symbols of fertility, found in the Barma Grande.

Venus figure

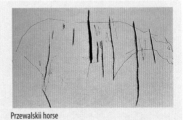

Przewalskii horse

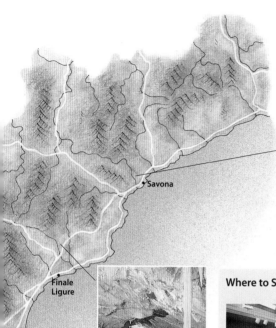

Arene Candide
The "white sands" cave (a sand dune once covered it) is closed to the public. Finds from it are in the archeological museum at Pegli near Genoa.

Grotte di Toirano
In the Grotta della Bàsura are hand-, knee- and footprints of Cro-magnon men, women and children.

Where to See Prehistoric Liguria

The interior of the Balzi Rossi museum

Some of Liguria's most significant prehistoric sites are also fascinating places to visit, in particular the site of the Balzi Rossi, with its museum *(see p173)*, and the Grotte di Toirano *(see pp150–51)*, with their superb formations of stalactites and stalagmites. Breathtaking hikes can also be taken along the Alpine paths of the Vallée des Merveilles and Monte Bego, which lie just across the border in France.

Hikers in the Vallée des Merveilles

The Caves of Liguria

The women of Liguria's most ancient ancestor died in the Grotta del Principe around 240,000 years ago. The great cave complex of Balzi Rossi, however, continued to be used by Neanderthal man even after that. Groups of hunter-gatherers lived in many other Ligurian caves, too: at Arma di Taggia near San Remo, and in the Grotta delle Fate at Toirano near Finale Ligure. With the passing of millennia, our closest ancestor (Homo sapiens sapiens) settled in Liguria, where traces of his presence have been found at Balzi Rossi, at Toirano and in the grotto of Arene Candide in Savona province, where archaeologists found 20 graves, including the famous tomb of the Giovane Principe (Young Prince).

Ruined Roman villa at Alba Docilia, now Albisola

Roman Liguria

The focus of the Romans was to establish landing stages for merchants and ships, but they did not have an easy time establishing their presence in Liguria. Genoa was one of the few places that fell to the Romans without conflict; it was incorporated into the Roman empire in the 2nd century BC.

The toughness of the Ligurians attracted the Carthaginians (under the command of Hannibal and his brothers Hasdrubal and Mago), who co-opted as allies the tribes of the Intumeli and Ingauni. In 205 BC, the Carthaginians besieged and destroyed Genoa. The Romans prevailed, however and, once the Carthaginians had been driven back, they continued their expansion, attacking Gallic tribes and extending the road network, which became a vital means of communication within the empire. The Via Postumia reached Roman Genua (Genoa) from Mediolanum (Milan) in 148 BC, although the road of greatest significance was the Via Julia Augusta, which was laid along the coast; the modern Via Aurelia follows its route.

As they conquered territory, the Romans also colonized it, gradually establishing a whole series of towns, along the coast. The most important of these Roman settlements were: Portus Lunae (Luni), Ingaunum (Albenga), Alba Docilia (Albisola), Genua (Genoa), Portus Delphini (Portofino) and Segesta Tigulliorum (Sestri Levante). Roman Liguria, however, was never more than a backwater: the result of its distance from the main routes of communication through Italy, and the fact that the Romans' most important ports were elsewhere.

Barbarian Invasions

The armies of the Visigoths under Alaric reached Liguria from North Africa in AD 409, and after that the region was raided by the Goths and their allies, the Heruli. Armies came and went, while both the political and military situation in the whole Italian peninsula was in a constant state of flux. In AD 536 Italy was invaded by the

Rotarius, king of the Longobards, who reached Liguria in 641

forces of the Eastern Empire, under the leadership of Justinian I. They eventually overcame the Goths, and a fairly peaceful period under Byzantine rule followed. Bishoprics had already started to emerge in the 5th century, and continued to be created under the Byzantines, including that of Albenga. Liguria was given the name of *Provincia*

205 BC Genoa, allied to Rome, is destroyed by the Carthaginians

Portrait of Hannibal

4th century Liguria becomes *Provincia Maritima Italorum*, part of the Byzantine empire

100 BC

AD 400

600

AD 409 Invasion of Visigoths under Alaric

Alaric's coat of arms

641–643 Lombard conquest by troops led by Rotarius

Maritima Italorum by its new rulers.

The period of Byzantine rule came to a close with the arrival in 641 of the Lombards, led by King Rotarius. The towns of Liguria became part of a Frankish territory which included tracts of land which now form part of Tuscany. The Saracens made incursions in 901, often from bases in the south of France. Later in the 10th century, during the reign of Berengarius, northeast Italy was divided into three: *Obertenga*, to the east, included Genoa, *Aleramica*, in the centre included Albenga, and *Arduinica*, to the west, included Ventimiglia. The families that had control of these territiories (such as the Del Carretto) found themselves in a powerful position that lasted for centuries.

Battle with the Saracens, a 14th-century miniature

The Rise of Genoa

Around the year 1000, the golden age of the free communes dawned. Their main activities revolved around maritime trade and the arming of commercial or military fleets. In this era of economic and political development, Genoese predominance became increasingly noticeable, though life was not entirely peaceful. In the mid-12th century, the city built a new wall to protect it against the ravages of Emperor Frederick I, known as Barbarossa. Nevertheless, after the independence of the Genoese commune was recognized, it began to compete with Pisa for control of the Mediterranean islands of Corsica and Sardinia. Genoese ships from the ports of Noli and Savona also took part in the Crusades.

Genoa expands along the Coast

Besides its growing power at sea, Genoa also sought to expand its sphere of influence, both commercially and militarily, on dry land; they gained control of cities, valleys and the mountain passes linking the coast to the Po valley, and even extended their dominion along the banks of that great river – a move crucial to a republic dependent on agricultural provisions.

After a century of clashes, battles and alliances, by 1232 virtually the entire Riviera di Levante coast was effectively under Genoese control. Among the cities which clashed most violently with Genoa were Ventimiglia (which fell in 1262) and Savona, which, following a long fight for independence, capitulated in 1528.

The port of Genoa as portrayed in a 16th-century painting

890 Beginning of raids by Saracens based in France

984 Benedictines rebuild the Abbey of San Fruttuoso

1099 The "Compagna", a pact between the districts of Genoa, is set up

1133 Genoa becomes the seat of a bishopric

800

1000

935 Sacking of Genoa by the Arabs

Cross of a knight who took part in the first Crusade

1097 Genoa contributes ten galleys to the first Crusade

1162 The Holy Roman Emperor recognizes the autonomy of Genoa

Genoa's Golden Age

The enterprising trading activities of Genoa's great shipowning families made the city into a Mediterranean power from the beginning of the 12th century. The exploits of aristocratic dynasties such as the Doria family took the Genoese to all corners of the known oceans. The growth in Genoa's power was consolidated with increasingly close links to other cities in Liguria, which were often in Genoese control, and to the area around Asti (in Piedmont) and Provence, indispensable suppliers of salt, grain and agricultural produce. Simone Boccanegra became Genoa's first lifetime Doge in 1339, although the most powerful institution during this period was the Banco di San Giorgio (Bank of St George). In a city riven by violent struggles between rival factions, the bank maintained a neutral position. At that time, thriving commercial houses from all over Europe were represented in Genoa, and the emissaries of the Banco di San Giorgio became familiar figures in treasuries all over Europe.

The Mediterranean (1250)
— Genoese trade routes
⋯ Pisa trade routes
— Venetian trade routes

Oberto Doria, founder of the illustrious Genoese dynasty, acquired the town of Dolceacqua in 1270.

The Pisan fleet consisted of 72 galleys. The defeat of Pisa was dramatic: 5,000 men died and 11,000 prisoners were taken in chains to Genoa.

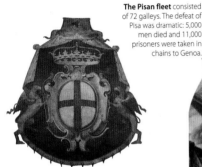

Rivalry with Pisa and Venice
Genoa struggled against two rival powers, Pisa and Venice. Pisa was defeated at Meloria but, with the advance of the Turks, Genoa saw her possessions in the East increasingly under threat, and the republic's rivalry with Venice intensified.

Genoa expands its rule along the coast
Many cities along the Riviera di Ponente were in Genoa's orbit at the time, including Albenga, which was forced to sign increasingly restrictive pacts, until its final subjugation in 1251. Ventimiglia yielded in 1261, followed in 1276 by Porto Maurizio. Left is an engraving (1613) by Magini of ships off the western riviera.

Genoa and the Crusades

During the 250 years of the Crusades, the maritime republics vied for supremacy in the struggle over trade routes, colonies and beneficial alliances. The two Crusades that brought about the conquest of Jerusalem saw the Genoese take an active role in the naval front line, with their *condottiero* Guglielmo Embriaco. In the ports of Acre and Haifa (in modern Israel), Genoese merchants built homes and warehouses, as well as churches. At its peak, the city of Acre had 50,000 inhabitants and 38 churches; it was the last place in the Holy Land to be conquered by the Arabs, in 1291. When the Christian kingdoms present in the Holy Land found themselves in trouble, Genoa frequently allied itself to the Knights of St John, the Armenians and even the Tartars in the fight against Venice, Pisa, the Templars and the Mameluks of Egypt.

The taking of Jerusalem in the First Crusade (1096–99)

The Meloria rocks (after which the battle was named) lie off Livorno, some 7km (4 miles) offshore.

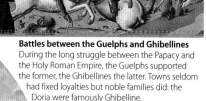

Battles between the Guelphs and Ghibellines
During the long struggle between the Papacy and the Holy Roman Empire, the Guelphs supported the former, the Ghibellines the latter. Towns seldom had fixed loyalties but noble families did: the Doria were famously Ghibelline.

The Battle of Meloria

One of the events that confirmed Genoese dominance in the Mediterranean was the Battle of Meloria, which saw Genoa fight and defeat her rival Pisa over possession of Corsica. In August 1284, a Genoese fleet under the command of Oberto Doria, took up position close to Porto Pisano. The battle was violent and the victor uncertain until the arrival of a second group of Genoese galleys, which took her adversary by surprise. Shown here is Battle of Meloria by Giovanni David, in Genoa's Palazzo Ducale.

The Genoese fleet was made up of 93 galleys.

Meloria was also the setting for another battle, in 1241, in which the Pisans, allied to Holy Roman Emperor Frederick II, defeated the Genoese.

Banco di San Giorgio
Founded in the early 1400s, the Bank of St George not only ran the domestic treasury, but was also directly involved with Genoa's colonies, such as Famagusta, in Cyprus. Shown here, an "8 Reali" coin minted by the bank.

Andrea Doria in a portrait by Sebastiano del Piombo

Clashes with other Maritime Republics

The centuries that witnessed the great geographical and commercial expansion around the Mediterranean of Italy's maritime republics, also saw Genoa extend its tentacles in all directions. With the Crusades – from the first, which brought about the capture of Jerusalem, to the ill-fated expedition of King Louis IX of France to North Africa – Genoa acquired ports and also *maone* (associations involved in the financing of commercial enterprises), in all corners of the Mediterranean. She then extended her sphere of influence towards the east and the ports of the Black Sea, important trading stations on the Silk Road.

It was a time of increasingly tough alliances and clashes:

Emperor Charles V, allied to Andrea Doria

although Genoa succeeded in eliminating Pisan influence from the Tyrrhenian Sea and from its major islands, taking decisive control of Corsica and defeating Pisa at the Battle of Meloria in 1284, the conflict with Venice was more protracted.

The Genoese defeated the Venetian fleet in the Battle of Curzola in the Adriatic in 1298, but were unable to reap the fruits of this victory and turn the situation in the East to their advantage. Turkish pressure led to an alliance with Venice (1343) which was of brief duration. The last war between Genoa and Venice (a result of both cities setting their sights on Cyprus) was decisive. The battles of Pola (1379) and Chioggia (1380) led to the Pace di Torino (Peace of Turin), which heralded the final decline of Genoese hegemony.

The Republic of Genoa

The period of the great continental struggles between the papacy and the Holy Roman Empire by no means spared Genoa and other Ligurian cities. The international nature of the struggle meant that foreign princes – such as the Visconti of Milan, summoned by the Ghibellines of the Riviera di Ponente, or Robert of Anjou, who intervened in favour of the Guelphs – got involved in Liguria's local conflicts.

During this period, Genoa was governed for almost two centuries by life-appointed doges, a position inaugurated in the 14th century. In 1522, however, their relatively peaceful rule over Genoa was shattered

---

1245–1252 Construction of the basilica dei Fieschi di San Salvatore

1252 The *genovino* is coined, Europe's first gold coin

1284 Victory of Genoa over Pisa at Meloria

Battle of Meloria

1339 Simone Boccanegra becomes the first doge of Genoa

1250   **1300**   **1350**

1251 Savona is attacked by Genoa

1262 Ventimiglia, defeated, comes under Genoese influence

1298 Genoese victory over Venice at Curzola

1361 San Remo becomes a free commune

by the arrival of Spanish troops. Andrea Doria later put the city under the protection of Charles V, King of Spain and Holy Roman Emperor – a demonstration of how power in the city had shifted. Andrea Doria was a talented soldier and admiral, and a member of one of Genoa's great families *(see p83)*; he was named lord of the city in 1528.

In 1553, for reasons connected to the wars between France and Spain, the French decided to land on Genoa-dominated Corsica, intending to establish a base in the Mediterranean Sea. Many Genoese fortresses fell, but a peace treaty eventually forced the French to withdraw.

This was not the end of trouble in Corsica, however. The defeat of the Ottoman fleet at the Battle of Lepanto in 1571 led to instability (and also pirate raids) in the Mediterranean. The 17th century saw numerous revolts by the Corsicans, as well as renewed attempts by the colonial power to impose its authority. But the decline of Genoa, along with widespread dissatisfaction among Corsicans, provoked yet more revolts in the early 18th century, eventually resulting in the annexation of Corsica to France.

Columbus, a native of Genoa

Other Ligurian Cities Develop

Albenga, which had long sought to resist the power of Genoa, finally came under Genoese control following a clash between Guelphs and Ghibellines. The town of San Remo was acquired by the Doria family but managed to liberate itself in 1361, becoming a free commune within the Genoese republic.

After years of autonomy, Savona was defeated by the Genoese in 1528 and the conquerors' first action was to rebuild the port. A great new fortress, Il Priamàr, was built, but the local population went into decline. La Spezia, subject to Genoa and, from 1371, seat of the Vicariate of the Riviera di Levante, was fortified at the end of the 14th century and remained under the control of the Genoese until the early 19th century.

Smaller towns also managed to find a role for themselves in a region dominated by the Genoese. Camogli, Portofino and Chiavari all lived off the sea, and their shipyards prospered.

A 16th-century view of the Battle of Lepanto

1407 Founding of the Banco di San Giorgio	**1451** Christopher Columbus is born in Genoa	**1522** Birth of the Republic of Genoa	**1543** Construction of La Lanterna, which becomes the symbol of the city of Genoa
1400	**1450**	**1500**	
1458 Brief period of French rule over Genoa begins	**1492** Colombo discovers America	**1528** Andrea Doria comes to power	

Caravel

The bombardment of Genoa by the French fleet in 1684

The Decline of Genoa

Two important constitutions were established in Genoa in the 16th century: one by Andrea Doria, in 1528, and another in 1576, which created the hierarchical structures that were to rule the city. But, as time went by, Genoa became decidedly more important for the financial power wielded by its banks than for its political or military strength. A striking sign of the diminished political role of "Genoa La Superba" (Genoa the Proud) was the 1684 bombardment of Genoa by the French fleet under Louis XIV.

With the decline in Genoese power, a series of autonomous political entities arose in the region, such as the Magnifica Comunità degli Otto Luoghi ("magnificent community of eight towns"), set up in 1686 around Bordighera. However, in a Europe in which the role of nation states was increasing in importance, there was no longer much room for such autonomous powers. The rich families of

Genoa increasingly moved away from commerce in order to concentrate more on financial investments.

The 17th and 18th centuries passed with no great incident, though Corsica was finally sold to the French in 1768. Liguria also found itself in conflict with the expansionist policies of Piedmont. Occupied in 1746 by the Austrians and the Piemontese, Genoa responded with a revolt provoked by the gesture of a young boy named Balilla, who sparked off an insurrection by hurling a stone at an Austrian cannon.

Piemontese Liguria

The arrival of Napoleon Bonaparte's French troops in Italy completely upset the political equilibrium of Liguria. In 1794 the troops of Massena and Bonaparte conquered the mountain passes which gave access to Italy. Three years later the Republic of Liguria was established, becoming part of the Napoleonic empire in 1805. Napoleon's defeat at Waterloo and the Congress of Vienna in 1815 finally put an end to the independence of Genoa and Liguria: the region was assigned to Piedmont and became part of the Kingdom of Sardinia, governed by the House of Savoy.

Genoese-born Giuseppe Mazzini

The only port of any size in the Kingdom of Savoy, Genoa was linked to Piedmont and to France by new communication routes. The city was also greatly altered by House

1576 Second constitution of Genoa

1686 The Magnifica Comunità degli Otto Luoghi is set up around Bordighera

1768 Permanent loss of Corsica

1550   **1600**   **1650**   **1700**   **1750**

Louis XIV, king of France

1684 The French fleet bombards Genoa, causing considerable damage

1746 Balilla sparks off a popular revolt against the Austro-Piemontese of Savoy architects. In 1828 Carlo Barabino built the Teatro Carlo Felice and, in 1874, construction of the new port of Genoa began. (It was greatly enlarged again in 1919 and in 1945.)

Perhaps due to Liguria's traditional resentment of Piedmont, the Risorgimento movement, which sought a united Italy, was particularly strong and heartfelt in Liguria. Giuseppe Mazzini, one of the key leaders, was born in Genoa, and it was from Quarto (now a Genoese suburb) that Garibaldi's "Thousand" set sail for the south in 1860. Eventually, a united Kingdom of Italy, which Liguria joined in 1861, was formed.

Tourism and Liguria Today

The building of the railway line along the coast, following the line of the Via Aurelia, represented a crucial stage in the future development of the region. The smaller towns, such as Bordighera, San Remo, Alassio, Santa Margherita and Lerici, became popular destinations with a growing number of visitors, largely the wealthy and the aristocratic of Europe. In the 1930s Genoa was reshaped by Mussolini-era demolition in the heart of the historic centre. Further modifications were carried out in the 1960s and 1970s.

The ports and harbours of Liguria were badly damaged during World War II and, in the valleys and the mountains of the Apennines, the Resistance fought hard against German occupation. Postwar

The architect Renzo Piano

Liguria has seen attempts to develop the region's industry, and to adapt its ports to the needs of tourism. Many industries have faced crisis, however, and Liguria has had more success in the field of agriculture, in particular the cut-flower industry.

Tourism is also, of course, of prime importance economically. The building of the motorway in the 1960s has increased the speed of development on both sides of the Riviera, which are crowded with visitors for most of the year. As the coast has become more prosperous and, in some cases, very rich (as in Portofino), so the neglected villages of the interior have met a rather different fate:many people have moved away, while there has also been a historic lack of investment in the interior.

Genoa, on the other hand, has been the focus of attention for more than a decade. The port was revamped (with the help of local architect Renzo Piano) in the run-up to the celebrations in honour of Columbus's "discovery" of America, and more money poured in prior to Genoa's year as Europe's City of Culture (2004).

Train at the Corniglia station, Cinque Terre

1782 Niccolò Paganini is born in Genoa	1805 Giuseppe Mazzini is born in Genoa	1828 Carlo Barabino designs Teatro Carlo Felice in Genoa	1874 Construction of a new port at Genoa begins	1940–45 Genoa is badly damaged by bombing in World War II	2004 Genoa is European City of Culture	2007 The 10th Annual Genoa Film Festival is held in July
1800		**1850**	**1900**	**1950**	**2000**	
1797 The Republic of Liguria is established	1815 Liguria becomes part of the Kingdom of Sardinia	1860 The expedition of the Thousand departs from Quarto	*Garibaldi departing from Quarto*	1992 Columbiadi (Columbus celebrations) held in Genoa	*Logo of the Colombiadi*	

GENOA
AREA BY AREA

Genoa at a Glance

The capital of Liguria, "Genova la Superba" (Genoa the Proud) has enjoyed a dominant role in the region, both commercial and political, for centuries. It is a fascinating city in a spectacular site and with many important monuments. First built by the sea, around the basin of the Porto Antico (the old port), the city could only then expand upwards. A labyrinth of medieval *carruggi*, Liguria's distinctive narrow alleys, was created up the steep hills behind the port, followed by new streets laid out in the 16th and 17th centuries, lined with grand palazzi built for Genoa's merchant families. The 19th-century and modern quarters of the city climb steeply again, adapting to the rising terrain. This scenic but inflexible landscape has created the need for various funiculars and lifts, some of which provide fantastic views. The current dynamism evident in Genoa is thanks largely to the Columbus celebrations of 1992 and the city's status, in 2004, as European City of Culture.

Palazzo Reale *(see p81)*, built in the 17th century, belonged to the Balbi family, to the Durazzos and finally to the Savoys, and is now the seat of the Galleria Nazionale.

Palazzo Doria Pamphilj *(see pp82–3)* was the private residence of the great 16th-century admiral and politician Andrea Doria. It still has apartments decorated for him and paintings he commissioned from artists such as Perin del Vaga and Sebastiano del Piombo.

Il Centro Storico
(see pp53–69)

The Aquarium *(see pp66–7)*, first opened in 1992 in the attractive setting of the Porto Antico, has become one of the most popular tourist destinations in Italy. It is extremely well laid-out, and features a rich variety of animal and plant life.

| 0 metres | | 400 |
| 0 yards | | 400 |

Further Afield
(see pp84–93)

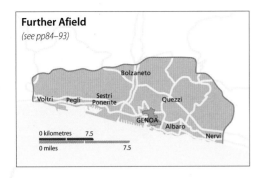

Via Garibaldi *(see pp72–3)* was laid out in the 1550s as a residential quarter for the chief aristocratic families of Genoa. Celebrated for centuries by travellers, its impressive architecture has remained remarkably well preserved.

San Lorenzo *(see pp56–7)* is Genoa's cathedral, built from the 11th to the 13th centuries in Romanesque-Gothic style. There is fine sculpture both inside and out, and the chapels of Lercari and San Giovanni Battista are of special interest.

Le Strade Nuove
(see pp70–83)

Palazzo Ducale *(see p58–9)* was the principal seat of the Doge of Genoa, and was enlarged to majestic dimensions in the 16th century. Today, the spacious palazzo is used for major exhibitions.

IL CENTRO STORICO

The old heart of the city is grouped around the Porto Antico and is made up of a hilly network of small piazzas, alleys and staircases. It is the largest medieval centre in Europe and is exceptionally well preserved, despite persistent neglect in some parts. The area is home to the cathedral of San Lorenzo and the Palazzo Ducale, the seat of power for centuries. Both public and private wealth has left its mark in the old town: Palazzo San Giorgio and the Loggia dei Mercanti on the one hand, the Doria family mansions in Piazza San Matteo and Palazzo Spinola on the other. The relationship between the old town and the port has been a centuries-old problem, largely due to the lack of integration between the two, which was further complicated in the 20th century by the building of a flyover. A chance to redeem the area and re-establish links with the seafront came in the 1990s: old buildings, such as the Teatro Carlo Felice, were restored, and new projects, including Renzo Piano's port buildings, were launched.

*See also Street Finder,
maps 5 & 6*

0 metres	400
0 yards	400

Sights at a Glance

Historic Buildings
⑩ Porta Soprana (or di Sant'Andrea)
⑪ Casa di Colombo
⑲ Loggia dei Mercanti

Historic Streets and Piazzas
④ Piazza De Ferrari
⑮ Porto Antico pp64–5
⑱ Piazza Banchi
㉒ Piazza San Matteo

Museums and Galleries
⑤ Accademia Ligustica di Belle Arti
⑧ Museo Civico di Storia Naturale
  Giacomo Doria
⑫ Museo di Sant'Agostino
⑯ Aquarium pp66–7
⑳ Palazzo Spinola di Pellicceria

Theatres
⑥ Teatro Carlo Felice

Churches
① San Lorenzo pp56–7
③ Il Gesù (or Sant'Ambrogio)
⑦ Santo Stefano
⑨ Basilica di Santa Maria Assunta
  in Carignano
⑬ San Donato
⑭ Santa Maria di Castello
㉑ Santa Maria delle Vigne

Palazzi
② Palazzo Ducale
⑰ Palazzo San Giorgio

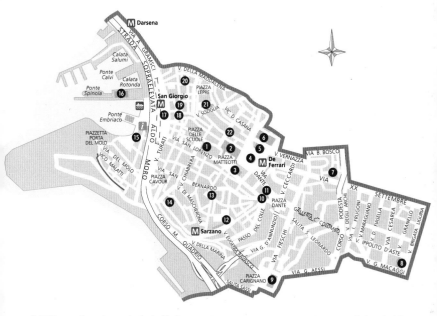

◀ A 19th-century lion sculpture at the church of San Lorenzo

For map symbols see back flap

Street-by-Street: Around Piazza Matteotti

Within the dense warren of the Centro Storico, the square overlooked by the cathedral, Piazza San Lorenzo, and Piazza Matteotti, in front of the Palazzo Ducale, create welcome open spaces. Nearby is Piazza De Ferrari, a 19th-century project developed to link the old city with the western, modern and industrial part of Genoa. Within this maze of streets there is almost no sense of the nearby sea, except when you get a sudden glimpse of a blue horizon. There are numerous places and monuments of interest in this area: churches of ancient origin such as Santa Maria di Castello, Santa Maria delle Vigne and Sant'Agostino; a variety of public spaces (Piazza Banchi, Piazza San Matteo, Via di Sottoripa); as well as public and private buildings, including the supposed birthplace of Christopher Columbus, the aristocratic Palazzo Spinola di Pellicceria, and Palazzo San Giorgio, from whose frescoed façade there are beautiful views of the sea.

★ Piazza San Matteo
At the heart of the district that was home for centuries of the Doria family, this medieval piazza preserves its original appearance. The beautiful church of San Matteo is also medieval.

Palazzo Spinola

PIAZZA CAMPETT

VIA DI SCURRERIA

PIAZZA SAN MATTEO

SALITA S MATTE

VIA ARCIVESCOVADO

❶ **★ San Lorenzo**
The cathedral was surrounded by the medieval city until the building of Via San Lorenzo along the church's right-hand side and the addition of a flight of steps up to the façade, both dating from the mid-19th century.

The port, Piazza Banchi and Palazzo San Giorgio

VIA SAN LORENZO

PIAZZA MATTEOTTI

❷ **★ Palazzo Ducale**
The seat of the Doge of Genoa, this building was begun in the Middle Ages, but was much altered in the 16th and 18th centuries. The palazzo has two large courtyards and contains valuable works of art.

SALITA POLLAIUOLI

VICO TRE RE MAGI

⓬ **Museo di Sant'Agostino**
The cloisters of the ruined church of Sant'Agostino house a collection of sculpture and architectural relics from around the city, including this 17th-century *Madonna with Child* by Pierre Puget.

For hotels and restaurants in this region see pp180–81 and pp188–91

❸ Chiesa del Gesù

Reconstructed by the Jesuits in the late 16th century on the site of the older church of Sant'Ambrogio, the Gesù has a sumptuous interior reflecting Genoa's golden age. Inlaid marble, stuccoes and frescoes create an ornate setting for two important works by Rubens, the Flemish artist who painted for various Genoese nobles.

Locator Map
See Street Finder, maps 2, 3, 5 & 6

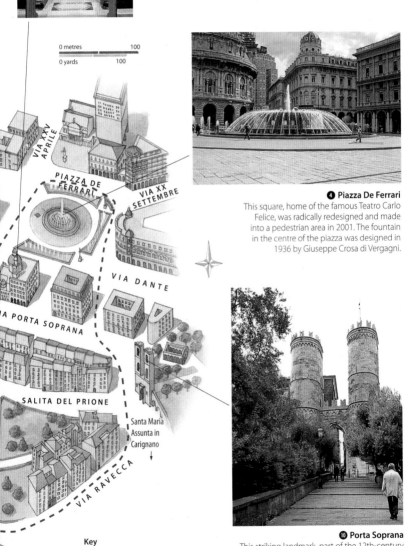

❹ Piazza De Ferrari

This square, home of the famous Teatro Carlo Felice, was radically redesigned and made into a pedestrian area in 2001. The fountain in the centre of the piazza was designed in 1936 by Giuseppe Crosa di Vergagni.

❿ Porta Soprana

This striking landmark, part of the 12th-century city walls, today marks the boundary between the Centro Storico and the modern city. Nearby is the Casa di Colombo *(see p60)*.

Key

— Recommended route

❶ San Lorenzo

The church of San Lorenzo (St Lawrence) was founded in the ninth century and was chosen as the cathedral because of its secure position within the city walls. Romanesque-style reconstruction began in the 12th century but was never completed. The cathedral's present, primarily Gothic appearance, including the lower part of the cheerfully striped façade, dates from the 13th century. Important alterations followed later, however, mainly in the 15th to 17th centuries: these include the rose window in the upper part of the façade, the Renaissance cupola by Galeazzo Alessi and the beautifully frescoed Lercari chapel. The symbol of St Lawrence (Genoa's patron saint, along with St John the Baptist) is the purse, a fact that prompts much teasing of the Genoese, who are famous for being frugal with money.

★ **Sculptures at Main Entrance**
Sculptures on medieval church doors introduced the faithful to important doctrinal subjects. Here, fine Romanesque bas-reliefs illustrate Stories from the life of Mary and the Tree of Jesse, on the jambs; and Christ blessing, the symbols of the Evangelists and the Martyrdom of San Lorenzo, in the lunette.

KEY

① **Marble pillars**

② **The rose window** was redone in 1869; of the original, from 1476, the symbols of the four Evangelists remain.

③ **The bell tower** was created from the right-hand tower in the 16th century.

④ **Dome by Galeazzo Alessi (1556)**

⑤ **The vault of the presbytery** and the apse bears two frescoes by Lazzaro Tavarone (*San Lorenzo and the Church treasury, Martyrdom of the Saint*, 1622–4); in the apse is a lovely 16th-century wooden choir.

⑥ **In the right-hand apse**, in the Senarega chapel, is a *Crucifix with Mary, John and St Sebastian* by Federico Barocci (1597).

⑦ **Romanesque blind arches**

⑧ **Black and white striped arches**

The Lions
Two 19th-century lion sculptures flank the main steps. A pair of Romanesque lions can also be seen on the edges of the façade.

★ Cappella di San Giovanni Battista

This chapel, dedicated to St John the Baptist, was the work of Domenico and Elia Gagini (mid-1400s). It is richly decorated with marble and topped with flamboyant Gothic detailing. Reliefs on the front of the chapel illustrate the life of the Baptist. Inside, are six wall niches with statues and the stone reliquary that once held the supposed ashes of the saint *(see below)*.

★ Museo del Tesoro

Opened in the 1950s, this unusual museum was the work of Caterina Marcenaro and Franco Albini, and is one of the most elegant of its kind. Built underground near the chancel, the wonderfully atmospheric museum is covered in Promontorio stone, the dark construction material typical of medieval Genoa. Within this charming framework, picked out by spotlights, are displayed objects brought back during the Republic's forays into the Holy Land. Among the highlights are the Sacro Catino, a 9th-century Islamic glass vessel, once believed to be the Holy Grail, used by Christ at the Last Supper; the Croce degli Zaccaria, a 12th-century Byzantine reliquary made of gold and gemstones; the cope of Pope Gelasio, in brocade fabric with gold and silver thread (15th century); and the elaborately embossed silver chest (12th century), which contains the supposed ashes of St John the Baptist, and which is carried in procession through the streets of Genoa on 24 June.

La Croce degli
Zaccaria

❷ Palazzo Ducale

Piazza Matteotti 9. **Map** 5 C3.
Tel 010 557 40 00. Exhibitions: **Open**
9am–7pm Tue–Sun. Shops: **Open**
daily. 🔲 palazzoducale.genova.it

This palazzo, constructed during the course of the Middle Ages, was given its name (meaning Doge's Palace) in 1339, when the election of Genoa's first doge, Simon Boccanegra, took place here. It was enlarged to its current size in the late 1500s by Andrea Vannone, a Lombard architect. Further major changes, the work of Neo-Classical architect Simone Cantoni, were made in the late 18th century following a fire. These included the erection of the façade overlooking Piazza Matteotti (another lively, frescoed façade faces Piazza De Ferrari), which features pairs of columns and is topped by statues and trophies.

Door knocker in the shape of a triton, Palazzo Ducale

The palazzo is organized around Vannone's attractive atrium, with a large, elegant, porticoed courtyard at either end. The staircases up to the first floor are lined with frescoes by Lazzaro Tavarone and Domenico Fiasella.

On the upper floor some of the public rooms are very fine: the **doges' chapel** was frescoed by Giovanni Battista Carlone

(1655) with scenes celebrating the glorious history of the city of Genoa; this theme continues in the decoration of the **Sala del Maggior Consiglio** and the **Sala del Minor Consiglio**. The **Salone**, designed by Simone Cantoni, features paintings by Giovanni David (c.1780), among others. Since extensive restoration in 1992, the palace has become a venue for major exhibitions. In addition, there are shops, bars and restaurants (including an expensive rooftop restaurant with panoramic views).

❸ Il Gesù (or Sant'Ambrogio)

Via Francesco Petrarca 1. **Map** 5 C4.
Tel 010 542 189. **Open** 10:30am–
noon, 4–7pm daily (9:30pm Sun).
📷 without permission.

This church, overlooking Piazza Matteotti, was built by the Jesuits. It was begun in 1589, over the existing church of Sant'Ambrogio, and given the name of il Gesù. The façade, following the original design by Giuseppe Valeriani, was finished only at the end of the 19th century.

The sumptuous Baroque interior consists of a single room topped by a dome. Multi-coloured marble decorates

St Ignatius Exorcising the Devil, by Rubens, Il Gesù

the floor, the pilasters and the walls of the side chapels. The upper parts of the walls have been finished with gilded stuccoes and frescoes by the artist Giovanni Battista Carlone (17th century).

The most valuable paintings in the church all date from the 17th century, including works by Guido Reni and a *Crucifixion* by Simon Vouet.

There are also works that were commissioned by the Pallavicino family from Peter Paul Rubens: a *Circumcision* (1605) and *St Ignatius Exorcising the Devil* (before 1620), both acknowledged masterpieces and precursors of the typical Baroque style.

❹ Piazza De Ferrari

Map 6 D4.

This piazza, with its large fountain, was created in the late 19th century with the aim of easing the flow of traffic between the Centro Storico and the western side of Genoa. Its design had to accommodate the existing buildings of the Accademia Ligustica di Belle Arti and the Teatro Carlo Felice, both built by Carlo Barabino in the 1820s. The new palazzi built around these two are eclectic in style.

The building of the theatre in 1991, the restoration of the fountain and other alterations,

One of the spacious interior courtyards of Palazzo Ducale

including those of 2001, have given the Piazza De Ferrari a major facelift.

❺ Accademia Ligustica di Belle Arti

Largo Pertini 4. **Map** 6 D3. **Tel** 010 581 957. **Open** 2:30–6:30pm Tue–Fri. 📷 by appt. 🅿 📷 without permission. 🆆 **accademialigustica.it**

Founded in 1751 by a group of aristocrats and scholars as a School of Fine Arts *(belle arti)*, the Accademia occupies a palazzo built for it in 1826–31 by Carlo Barabino. The museum on the first floor is home to paintings and drawings donated to the academy. Works of art from the 15th to 19th centuries are arranged chronologically: they include works by major Ligurian artists (Gregorio De Ferrari and Bernardo Strozzi among others) and artists who were active in Genoa (such as Perin del Vaga and Anton Raphael Mengs).

Polyptych of St Erasmus **by Perin del Vaga**

❻ Teatro Carlo Felice

Passo Eugenio Montale 4. **Map** 6 D3. **Tel** 010 538 11, ticket office 010 589 329 or 010 591 697. **Open** for performances. 📷 Mon, by appt. 📷 🆆 **carlofelice.it**

The Neo-Classical theatre designed in the 1820s by Carlo Barabino was virtually gutted by bombing in 1944, and only parts of the original façade survived. These give way to

The ultra-modern stage at the Teatro Carlo Felice

the modern part of the Teatro Carlo Felice, designed by Ignazio Gardella, Aldo Rossi and Fabio Reinhart in 1991. The theatre is dominated by a huge square tower pierced by small windows. Four sections of stage area are manoeuvred by a complex, state-of-the-art computerized system, making the theatre one of the most innovative in Europe.

❼ Santo Stefano

Piazza Santo Stefano 2. **Map** 6 E4. **Tel** 010 587 183. **Open** 3:30–6:30pm Tue–Sun (Sun am only in Aug).

Built at the end of the 12th century, the Romanesque church of Santo Stefano stands on the site of a Benedictine abbey. The church underwent major restoration after being damaged in World War II.

The façade features bands of black and white striped marble, typical of Pisan and Ligurian Romanesque, with a main door surmounted by an oculus and a mullioned window. The brick-built apse is particularly lovely, ornamented by blind arches with arcading above. The bell tower and the 14th-century lantern are also constructed in decorative brick.

Inside, in the presbytery, are a *Martyrdom of St Stephen,* a fine work by Giulio Romano (1524), and paintings by various Genoese and Lombard artists, among them Valerio Castello, Gregorio De Ferrari and Giulio Cesare Procaccini.

❽ Museo Civico di Storia Naturale Giacomo Doria

Via Brigata Liguria 9. **Map** 6 F5. **Tel** 010 564 567. **Open** 9am–7pm Tue–Fri, 10am–7pm Sat & Sun. 📷 📷 📷 by appt. 🆆 **museodoria.it**

Established in 1867 by Marchese Giacomo Doria, its director for more than 40 years, Genoa's Natural History Museum contains important zoological finds, many collected in the 19th century.

On the ground floor there are the rooms devoted to mammals and a series of reconstructed animal habitats.

A definite must-see is the Palaeontology Room, with its skeleton of *Elephus antiquus italicus*, an ancient elephant found near Rome in 1941. On the first floor are displays of reptiles, amphibians, birds, butterflies and insects.

The museum does a lot of educational work and has a full calendar of conferences and exhibitions.

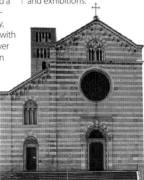

Santo Stefano, with its classic combination of black and white marble

❾ Basilica di Santa Maria Assunta in Carignano

Piazza di Carignano. **Map** 3 A4.
Tel 010 540 650. **Open** 7:30–11am,
4:30–6:30pm daily.

This fine Renaissance church, one of the city's most prominent landmarks, was designed for the hill closest to the centre of the city by Galeazzo Alessi, the great Perugian architect. Begun in 1549, it took 50 years to complete.

A monumental flight of steps, designed by Alessi but built in the 19th century, leads up to the broad façade, flanked by two elegant bell towers. Rising above is a high central cupola surrounded by four smaller domes.

The elaborate sculptural decoration on the façade, the work of Claude David (18th century), includes a statue of the Virgin Mary over the door and statues of saints Peter and Paul in the side niches. A balcony runs along the roofs and around the central dome, making the most of the church's wonderfully panoramic position.

Inside, the harmonious exterior motif of pilasters with Corinthian capitals continues. As in St Peter's in Rome, the four vast pilasters that support the cupola have niches containing statues: these include *St Sebastian* by Pierre Puget (1620–94). On the second altar on the right is a *Martyrdom of St Blaise* by Carlo Maratta (1625–1713), and in the sixth on the left a famous *Pietà* (c.1571) by Luca Cambiaso. Other paintings, some of which have been adapted to fit the church's particular setting, are by Domenico Fiasella and Guercino. The organ, dating from 1656, is remarkable.

The two majestic towers of Porta Soprana

Statue of the Virgin Mary in Santa Maria in Carignano

❿ Porta Soprana (or di Sant'Andrea)

Via Di Ravecca 47 nero. **Map** 6 D4.
Tel 010 246 53 46. **Open** 10am–6pm
Sat, Sun & hols. 📷 weekdays
only, groups only, by appt.
🚫 without permission.

This gate corresponds to an opening made in the walls in the 9th century to connect Genoa to the east; the actual structure, however, was part of a ring of walls built in 1155 to defend Genoa from possible attack by Emperor Frederick I, known as Barbarossa *(see p91)*. It is similar to the Porta di Santa Fede, on the other side of the city. Restoration carried out in the 19th and 20th centuries has liberated the historic gate of the structures added to it over the centuries, and exposed the pointed arch flanked by a pair of imposing cylindrical battle-mented towers. These are ornamented by delicate arcading and cornicing.

⓫ Casa di Colombo

Piazza Dante. **Map** 6 D4.
Tel 010 246 53 46. **Open** 10am–6pm
Sat, Sun & hols.

Tradition has it that this modest house near Porta Soprana was the childhood home of Christopher Columbus, the world-famous navigator who was born in Genoa in 1451.

The house that visitors can tour today is, in fact, an 18th-century reconstruction: the original house was destroyed by cannon fire during a French bombardment in 1684. Restoration carried out on the building in preparation for

The supposed birthplace of famous explorer Christopher Colombus

the Columbus celebrations of 1992 extended to the adjacent 12th-century **Chiostro di Sant'Andrea** (cloister of St Andrew), all that is left of a Benedictine monastery that was demolished at the beginning of the 20th century, along with many of the other buildings in the area.

⑫ Museo di Sant'Agostino

Piazza Sarzano 35 rosso. **Map** 5 C5. **Tel** 010 251 12 63. **Open** 9am–7pm Tue–Fri, 10am–7pm Sat & Sun. 🖾 🖾 🕭 🖾 museidigenova.it

This 13th-century monastic church was a lucky survivor of World War II bombing, which badly damaged Piazza Sarzano. The façade, with its black and white stripes, is typically Ligurian, while the elegant bell tower is coated with colourful majolica tiles. While the church functions now as an auditorium, the

Funeral monument of Margaret of Brabant

former Augustinian monastery buildings that are adjacent – including the two cloisters (a triangular one, dating from the 14th and 15th centuries, and a rectangular, 18th-century one) – have been skilfully adapted to house the **Museum**. The focus of the collection are the sculptures brought here from sites (including demolished churches) all over the city, but there are also detached frescoes, architectural fragments and examples of Genoese art from the Middle Ages to the 18th century.

There are two particularly important sculptures in the collection. One of these is the remains of the funerary monument of Margaret of Brabant, sculpted in honour of the wife of emperor Henry VII, who died in 1311 while visiting Genoa. The work was sculpted in Pisa in 1313–14 by Giovanni Pisano, one of the most famous sculptors in Italy at that time. The other is a particularly

moving *Penitent Madonna*, by Antonio Canova (1796).

⑬ San Donato

Piazzetta San Donato 10. **Map** 5 C4. **Tel** 010 246 88 69. **Open** 8am–noon, 3–7pm Mon–Sat, 9am–12:30pm, 3–7pm Sun. **Closed** 16–31 Aug. 🖾

The church of San Donato, built during the 12th century, is one of the best examples of Romanesque architecture in Genoa.

The building's most striking and interesting feature, which is characteristic of early Romanesque architecture, is the splendid octagonal bell tower, erected over the church crossing; its three levels (the third is a 19th-century addition) are each pierced by windows. The tower was chosen as a model by the designers of the north tower of San Benigno, the so-called "Matitone" (great pencil) in the Porto Antico *(see pp64–5)*.

The façade carries some noticeable features dating from late 19th-century alterations, when the rose window was added, but the main doorway is original and of particular beauty; it incorporates a Roman architrave in the moulding.

The tall, striking bell tower of San Donato

On the right-hand side of the church, look out for a shrine with a statue of the *Madonna and Child* (18th century); it is one of many erected in the Centro Storico.

The charming interior has a nave and two aisles, with Corinthian columns and a gallery of windows above; some of the columns are Roman.

A *Madonna and Child* (1401) by Nicolò da Voltri is on the altar in the right-hand apse and, in the chapel of San Giuseppe in the left-hand aisle, there is a beautiful panelled triptych by the Flemish painter Joos van Cleve; this depicts an *Adoration of the Magi* (c.1515) in the central panel.

Contemporary Art at Villa Croce

Villa Croce, surrounded by palms

Via Jacopo Ruffini 3. **Tel** 010 580 069. **Open** 9am–1pm Tue–Fri, 10am–1pm Sat; temporary exhibitions: 9am–6:30pm Tue–Fri, 10am–6:30pm Sat & Sun. 🖾 🖾 (free on Sun). 🖾 🖾 🖾 museidigenova.it

The Museo d'Arte Contemporanea, in the residential district of Carignano, south of the city centre, is surrounded by a large park overlooking the sea. It occupies a lovely, late 19th-century classical-style villa, which was donated to the city by the Croce family in 1951. The museum currently possesses some 3,000 works, which document in particular Italian graphic arts and abstract art from 1930 to 1980 (including work by Fontana and Licini). There are also examples of work by young regional artists. The museum promotes young talent by collecting works, organizing exhibitions and assembling a digital archive of material related to local arts.

⑭ Santa Maria di Castello

Salita Santa Maria di Castello 15.
Map 5 B4. **Tel** 010 254 95 11. **Open**
Church & Museum: 9:30–12:30am,
3:30–6:30pm daily.

This church rises on the site of the Roman *castrum*, or fort, around which the earliest parts of the city were constructed. Among the most illustrious of old Genoese churches, it was built in the 12th century on the site of an earlier place of worship, at a time when Romanesque buildings were appearing all over the city.

In the mid-15th century the church was entrusted to the Dominicans, who added monastic buildings, including three cloisters. The latters' decoration was commissioned by the Grimaldi family (in line with the huge increase in private patronage at that time in Genoa) and turned the complex into a point of reference for artists in the city. In the centuries to come, other aristocratic families commissioned the decoration of the church's side chapels.

The stone façade is crowned by a cornice of blind arches. The central doorway incorporates a Roman architrave, and there are other Roman elements inside: several of the Corinthian capitals which adorn the red granite columns in the nave came from Roman buildings; and in the

The Loggia dell'Annunciazione, Santa Maria di Castello

Cappella del Battistero is a sarcophagus of Roman origin. The apse, the chapels and the dome are the result of changes made from the 15th to the 18th centuries. In the chapel in the left transept is a *Virgin with the saints Catherine and Mary Magdalen and the effigies of St Dominic* by il Grechetto (1616–70). The high altar has a splendid late 17th-century marble sculpture of the *Assumption*.

Among the monastic buildings, the second cloister is of special note. Here, the lower of the two loggias, the **Loggia dell'Annunciazione**, features roundels with *Sibyls* and *Prophets* (15th century) in its vault, and a charming fresco of the *Annunciation* by Justus von Ravensburg, signed and dated 1451.

There is a small **museum**, with works such as *Paradise* and *The Conversion of St Paul* by Ludovico Brea (1513); an *Immaculate Conception*, a wooden sculpture by Maragliano (18th century); and a *Madonna and Child* by Barnaba da Modena (14th century).

Next to the church stands the 12th-century **Torre degli Embriaci**, evidence of the medieval power of the aristocratic Embriaci family, who lived in this quarter.

⑮ Porto Antico

See pp64–5.

⑯ Aquarium

See pp66–7.

The frescoed façade of Palazzo San Giorgio

⑰ Palazzo San Giorgio

Via della Mercanzia 2. **Map** 5 B3.
Tel 010 241 26 25/27 54. **Open** phone to check opening hours of exhibitions, or ask at the tourist office.

This palazzo is traditionally identified as the place in which Marco Polo was imprisoned following the Battle of Curzola (between the Venetians and the Genoese) in 1298. While here, Polo met a writer from Pisa called Rustichello, with whom he joined forces after their release to write *Il Milione* ("The Travels"). The palazzo is made up of two distinct parts: a medieval part turned towards the city, which was built in 1260

Detail of the façade of Palazzo San Giorgio

as the seat of the government (the Capitani del Popolo) and later became the Banco di San Giorgio (1407); and a second part, a huge 16th-century extension built to overlook the port. The fresco decoration on the latter's façade (1606–8), by Lazzaro Tavarone, was discovered only during restoration work in the 1990s.

The expansion of the palazzo, which involved major restructuring of the medieval section (later heavily restored in the 1800s), was required because of the rise in power of the Banco di San Giorgio. The bank administered the proceeds from taxes collected by the Republic and also ran the Republic's colonies; it was, in effect, responsible for much of Genoa's prosperity in the 15th century. Today, the palace houses the offices of the harbour authorities.

Inside, the **Salone delle Compere** is decorated with 16th-century statues of the Protettori del Banco (protectors of the bank) and the *Arms of Genoa with the symbols of Justice and Strength* by Francesco De Ferrari (1490–91).

The **Sala dei Protettori** features a monumental hearth by Gian Giacomo Della Porta (1554). You can also visit the Manica Lunga, a 128-m (420-ft) long corridor which once served as a dormitory for Benedictine monks, and the Sala del Capitano del Popolo.

⑱ Piazza Banchi

Map 5 B3.

Along harbourside Piazza Caricamento, flanked on one side by Palazzo San Giorgio, runs **Via Sottoripa**. Dating from the 12th century, this charming arcaded street was designed so that its shops could make the most of their proximity to the buzzing port area. Today, as it did in the past, the street houses various specialist foods shops, and there are snack bars, too.

From here, Via al Ponte Reale leads to **Piazza Banchi**, the commercial core of the city up until the 18th century, and a crucial crossroads of major lines of communication between the city and the port. By the Middle Ages there was already a thriving grain market in the piazza, and money-changers also set up their stalls here, attracting merchants from all over the world; the piazza is named after the money-changers' tables. Later, money-changers and other traders did business in the 16th-century **Loggia dei Mercanti**.

The church of **San Pietro in Banchi**, founded in the 9th century, was destroyed by a fire which damaged the square in 1398, but rebuilding work didn't begin until the 16th century. The project was managed by Bernardino Cantone, who used a form of self-financing which involved the construction and the subsequent sale of several shops at ground level. As a result, the church is raised up on a terrace and is reached by means of a scenic flight of steps. It has a central plan with an octagonal dome with three pinnacles (four were originally planned). The façade bears frescoes by Giovanni Battista Baiardo (c.1650), which were restored in the 1990s.

The Loggia dei Mercanti, with stalls in front, in Piazza Banchi

⑲ Loggia dei Mercanti

Piazza Banchi. **Map** 5 B3. **Open** for exhibitions; contact the tourist office for details.

This elegant Renaissance loggia was built in Piazza Banchi in the late 16th century, to a design by Andrea Vannone, in order to accommodate the work of the city's money-changers. The loggia was a typical element of buildings intended for commerce during the Middle Ages, and there are many examples in the old city.

The loggia in Piazza Banchi is built on a rectangular plan and has a single barrel vault supported by arches resting on paired columns; its openings were glassed in during the 19th century. The exterior features a sculptured frieze (16th century) by Taddeo Carlone, and the interior a fresco of the *Madonna and Child and saints John the Baptist and George* by Pietro Sorri (1556–1621).

In 1855, the loggia became the seat of the first trade Stock Exchange in Italy; it is now used as a site for exhibitions.

Piazza Banchi, overlooked by San Pietro in Banchi

⑮ Porto Antico

The old port was the obvious venue for the staging of the Columbus celebrations of 1992, and these provided a perfect opportunity to restore the link between the port, for centuries detached from the rest of the city, with the Centro Storico. This project was undertaken by local architect Renzo Piano, who also transformed the district into an attraction in its own right, by restoring disused buildings such as the 19th-century cotton warehouses – now a multiplex cinema and exhibition centre – and by constructing landmarks such as Bigo and the Aquarium, the design of which includes maritime motifs, emphasizing the history of this district.

Porta del Molo
Also known as Porta Siberia, this gate was built in 1553 by Galeazzo Alessi. It was designed as a defensive bulwark for the port and as a place for the collection of taxes.

★ Il Bigo
Inspired by the masts of a ship and designed by Renzo Piano, the Bigo features a revolving panoramic lift. From a height of 40 m (130 ft), this offers great views over the port and city.

KEY

① **Museo Nazionale dell'Antartide Felice Ippolito** is housed in the restored Millo building (1876). This museum features faithful re-creations of polar animal habitats and also scale models of the Italian base in Antarctica (Baia Terra Nova).

② **Boat trips** are the only way to reach certain areas otherwise closed to visitors. From the quays of Porto Antico, boats offer guided tours lasting around 45 minutes. The bustle and activity of the port are fascinating and there is a breathtaking panorama of the city from the sea.

③ **La Città dei Bambini** is the foremost educational/entertainment centre in Italy, aimed at children. The high-tech hands-on "play and learn" park includes two different routes, aimed at 3–5-year-olds and 6–14-year-olds.

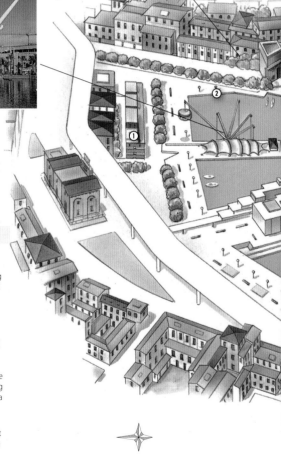

0 metres		100
0 yards		100

Biosfera by Renzo Piano
Built in 2001, the Biosphere is a futuristic glasshouse containing all sorts of tropical plants, from mangroves to rubber and cocoa trees, as well as numerous types of ferns, some of which are extremely rare. There are butterflies and chameleons, too.

★ **Aquarium**
Another work by Renzo Piano, the Aquarium is the largest of its kind in Europe and attracts over one million visitors a year (see pp66–7).

La Lanterna

This is the symbol of Genoa, and the oldest working lighthouse in the world. The original lighthouse, dating from the 12th century, was destroyed by Louis XIII's French army. It was rebuilt in its current form, with two superimposed towers, in 1543, and its beam has a reach of 52 km (33 miles). There is a superb view from the top, if you can bear the 375 steps, and in 2006, the Museo della Lanterna opened in the adjacent fortifications.

⑯ Aquarium (Acquario)

The work of internationally renowned architect Renzo Piano (co-designer of the Pompidou Centre in Paris), with technical help from American architect Peter Chermayeff, the Aquarium is built within a ship anchored in the port. It is one of Europe's largest aquariums, with numerous tanks that are viewable from underwater level as well as from above. The aim is to help visitors to discover and marvel at different aspects of the sea and to promote understanding of the extent to which human life is linked to the oceans. There are spectacular reconstructions of diverse ecosystems on the planet, making it possible to observe animals, habitats and ocean floors at close quarters.

★ Hummingbird Forest
This area re-creates the luxuriant rainforest habitat of the smallest birds in the world. The hummingbird's signature features are its iridescent feathers, long bill and powerful wing-speed.

A Coral Reef in Madagascar
This colourful zone is testimony to how coral reefs make a rich and desirable habitat for countless species of fish, from moray eels to angel fish (seen here).

KEY

① Red Sea Tank

② **The Forest of Madagascar** reconstructs a tropical forest habitat of this island off the east coast of Africa. A paradise for naturalists, Madagascar teems with unusual plant and animal species. A terrarium nearby holds tortoises, turtles and iguanas native to the island.

③ **La Grande Nave Blu (Great Blue Ship)** is a real ship, acquired by the Aquarium in 1998. There are more than 20 tanks in around 2,500 sq m (27,000 sq ft) of exhibition space.

④ Level 2

⑤ Auditorium (3D films)

⑥ Cloakroom

⑦ Reception

⑧ Entrance on Level 1

★ Tactile Tank
One of the most popular attractions, this tank allows people to gently touch skate, gurnard and stingrays. The fish confidently approach the hands held out to stroke them.

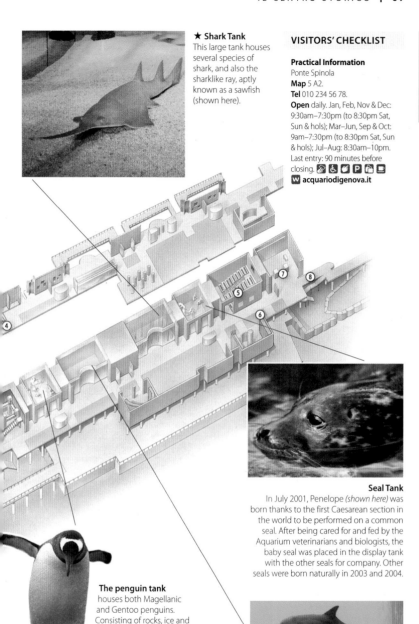

★ **Shark Tank**
This large tank houses several species of shark, and also the sharklike ray, aptly known as a sawfish (shown here).

Seal Tank
In July 2001, Penelope *(shown here)* was born thanks to the first Caesarean section in the world to be performed on a common seal. After being cared for and fed by the Aquarium veterinarians and biologists, the baby seal was placed in the display tank with the other seals for company. Other seals were born naturally in 2003 and 2004.

The penguin tank
houses both Magellanic and Gentoo penguins. Consisting of rocks, ice and water, the tank is visible from two levels, enabling the public to observe the penguins on the rocks as well as underwater.

Dolphin Tank
The resident dolphin Beta acquired two new companions in June 2006. Linda and Mateo are mother and son and used to live at the dolphinarium in Bruges, Belgium. These playful creatures are best admired during feeding time.

One of the sumptuous rooms in Palazzo Spinola di Pellicceria

⑳ Palazzo Spinola di Pellicceria

Piazza Pellicceria 1. **Map** 5 B2. **Tel** 010 270 53 00. **Open** 8:30am–7:30pm Tue–Sat, 1:30–7:30pm Sun & public hols. **Closed** 1 Jan, 1 Aug, 25 Dec. 📷 combined ticket for Palazzo Spinola & Palazzo Reale. 🎫 by appt. ♿ up to the 3rd floor. 📷 without permission. 📷 🌐 palazzospinola.it

With all the elegance and fascination of an old aristocratic mansion house, Palazzo Spinola is richly frescoed and has sumptuous furnishings and paintings. Built in the 16th century by the Grimaldi family, the palazzo passed to the Spinola family in the 18th century, and they eventually donated it to the state in 1958.

The first two floors house the **Galleria Nazionale di Palazzo Spinola**, in a manner that is sensitive both to the building and to the art collection. The rooms have been restored to their original style, with paintings arranged as if this were still a private home. Two important fresco cycles illustrate the two main phases in the history of the palazzo. One, by Lazzaro Tavarone, illustrates in two rooms *Exploits and Personalities in the Grimaldi family* (1614–24), while the

other decorates the Galleria degli Specchi (hall of mirrors) and salons, the work of Lorenzo De Ferrari for the Spinola family (1730–37). The Spinola donation includes works by Guido Reni, Anthony van Dyck and il Grechetto.

The **Galleria Nazionale della Liguria**, on the third floor, is reserved for works which were not part of the Spinola donation. These include fine works such as Antonello da Messina's *Ecce Homo* (c.1474), *an Equestrian Portrait of Gio Carlo Doria* (1606) by Rubens, and *Justice*, sculpted by Giovanni Pisano for the funerary monument of Margaret of Brabant *(see p61)*.

Ecce Homo by Antonello da Messina, Palazzo Spinola di Pellicceria

㉑ Santa Maria delle Vigne

Vicolo del Campanile delle Vigne 5. **Map** 5 C3. **Tel** 010 247 47 61. **Open** 8am–noon, 3:30–6:30pm daily. ♿ 🌐 basilicadellevigne.it

The area now occupied by the Piazza delle Vigne was planted with vines *(vigne)* in around the year 1000, but was later engulfed by the expanding city. The church of Santa Maria was founded in the same era, though the only Romanesque element to have survived is the bell tower. The church was otherwise completely rebuilt in Baroque style in around 1640, after the area around the apse had already been reconstructed in the 16th century at the behest of the local Grillo family. Further changes have been made since. The façade (1842) is the work of Ippolito Cremona.

The interior, with a nave and two aisles divided by broad arcades, is bathed in sumptuous gilding, stucco and fresco decoration, dating from different periods. The presbytery was frescoed in 1612 by Lazzaro Tavarone, with a *Glory of Mary*; the aisles and the octagonal cupola were painted by various artists from the 18th century

Slate ornamental panel showing St George and the Dragon

Door Carvings

A recurrent sight in the Centro Storico are the doorways featuring carvings sculpted from marble or the characteristic black stone of Promontorio (from the Lavagna area). These panels were the product of economic necessity and the scarcity of building space: in the 15th century, noble families were obliged to extend the use of the ground floors of their palazzi in order to accommodate shops, and they therefore wanted to create handsome new doorways that would make their own residences stand out. Famous sculptors (in particular, members of the Gagini family) developed this craft, often producing work of great skill. Among the most common subjects were the triumphs of the commissioning family or holy scenes such as St George killing the dragon. There are some examples in the Museo di Sant'Agostino.

One of the Doria palazzi in Piazza San Matteo

according to the wishes of the civic senate, was given to the admiral in 1528.

The small church of **San Matteo**, the family place of worship of the Dorias, built in 1125, was rebuilt in the late 13th century in Gothic style. Pilasters divide the black- and-white striped façade into three, corresponding to the aisles. The interior was altered in the 16th century for Andrea Doria, who is buried in the crypt, as is his ancestor Lamba Doria. Giovan Battista Castello, known as il Bergamasco, modified the nave and aisles and painted the nave vault (1557–9), a collaboration with Luca Cambiaso. The statues in the apse niches and the decoration of the presbytery and the cupola (1543–7) are by Angelo Montorsoli.

To the left of the church is a pretty cloister (1308), with pointed arches resting on slim paired columns.

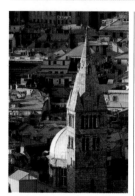

The Romanesque bell tower of Santa Maria delle Vigne

to the early 20th century. The church contains paintings by Gregorio De Ferrari, Bernardo Castello and Domenico Piola and a tablet depicting a *Madonna*, attributed to Taddeo di Bartolo (late 14th century).

㉒ Piazza San Matteo

Map 5 C3. Chiesa di San Matteo: **Tel** 010 247 43 61. **Open** 8am–noon, 4–5pm Mon–Fri, 9:30–10:30am, 4–5pm Sat & Sun. 🅿 donations. ♿ 📷 allowed inside.

From the 12th to the 17th centuries this lovely square was the headquarters of the powerful Doria family, which, in common with the other

powerful Genoese dynasties, gathered its political clique in a distinct area of the city. Despite changes to the palazzi facing the square, the piazza has kept its original compact form and a distinct charm, missing from other similar areas.

The buildings bear typical wall coverings of striped black and white marble, characteristic of Gothic civic buildings. Of particular note is **Palazzo di Lamba Doria**, at no. 15, named after the family member who defeated the Venetian fleet at Curzola in 1298; the typical structure of a medieval Genoese palazzo is still in evidence. Also noteworthy is **Palazzo di Andrea Doria**, at no. 17, which,

The 14th-century cloister attached to the church of San Matteo

LE STRADE NUOVE

Walking around the district known as Le Strade Nuove (or "new streets") – along Via Balbi and Via Garibaldi in particular – you are drawn back to the era of the 16th and 17th centuries, when Genoa dominated much of Europe in the field of finance. The "Genoese Century", or golden age, lasted from 1528 to 1630, when the power of several families was at its height. They poured their legendary wealth into new buildings and art commissions. The Centro Storico was not touched since they preferred to build anew – and magnificently – alongside,

adapting Renaissance designs to the uneven terrain. The artist Rubens held the palazzi on Via Garibaldi in such high esteem that he made detailed drawings for a 1622 publication. The palazzi typically have loggias and hanging gardens, designed to disguise the steep slopes, and are the work of several architects; foremost among them Galeazzo Alessi. He found an ideal model in the Palazzo Doria Pamphilj (built in 1529 for Andrea Doria), which continued to inspire the palaces built for the Balbi family in the 17th century.

Sights at a Glance

Historic Buildings
⑨ Albergo dei Poveri

Historic Streets and Squares
① Piazza Fontane Marose
③ Via Garibaldi
⑩ Via Balbi

Museums and Galleries
② Museo di Arte Orientale Edoardo Chiossone
⑤ *Palazzo Rosso pp76–9*
⑥ Galleria di Palazzo Bianco
⑭ Galata Museo del Mare

Palazzi
④ Palazzo Doria Tursi
⑪ Palazzo dell'Università
⑫ Palazzo Reale
⑮ Palazzo Doria Pamphilj or del Principe

Churches
⑬ San Giovanni di Pré and La Commenda
⑦ San Siro
⑧ Santissima Annunziata del Vastato

See also Street Finder, maps 2, 5 & 6

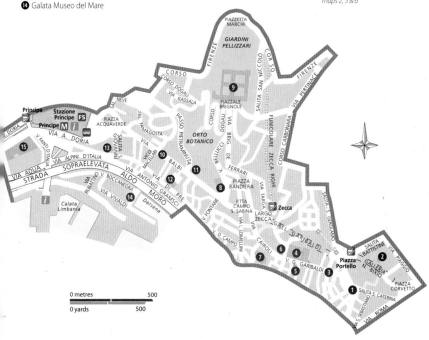

◀ Stunning interiors of the Santissima Annunziata del Vastato

For map symbols *see back flap*

Street-by-Street: Around Via Garibaldi

When Via Garibaldi was laid out in the mid-16th century, it was the first of the "new streets", and was known as La Strada Nuova. The mansions lining the street are wonderfully preserved, with sumptuous interiors, and often contain exceptional decoration or fine art collections, the fruits of shrewd collecting. Among the palazzi open to the public are Palazzo Doria Tursi (the largest in the street), which still serves as the town hall, and Palazzo Bianco and Palazzo Rosso, which house the Musei di Strada Nuova, the city's largest art gallery. Not far away is the church of San Siro, richly decorated in the 16th and 17th centuries and the first cathedral of Genoa.

Beyond Piazza Fontane Marose, the attractive square at one end of Via Garibaldi, is the Edoardo Chiossone museum *(see p74)*, a rare collection of oriental art that was assembled in the 19th century.

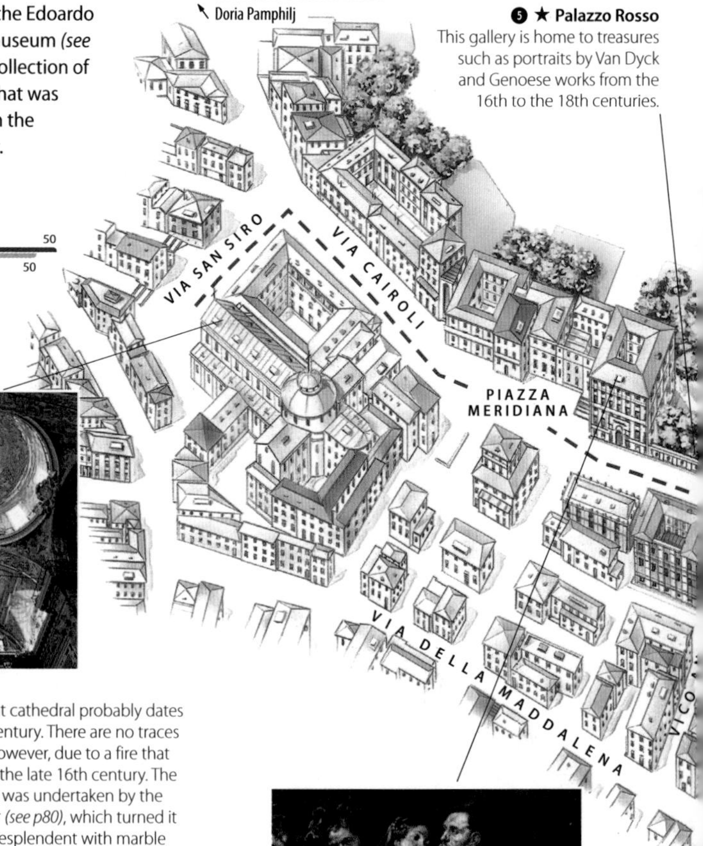

Santissima Annunziata del Vastato, Palazzo Reale, Palazzo Doria Pamphilj

❺ ★ Palazzo Rosso
This gallery is home to treasures such as portraits by Van Dyck and Genoese works from the 16th to the 18th centuries.

0 metres 50
0 yards 50

VIA SAN SIRO

VIA CAIROLI

PIAZZA MERIDIANA

VIA DELLA MADDALENA

VICO

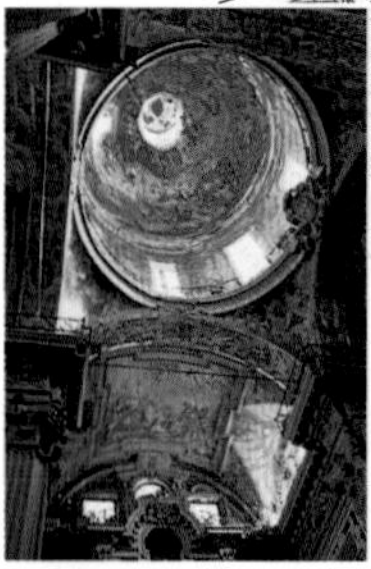

❼ San Siro
Genoa's ancient cathedral probably dates from the 4th century. There are no traces of its origins, however, due to a fire that destroyed it in the late 16th century. The reconstruction was undertaken by the Theatine Order *(see p80)*, which turned it into a temple resplendent with marble inlay and frescoes.

❻ ★ Palazzo Bianco
This gallery houses 13th–18th-century European paintings. The collection includes a large number of Genoese works, as well as some important Spanish, French and Flemish paintings, such as *Venus and Mars* by Rubens, shown here.

❹ Palazzo Doria Tursi
Three times the length of the other mansions in via Garibaldi, this 16th-century palazzo has an exquisite courtyard, with a double staircase leading up to an arcaded loggia.

❸ Via Garibaldi
Now pedestrianized, this street transports you back to the golden age of the Genoese aristocracy in the 16th and 17th centuries. The monumental façades loom high above you as you walk beneath.

Palazzo Podestà was begun in 1563. The façade is a delightful example of Genoese Mannerism.

Palazzo Doria has a lovely Baroque façade dating from 1563–67.

Key

— Suggested route

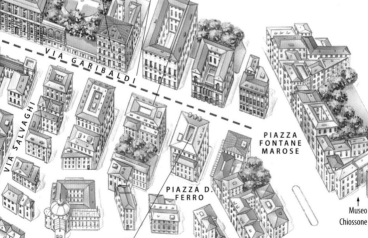

VIA GARIBALDI

VIA SALVAGHI

PIAZZA
FONTANE
MAROSE

PIAZZA D.
FERRO

Museo
Chiossone

Palazzo Carrega Cataldi
now houses the Chamber of Commerce.

❶ Piazza Fontane Marose

Map 6 D2.

This square owes its name to an ancient fountain *(fonte)*, which was recorded in a 13th-century document but destroyed in the 19th century. The piazza is attractive and free of traffic, but has an "assembled" look, the result of numerous changes in the layout and of the variations in street level.

Among the palazzi facing onto the square, the main one, at no. 6, is **Palazzo Spinola "dei Marmi"**, built in the mid-15th century and so-called because of its typically elegant covering of black and white striped marble *(marmo)*. The palazzo's design had to adapt to the extremely uneven terrain and pre-dates the building of the palazzi in Via Garibaldi.

The only building in the piazza contemporaneous with the buildings on Via Garibaldi is **Palazzo Interiano Pallavicini** (no. 2), which was constructed in 1565 by Francesco Casella.

Colour woodblock print, early 19th century, Museo Chiossone

❸ Museo di Arte Orientale Edoardo Chiossone

Villetta Di Negro, Piazzale Mazzini 4.
Map 6 D2. **Tel** 010 542 285.
Open 9am–7pm Tue–Fri, 10am–7pm Sat & Sun. **Closed** public hols. 🅿 🅰 ground floor. 🅦 **museidigenova.it**

Genoa's Museum of Oriental Art is set within the **Parco della Villetta Di Negro**, which was designed as a garden of acclimatization for exotic plants by the nobleman Ippolito Durazzo at the beginning of the 19th century. The gardens are still planted with the original mix of Mediterranean and exotic plants. The museum is housed in the villa at the top of the park that was built in 1971, as a replacement for an earlier villa, which was destroyed during World War II.

Sculpture at the Museo Edoardo Chiossone

What is one of Europe's foremost collections of oriental art is named after Edoardo Chiossone (1833–98), a Genoese painter and engraver who, from 1875–98, ran the Printing Bureau of the Ministry of Finance in Tokyo, designing banknotes for the Japanese government. He also became a respected portrait painter at the Japanese court, as well as an avid collector of oriental art.

Edoardo Chiossone bequeathed his collection of around 15,000 pieces to Genoa's Accademia Liguistica, where he had trained. These pieces, some of which are exceedingly rare, even in the Far East, include paintings, prints, lacquerware, enamels, sculptures, ceramics, textiles, and an exceptional collection of Samurai armour. Specific works include a *Seated Buddha*, a lacquered wood Japanese sculpture, from the Kamakura period; and Ukiyoe paintings, a genre which flourished in Japan from the middle of the 17th century, including works by the masters Harunobu, Shunsho and Utamaro.

The entrance to Palazzo Lercari Parodi on Via Garibaldi

❾ Via Garibaldi

Map 5 C2.

The French writer Madame de Staël (1766–1817) was so struck by the magnificence of this street that she called it *Rue des Rois* (street of kings). For the Genoese it was simply "la Strada Nuova delli Palazzi" (the new street of mansions). Its construction resulted from the creation of an oligarchy by the Genoese admiral Andrea Doria, supported by a few wealthy families devoted to lucrative commercial and financial activity. In the mid-16th century, these families abandoned the old town, where space was severely restricted, and created this handsome residential street. Designed by the treasury architect Bernardino Cantone, the palazzi were erected between 1558 and 1583. In the first section, you can see how the entrances to the palazzi run in parallel on both sides of the street, a sign of the planning involved in the layout. (The vast Palazzo Doria Tursi interrupts this symmetry.) Today, the palazzi are occupied mainly by offices, banks and museums.

At no. 1 is **Palazzo Cambiaso**, which fronts onto both Via Garibaldi and Piazza della Fontana Marose, creating a clever continuity between the two spaces. Nearby, at no. 3, is **Palazzo Lercari Parodi** (1571–8). Originally, this palazzo had loggias open to both the exterior and the interior, but today these are closed. The interior is unusual in that the rooms around the courtyard housed the servants' quarters while the public rooms were on the first floor; the opposite arrangement was more common.

At no. 4 stands **Palazzo Carrega Cataldi** (1561), by Bernardo Cantone and G. Battista Castello; its façade is a delightful fusion of frescoes and stuccowork.

At no. 7 stands lovely **Palazzo Podestà**, also built by Cantone and Castello. The façade has rich stucco decoration, echoed by an innovative interior with an oval atrium and a garden.

Genoa's coat of arms on the façade of Palazzo Doria Tursi

❹ Palazzo Doria Tursi

Via Garibaldi 9. **Map** 5 C2. **Tel** 010 557 21 93. **Open** 9am–7pm Tue–Fri, 10am–7pm Sat & Sun.

Constructed for Nicolò Grimaldi (so rich that he was nicknamed "monarca" by his fellow citizens), this enormous palazzo breaks the coherence maintained up to this point of Via Garibaldi. Constructed from 1569–79 by Domenico and Giovanni Ponzello, with the help of sculptor Taddeo Carlone, the palazzo was acquired in 1596 by the Doria family, in whose hands it remained until 1848, when it was bought by Emperor Vittorio Emanuele I and became the seat of the town council. The façade, with its imposing entrance, is distinctive for the varied colours of the stone: a mixture of white marble, local pink Finale stone and slate tiles. A high plinth unites the central section with two airy side loggias; the latter were built in the late 16th century for the Doria but they blend in so neatly with the whole façade that they may have been part of the original design.

Inside is one of the most magnificent courtyards in Genoa, with a grand staircase that splits elegantly into two after the first flight. The clock tower was added in 1820. Inside, the rooms flow harmoniously through the palazzo despite the uneven ground. Previously private rooms were opened up to the public as a museum in 2004. The highlights of the collection, which includes decorative and applied arts, coins and ceramics, are a 1742 violin owned by Nicolò Paganini, and various manuscripts relating to Christopher Columbus, including three signed letters.

❺ Palazzo Rosso

See pp76–7.

The grand interior courtyard of Palazzo Doria Tursi, with its lovely clock tower

Ecce Homo (1605) by Caravaggio in Palazzo Bianco

❻ Galleria di Palazzo Bianco

Via Garibaldi 11. **Map** 5 C2. **Tel** 010 557 21 93. **Open** 9am–7pm Tue–Fri, 10am–7pm Sat & Sun. **w** museidigenova.it

Palazzo Bianco, found at the end of Via Garibaldi, was built in the mid-16th century for the Grimaldi family. It was altered in 1714 for Maria Durazzo Brignole-Sale, who introduced a new white façade, perhaps to distinguish it from the nearby Palazzo Rosso, the first home of the Brignole family.

In 1888 the palazzo and its art collection, including collections assembled by later occupants of the palazzo, were donated to Genoa by Maria de Ferrari, Duchess of Galliera, the last descendant of the Brignole family (who also donated the Palazzo Rosso to the city).

The gallery offers an exhaustive tour of Genoese painting as well as many great European paintings from the 13th to the 18th centuries. Genoese artists represented include Luca Cambiaso, Bernardo Strozzi, Giovanni Benedetto Castiglione, known as il Grechetto, and Alessandro Magnasco, whose famous *Trattenimento in un Giardino di Albaro* (1735) is here.

There is also an important core of Flemish paintings, with works by Gérard David, Van Dyck and Rubens, as well as paintings by Murillo, Filippino Lippi, Caravaggio and Veronese.

❺ Palazzo Rosso

This palazzo, which owes its name to the reddish colour of its exterior (*rosso* means red), is the last of the sumptuous mansions on Via Garibaldi, and one of the main noble residences in Genoa. It was built by Pierantonio Corradi for the Brignole-Sale family in the 1670s, then at the height of its power; the two main floors were intended for the art collector brothers Gio Francesco and Ridolfo, and their heirs. When the Duchess di Galliera, Maria Brignole-Sale De Ferrari, gave the palace to the city in 1874 she included its rich art collection. Palazzo Rosso was damaged during World War II, but Franco Albini's restoration in the 1950s successfully recaptured the majesty of the original building. Inside, the frescoes and gilt and stucco work are as much to be admired as the art. See pp78–9 for a detailed description of the exhibits.

Ceiling frescoes by Gregorio De Ferrari in Room 28 were destroyed by bombs that fell in 1942.

★ Portraits by Van Dyck
Fine portraits of the Brignole-Sale family by Van Dyck in Room 29 include this picture of Anton Giulio, which pictures the 22-year-old frozen in a pose hitherto reserved for sovereigns, a superb affirmation of his social status.

★ Allegory of Spring by Gregorio De Ferrari
When Gregorio De Ferrari painted this allegory (1686–7) in the Sale delle Stagioni, he used the scene in which Venus seduces Mars. This masterpiece of Baroque "illusionism" was the fruit of the collaboration between De Ferrari and artists skilled in perspective and stuccowork.

Entrance

Portrait of a Young Man by Albrecht Dürer
This work, dated 1506, can be found in Room 13. It was produced during Dürer's second trip to Italy. In abandoning the traditional sideways profile, the subject is brought into more direct contact with the onlooker.

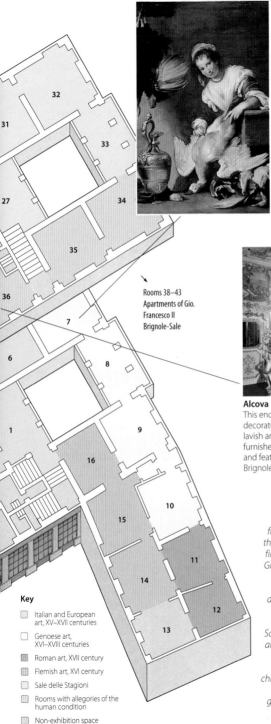

VISITORS' CHECKLIST

Practical Information
Via Garibaldi 18
Map 5 C2.
Tel 010 247 63 51.
Fax 010 247 55 57.
🅦 **museidigenova.it**
Open 9am–7pm Tue–Fri,
10am–7pm Sat & Sun.

The Cook by Bernardo Strozzi
Local artist Strozzi (1581–1644)
displays great virtuosity with his
brushwork in this canvas, inspired
by Flemish models and the
naturalism of Caravaggio (Room 7).

Alcova
This enchanting 18th-century room is
decorated with frescoes enclosed by
lavish amounts of gilt and stuccowork. It is
furnished with a large bridal bed (c.1780)
and features pastel portraits of the
Brignole-Sale family.

Rooms 38–43
Apartments of Gio.
Francesco II
Brignole-Sale

Gallery Guide
*The main artworks are distributed
between 33 rooms on the two main
floors (an additional 19 rooms are on
the mezzanine and third floor). On the
first floor are works by Guido Reni and
Guercino, as well as by Genoese artists
such as Bernardo Strozzi. On the
second floor, the magnificently
decorated rooms are a big attraction,
particularly the Sale delle Stagioni,
along with the portraits of Brignole-
Sale by Anthony Van Dyck. The gallery
also has the finest library of art history
in Liguria, as well as an education
centre that organizes activities for
children. The 2004 renovations restored
the third-floor rooms to their former
glory as the apartment of the director
of the civic museums, Caterina
Marcenaro (1906–76).*

Key

- ⬜ Italian and European
  art, XV–XVII centuries
- ⬜ Genoese art,
  XVI–XVIII centuries
- ⬛ Roman art, XVII century
- ⬛ Flemish art, XVI century
- ⬜ Sale delle Stagioni
- ⬛ Rooms with allegories of the
  human condition
- ⬛ Non-exhibition space

Exploring Palazzo Rosso

The main museum takes up two floors, and occupies rooms which are still decorated with antique furniture, sculptures, mirrors and porcelain. On the upper floor (the only one to have been lived in) are rooms frescoed by the great painters of the 17th century in Liguria, magnificent examples of Baroque decoration. The paintings of the Brignole-Sale family, which form the core of the art collection, are primarily works by Italian and Flemish masters and the Genoese school, reflecting the taste prevalent in the centuries during which the collection was formed. Palazzo Rosso combines beautifully and seamlessly the role of a noble residence with that of a gallery of art assembled by a family of Genoese patricians.

Judith and Holofernes by Paolo Veronese, displaying great mastery of colour

Rooms 1–6: Italian and European Painting, 15–17th Centuries

The collection of paintings was assembled by the Brignole-Sale family, whose acquisitions lasted for more than two centuries. The marriage between Giovan Francesco Brignole-Sale and Maria Durazzo strengthened the collection further.

Room 1 has a fine *Portrait of Maria Brignole-Sale* (1856), one of many family portraits. In Room 2, in addition to the *Madonna with Child, St Joseph and St John as a Child* by an artist of the Perin del Vaga school, is a *Portrait of a Man* (15th century) thought to be by Michele Giambono or Gentile da Fabriano.

Room 3 is dedicated to the Venetian school from the 16th century, with works by Tintoretto and Paolo Veronese, such

as the latter's *Judith and Holofernes*. Other works here are by Paris Bordone and Alessandro Bonvicini (also known as il Moretto). The painting *Madonna and Child, St John the Baptist and Mary Magdalen* (1520–22) by Palma il Vecchio, is a beautiful work featuring a lovely use of colour.

Room 4 has 17th-century paintings of the Emilian school, among them an *Annunciation* by Ludovico Carracci, a key figure in the Bolognese school, along with his cousins Agostino and Annibale. Among Carracci's pupils was Guido Reni, whose *St Sebastian* (1615–16) reveals his ability to depict a range of emotions through measured, classical painting. The works of Giulio Cesare Procaccini are also of interest.

The intense *St Sebastian* by Guido Reni, on display in Room 4

Room 5 contains works by Guercino (1591–1666), including the fine *Dying Cleopatra*, bought by one of the Durazzo family in 1648. By the same artist is *God the Father with Angel* (c.1620), once part of an altar painting entitled *Vestizione di San Guglielmo*, now in the Pinacoteca Nazionale di Bologna, and the *Suicide of Catone Uticense* (1641).

Room 6 is devoted to 17th century Neapolitan painting, including several works by Mattia Preti, such as *The Resurrection of Lazarus* (1630–40), which employs a dramatic use of light and shade.

Rooms 7–10: Genoese Painting from the 16–18th Centuries

These rooms document the richness and high quality of the works produced by the Genoa school during the city's so-called golden age, a period of great economic and cultural fervour that lasted from the 16th to the 18th centuries.

Room 7 is dedicated to local artist Bernardo Strozzi (1581–1644). His paintings range from the youthful *La Carità* to two devotional paintings depicting *St Francis* and magnificent works from his mature phase, such as a *Madonna* with Child and San Giovannino, showing the clear influence of Caravaggio, and *The Cook*, showing a Flemish influence.

In Room 9 are paintings by Sinibaldo Scorza (1589–1631) and Giovan Battista Castiglione, known as il Grechetto (1610–65). Scorza was primarily a painter of landscapes and animals, while il Grechetto, a draughtsman and engraver, dealt with pastoral themes. He was a brilliant interpreter of biblical scenes: his *Flight of the Family of Abraham* (1630s) is a good example.

Room 10 is dedicated to Genoese artists of the 17th and 18th centuries, including Pellegro Piola, Giovanni Bernardo Carbone and Bernardo Castello, specialists in depictions of idyllic landscapes.

Rooms 11–12: Roman Painting from the 17th Century

Among the works in Room 11 is an exquisite *Madonna with Child in a Landscape* (1615–20), by Orazio Gentileschi, a friend and follower of Caravaggio. The painting is reminiscent of late-medieval works, especially in its portrayal of the Virgin Mary, who is sitting on the ground, a detail that underlines her humility.

In Room 12 is Andrea Sacchi's *Dedalus and Icarus*. Despite the strong chiaroscuro effect, this painting represents Sacchi's successful break from Caravaggio-esque influences.

Ludovico Carracci's *Annunciation*, which can be admired in Room 4

Rooms 14–16: Dürer & Flemish Painting from the 16th Century

The undisputed masterpiece of Room 14 is Albrecht Dürer's *Portrait of a Young Man* (1506). Part of the Vendramin Collection in Venice during the 16th century, the painting came to Genoa via Giuseppe Maria Durazzo, who acquired it in 1670 and passed it on to his daughter Maria, wife of Gio. Francesco II Brignole-Sale. The painting was subject to excessively vigorous cleaning in the 20th century, which has led to some damage. It remains, however, a great example of the Nuremberg artist's activity while in Italy. Also in Room 14

is Hendrick Avercamp's delightful *Winter Landscape with Ice Skaters*.

One of the highlights in Room 16 is Jan Wildens's *July: Hay Gathering* (1614), part of the artist's series of 12 months (eight of which are held in Genoese museums). The large dimensions of the paintings suggest that they were probably commissioned and created with the aim to decorate the mansions of the Genoese nobility. Cornelis de Wael's *Fight Between Infantry and Cavalry* also hangs in Room 16.

Rooms 27–33: Rooms of the Four Seasons and Loggias

Room 28 originally bore frescoes of the *Myth of Phaethon* by Gregorio De Ferrari. They were destroyed during World War II, although the preparatory drawings were fortunately saved. His work does survive, however, in the subsequent rooms. Frescoes on the ceiling in the next four rooms (29–32), completed in 1687–89, depict the Allegories of the Four Seasons: *Spring and Summer* are by Gregorio De Ferrari, and *Autumn* and *Winter* by Domenico Piola (assisted by perspective painters Enrico and Antonio Haffner). These superb works use complex iconograpy to exalt the glory of the Brignole-Sale family, taking the form of illusionistic art that weaves

Geronima Brignole-Sale and her Daughter Aurelia, by Van Dyck

Loggia delle Rovine (or Loggia di Diana), frescoed by Piola

together fact and fiction by superimposing stuccoes over frescoes.

This decorative cycle culminates in the Loggia delle Rovine (or Loggia di Diana) by Paolo Gerolamo Piola. Fine portraits are displayed in these same rooms. The works by Van Dyck (highlights include the portraits of *Anton Giulio Brignole-Sale, Paolina Adorno Brignole-Sale* and *Geronima Brignole-Sale and her Daughter Aurelia)* were commissioned in the first half of the 17th century by Gio. Francesco II Brignole-Sale. It was the first major demonstration of the economic power that the family had acquired.

Rooms 34–37: Rooms with Allegories of Human Life

These rooms were frescoed in 1691–92 by Giovanni Andrea Carlone, Bartolomeo Guidobono, Carlo Antonio Tavella and Domenico Parodi. The paintings depict the allegories of the *Life of Man* (Room 34), the *Liberal Arts* (35) and *Youth in Peril* (37).

Room 36, Alcova, is a delightful space, decorated and furnished in full 18th-century style: delicate perspective wall paintings by Andrea Leoncino adorn the walls and the ceiling. The bridal bed was made by Gaetano Cantone in 1783.

The richly decorated interior of the church of San Siro, once Genoa's cathedral

❼ San Siro

Via San Siro 3. **Map** 5 B2.
Tel 010 246 16 74. **Open** 7:30am–noon, 4–7pm daily.

A church of ancient foundation, San Siro was mentioned in documents in the 4th century. It was Genoa's cathedral until the 9th century, when that title passed to San Lorenzo.

Following a fire in 1580, San Siro was reconstructed under the supervision of the Theatines, an order of Italian monks established to oppose the Reformation by raising the tone of piety in the Roman Catholic church. The church's current appearance dates from this period, though the façade was the work of Carlo Barabino (1821).

Inside, there are three broad aisles with frescoes and stuccoes by Giovanni Battista and Tommaso Carlone respectively (second half of the 17th century). In the presbytery, adorned with multicoloured marbles, is a monumental high altar in bronze and black marble, a fine work by Pierre Puget (1670). Also of interest in the church is an *Annunciation* by Orazio Gentileschi (1639).

Several side chapels were decorated by Domenico Fiasella, Domenico Piola and Gregorio De Ferrari, who also painted the canvases in the church sacristy.

❽ Santissima Annunziata del Vastato

Piazza della Nunziata 4.
Map 5 B1. **Tel** 010 246 55 25.
Open 9am–noon, 3–7pm daily. **Closed** during services. 🖾

The name of this church combines the two names, one past and one present, of the square that it looks onto. Now Piazza della Nunziata, the square was originally Piazza del Vastato, a name derived from *guastum* or *vastinium*; these terms referred to the fact that the district, which was not enclosed within the city walls, was free from the restrictions which could prevent its use by the military.

The original church dates from 1520, but it was rebuilt in the 16th and 17th centuries for the powerful Lomellini family. The façade has two bell towers, with a 19th-century pronaos (portico).

The rich interior decoration is thought to be the work of the brothers Giovanni and Giovan Battista Carlone in 1627–8, involving other important artists such as Gioacchino Assereto, Giovanni Andrea Ansaldo and Giulio Benso over the ensuing decades. The central nave is dedicated to glorifying the divinity of Christ and of the Virgin Mary. In the vaults of the transepts, frescoes by Giovanni Carlone depict the *Ascension* and *Pentecost*; the *Assumption of Mary* in the cupola was painted by Andrea Ansaldo and later restored by Gregorio De Ferrari.

In the side aisles are frescoed scenes from the Old and New Testaments. The frescoes in the presbytery and the apse (*Annunciation and Assumption*), by Giulio Benso, are placed within a grandiose painted architectural framework.

❾ Albergo dei Poveri

Piazzale Brignole 2. **Map** 2 E1.

The grandiose white façade of the vast Albergo dei Poveri, with the Genoa city coat of arms at the centre, dominates your vision as you approach along Via Brignole De Ferrari. One of Italy's earliest charitable institutions, providing food, lodging and medical care for the poor and sickly, it was established in the 1600s under the patronage of Emanuele Brignole.

The former poorhouse, an emblem of the munificence of the city's nobility, is laid out around four courtyards, with a church at the centre. Works of art housed here include paintings by Giovan Battista Paggi, Pierre Puget and Domenico Piola. The building has been taken over recently by the University of Genoa, but may be open to the public in the future.

Nearby are the **Salita di San Bartolomeo del Carmine** and the **Salita San Nicolò**, perfectly preserved narrow uphill streets (*creuze*) that were once in the outskirts but have now been absorbed into the city centre.

The imposing façade of the Albergo dei Poveri

The internal courtyard of one of the majestic palazzi on Via Balbi

❿ Via Balbi

Map 2 E2.

This street, leading from Piazza della Nunziata, was one of the original Strade Nuove. Created in 1602 by Bartolomeo Bianco for the powerful Balbi family, its building was the result of a deal between the Balbi and the government, which ostensibly aimed to improve traffic flow in the area. (Ironically, Via Balbi can occasionally be clogged with traffic, though efforts have been made to rectify this.) By 1620, seven palazzi had been built, creating the Balbi's very own residential quarter. Sadly, none of the palazzi are open to the public.

At no. 1, **Palazzo Durazzo Pallavicini** (1618), one of the many residences to have been designed by Bianco, has a lovely atrium and a superb 18th-century staircase. **Palazzo Balbi Senarega**, another Bianco work at no. 4, is now a university faculty. Inside are fine frescoes by Gregorio De Ferrari.

⓫ Palazzo dell'Università

Via Balbi. **Map** 2 E2. **Tel** 010 209 91. **Open** 7am–7pm Mon–Fri; 7am–noon Sat.

Perhaps the most famous building on Via Balbi, this palazzo was built as a Jesuit college in 1634–36 to a design by Bartolomeo Bianco. It has functioned as the seat of the University of Genoa since 1775. Today it houses the rectorate and several faculties. Like the palazzi in Via Garibaldi (especially Palazzo Doria Tursi), this palazzo has the familiar succession of atrium, raised courtyard and hanging garden. The courtyard, with paired columns, is beautiful and airy. In the **Great Hall** (Aula Magna) there is a series of six statues personifying the theological and cardinal virtues by Giambologna (1579).

The **Biblioteca Universitaria** (university library), occupies the adjacent former church of saints Gerolamo and Francesco Saverio: the apse, with some fine frescoes by Domenico Piola, has been transformed into a reading room.

Vase on display in Palazzo Reale

⓬ Palazzo Reale

Via Balbi 10. **Map** 5 A1. **Tel** 010 271 02 36. **Open** 9am–1:30pm Tue, Wed; 9am–7pm Thu–Sun. Ticket office closes 30 minutes before closure. **Closed** 1 Jan, 1 May, 25 Dec. 🖼 combined ticket valid for Palazzo Reale and Palazzo Spinola. 🅦 **palazzorealegenova.it**

Constructed for the Balbi family in 1643–55, this fine palazzo was rebuilt for Eugenio Durazzo only 50 years later. Its new designer, Carlo Fontana, opted for a Baroque mansion, modelled on a Roman palazzo. The building acquired its present name in 1825, when it became the Genoa residence of the royal House of Savoy. Fontana's internal courtyard is striking: a combination of delightful architecture in red and yellow and fine views over the port. The superb mosaic pavement in the garden came from a monastery. The palazzo's magnificent rooms, decorated in the 18th and 19th centuries by the Durazzo family and by the Savoys, now form part of the **Galleria Nazionale**. They contain furniture, furnishings and tapestries, along with frescoes, paintings and sculpture.

The 18th-century rooms include the lavish and breathtaking Galleria degli Specchi (hall of mirrors), with a ceiling frescoed by Domenico Parodi. Rooms created by the Savoys include the Sala del Trono (throne room), Sala delle Udienze (audience chamber) and the Salone da Ballo (ballroom). The most valuable works of art in the museum include paintings by Luca Giordano, Van Dyck, Bernardo Strozzi, il Grechetto and Valerio Castello; and sculptures by Francesco Schiaffino and Filippo Parodi.

The splendid Galleria degli Specchi in Palazzo Reale

Loggias on Piazza della Commenda

⓭ San Giovanni di Pré and La Commenda

Piazza della Commenda 1. **Map** 2 D2. **Tel** 010 265 486. **Open** Upper church: 10am–5pm Tue–Fri, 10am–7pm Sat & Sun. Lower church: By appt only. ✗ without permission.

A stone's throw from the main railway station, the church of San Giovanni di Pré was founded in 1180 by the Knights of the Order of St John. The original Romanesque church was largely rebuilt in the 14th century. The bell tower, adorned with a pyramidal spire, was left untouched and it is very attractive.

The main church consists, in fact, of two churches, one above the other. The lower one, which was always intended for public worship, has three aisles with cross vaults. The upper church was used by the Knights of the Order and opened to the public only in the 18th century. To do this, the church had to be re-oriented in the opposite direction, an entrance made in the apse and a second, artificial apse created from the opposite end. The upper church is similar in style to the lower church, though it is larger. Heavy columns support Gothic arches between the aisles and ribbed vaults, the bare stone making the interior very atmospheric. There are paintings by Giulio Benso, Bernardo Castello and Lazzaro Tavarone.

La Commenda, next door, was founded by the Knights of St John in the 11th century to provide lodgings for pilgrims waiting to sail to the Holy Land; it also functioned as a hospital.

Its portico, topped by two loggias, faces onto Piazza della Commenda. There are wonderful frescoes on the third floor. The complex was rebuilt in the 16th century, but restoration work in the 1970s revived its Romanesque appearance. Exhibitions and cultural events are held here.

A short walk eastwards, along Via di Pré (derived from "prati", meaning fields, a reminder of how rural this area once was), brings you to the **Porta dei Vacca** (or **Santa Fede**), a Gothic arch (1155) much altered by the addition of subsequent buildings.

⓮ Galata Museo del Mare

Calata De Mari 1, Darsena. **Map** 2 D3. **Tel** 010 234 5655. **Open** Nov–Feb: 10am–6pm Tue–Sun (to 7:30pm Sat & Sun); Mar–Oct:10am–7:30pm Tue–Sun; Aug daily. Last entrance: 60 mins before closure. ✗ 📷 (electronic guide for the blind available). ♿ P 📷 🖥 🌐 **galatamuseodelmare.it**

Completed in 2004 and intrinsic to the revival of Genoa's port area, this museum of the sea is the largest museum of its kind in the Mediterranean. The complex combines 16th-century and Neo-Classical architecture with a stylish glass, wood and aluminium structure. It is located in the Darsena port area, alongside the Stazione Marittima and the historic Galata shipyards.

The museum illustrates Genoa's longstanding relationship with the sea, from the Middle Ages to the present. The star exhibit and focal

point is a beautifully restored 16th-century Genoese galley, eye-catching behind its glass veil, lit up at night and visible across the whole bay. As well as a fine display of maps and sailing instruments, the museum houses an original 17th-century launching berth and a reconstructed 17th-century pirate ship, which visitors can board.

Fully interactive, the museum enables visitors to taste life at sea at first hand: you can even experience what it is like to cross the Cape Horn in a storm.

The magnificent Fountain of Neptune, in the gardens of Palazzo Doria Pamphilj

⓯ Palazzo Doria Pamphilj or del Principe

Piazza del Principe 4. **Map** 1 C1. **Tel** 010 255 509. **Open** 10am–5pm Fri–Wed. **Closed** 1 Jan, Easter, 1 May, Aug, 25 Dec. ✗ 📷 book ahead. ♿ 📷 ✗ 🌐 **palazzodelprincipe.it**

Constructed by Andrea Doria when he was at the height of his political power, this palazzo was conceived as a truly magnificent, princely residence, a demonstration of the admiral's power. It is still owned by the Doria Pamphilj family.

The building was begun in around 1529 and incorporated several existing buildings. When Charles V came as a guest in 1533, the decoration was largely complete. The principal artist

Andrea Doria

This portrait of Andrea Doria (1468–1560), painted by Bronzino after 1540, and now in Palazzo Doria Pamphilj, is fitting: posing, despite his advanced years, in a heroic attitude, semi-nude, as the god of the sea, Neptune. Two fundamental themes in his life are concentrated in this work: the sea and the arts. A member of one of the most powerful families in Genoa, he did not, however, have an easy life. He made a successful career through warfare: initially serving the pope, then the king of France and, finally, emperor Charles V. A soldier and admiral of huge talent, he was one of the few to defeat feared pirates operating in the Mediterranean, to such an extent that he gained the deep respect of the Genoese, who declared him lord of the city in 1528. From this position of power he established an aristocratic constitution which lasted until 1798. He spent many years in his palazzo, built with the help of some of the great artists of the Renaissance.

Andrea Doria as Neptune by Bronzino

involved was Perin del Vaga (c.1501–47), a pupil of Raphael summoned to Genoa by Andrea Doria.

A marble entrance by Silvio Cosini gives way to an atrium, decorated with frescoes (1529) by Perin del Vaga showing *Stories of the kings of Rome and Military Triumphs*. On the upper floor, between the public rooms, the **Loggia degli Eroi** has a stuccoed ceiling by del Vaga and Luzio Romano. Along the internal wall, frescoes by del Vaga depict 12 ancestors of the Doria family. Following lengthy restoration work in the loggia, the splendour of the frescoes' original colours has been greatly revived. The **Salone dei Giganti**

has a ceiling fresco by del Vaga showing *Giants struck by Jove* (1531). Fine tapestries depicting the *Battle of Lepanto*, in the **galleria**, were made in Brussels in 1591 to a design by Luca Cambiaso.

As well as bringing new life to the palazzo's decoration, restoration work has also made it possible for the public to visit the private apartments of Andrea Doria and his wife.

Around the palazzo, from the water's edge to Monte Granarolo to the rear, there was an enchanting garden, much altered in the 19th and 20th

centuries to make way for a section of railway line and several road junctions. Damage during World War II didn't help, and there is now a project to return the garden to its 16th-century appearance. The garden's two main landmarks are the **Fontana del Tritone** by Montorsoli (a pupil of Michelangelo) and the **Fontana di Nettuno** by Taddeo Carlone, both made in the 16th century.

The nearby **Stazione Marittima**, a 1930s departure point for transatlantic liners, was created out of the Doria's private quay.

Detail from the Fontana del Tritone

The beautifully restored frescoes by Perin del Vaga in the Loggia degli Eroi

FURTHER AFIELD

Genoa sprawls westwards and eastwards from the city centre, taking in the Circonvallazione a Monte (mountain by-pass) and the old city walls and forts, as well as the towns annexed to the city with the creation of Greater Genoa in the 1920s. From Voltri, on the Riviera di Ponente to the west, to Nervi, on the Riviera di Levante to the east (the limits of Genoa's administrative territory), the steep landscape and beautiful coastline conceal all kinds of surprises: from the splendid 19th-century park of Villa Durazzo Pallavicini, at Pegli, to the sanctuaries just above Genoa, famous for their nativity scenes and the focus of pilgrimages. Genoa's city walls, which circle the regional capital some distance from the centre, date from the 17th century and

feature magnificent fortresses, still in a perfect state of preservation. Then there are medieval jewels such as the church of San Siro di Struppa, standing alone among vineyards and gardens.

One sight that should not be missed is the Neo-Classical cemetery at Staglieno, regarded as one of Genoa's major attractions. East of the city centre, the residential district of Albaro is full of graceful villas set into an urban context, while Boccadasse is a picturesque, well-preserved fishing village, popular with visitors and locals alike. Nervi is a famous bathing resort with beautiful Art Nouveau buildings, a municipal park created out of the gardens of three villas, and the Passeggiata Anita Garibaldi, one of the loveliest coastal walks in Italy.

Sights at a Glance

Historic Buildings
6 Castello D'Albertis
9 City Walls
   and Fortresses

Residential Districts
1 Voltri
2 Pegli
12 Albaro
13 Boccadasse
14 Nervi

Churches and Sanctuaries
4 Basilica di San Francesco
   di Paola
5 Santuario di Oregina
7 Santuario della Madonnetta
8 San Bartolomeo
   degli Armeni
11 San Siro di Struppa

Parks and Gardens
3 Parco Durazzo Pallavicini

Cemeteries
10 Cimitero di Staglieno

Key

■ Central Genoa
□ Greater Genoa
═ Motorway
▬ Main road
═ Minor road
— Railway line
— Walls

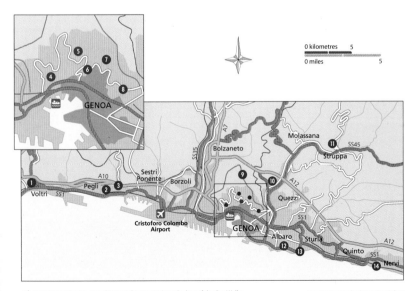

◄ Castello MacKenzie, one of Genoa's fortresses along the line of the City Walls   **For map symbols** see back flap

The Villa Brignole-Sale, surrounded by an English garden, at Voltri

❶ Voltri

Road Map D3. **FS** Genoa–Savona line 🚌

One of the most important towns in Greater Genoa, Voltri is more or less a continuation of the periphery of the city. The main sight of interest here is the **Villa Brignole-Sale**, also called the Villa della Duchessa di Galliera. Originally built in the 17th century, what you see was largely created in the 18th century. The palace became the home of Maria Brignole-Sale, Duchess of Galliera, in 1870. Her most striking contribution was the creation of an English-style garden, complete with pine trees, holm oaks and a deer park.

The park extends for over 32 ha (80 acres) and is scattered with romantic follies and farm-houses. While the villa, with its lavish interior, is not open to the public, the grounds are a public park.

On the left of the villa, in a beautiful panoramic position, stands the **Sanctuary of Nostra Signora delle Grazie**. The Duchess of Galliera had it restored in Gothic style. She was buried here in 1888.

❷ Pegli

Road Map D3. **FS** 🚌

Annexed, like other nearby towns, to the city of Genoa in 1926, Pegli owes its fame to the aristocracy of Europe. From the end of the 19th century onwards, this was the aristocrats'

preferred holiday place; it was also a popular retreat for the Genoese. Two villas hint at its former elegance.

Villa Durazzo Pallavicini, surrounded by a splendid park bursting with fanciful pagodas, arches and other follies *(see pp88–9)*, is the home of the **Museo Civico di Archeologia Ligure**. Objects from the paleontological, prehistoric, Etruscan and Roman eras are displayed alongside the collection of antique vases given to the city in 1866 by Prince Otto of Savoy.

Among the more interesting finds are tools from the caves at Balzi Rossi *(see p173)* and the earliest known statue-stele from Lunigiana (c.3000 BC).

The 16th-century Villa Centurione Doria, featuring frescoes by Lazzaro Tavarone, is now home to the **Museo Civico Navale**. This traces Genoa's seafaring history using a fascinating array of objects. These include a portrait of Christopher Columbus by Ghirlandaio, models of three caravels, ship instruments such as astrolabes, and a famous view of Genoa by De Grassi, dating from 1481.

🏛 **Museo Civico di Archeologia Ligure**
Via Pallavicini 11. **Tel** 010 698 10 48. **Open** 9am–7pm Tue–Fri; 10am–7pm Sat, Sun & public hols. 🅿 ♿ 📷 📶
W museoarcheologico.it

🏛 **Museo Civico Navale**
Piazza Bonavino 7. **Tel** 010 696 98 85. **Open** 9am–1pm Tue–Fri; 10am–7pm Sat &Sun. 🅿 ♿
W museonavale.it

❸ Parco Durazzo Pallavicini

See pp88–9.

Ex votos in the Basilica di San Francesco di Paola

❹ Basilica di San Francesco di Paola

Salita San Francesco di Paola 44. **Map** 1 C1. **Tel** 010 261 228. 🚌 32, 35. **Open** Apr–Sep: 7:30am–noon, 3:30–7pm daily; Oct–Mar: 7:30am–noon, 3:30–6pm daily. ♿

This sanctuary is at one extreme of the Circonvallazione a Monte, the charming but tortuous panoramic road that snakes across the slopes just above the city. From the church courtyard, built on a rocky outcrop that dominates the district of Fassolo, visitors can enjoy a marvellous view of Genoa's Porto Antico, which can be

Overlooking Pegli, with the airport in the background

reached via a brick-paved road lined with the stations of the Cross.

Dating from the early 16th century, the basilica took on an important role during the following century, when its patrons included powerful families such as the Doria, the Balbi and the Spinola. Also known as the Sanctuary of Sailors, the church contains numerous mariners' ex votos. Stuccoes and multicoloured marble embellish the spacious interior, and the side chapels contain some important works of art. In the third chapel on the right is a *Nativity* by Luca Cambiaso (1565), while the chapel at the end of the left aisle contains a *Washing of the Feet* signed by Orazio De Ferrari. Anton Maria Maragliano, one of the most active sculptors in Liguria in the 17th century, was responsible for the wooden statue of the Virgin Mary in the apse.

Detail from the funerary monument of Alessandro de Stefanis

❺ Santuario di Oregina

Salita Oregina 44. **Map** 2 D1. **Tel** 010 212 024. 🚌 39, 40. **Open** 8am–noon, 4–7pm daily. **Closed** Sun pm; afternoons in Aug.

The history of this sanctuary is linked with worship of the Madonna di Loreto. It stands at the top of a flight of steps, preceded by a tree-filled square, in a gorgeous panoramic position looking over the city and the sea.

A group of monks singled out this area, which still had a strongly rustic character at the time, as a place of hermitage in 1634. They immediately built a simple chapel here, but this was taken over by the Franciscan Friars Minor in the following year.

The sanctuary, as it appears today, was built in 1650–55, with further modifications being made in 1707, including the addition of a dome and changes to the façade, some of which echoed motifs already used inside the church. The upper part of the façade features pilasters, Corinthian columns, a large window and a curvilinear pediment with stuccoes, following the dictates of Ligurian Baroque churches in hilly areas.

Inside the sanctuary, as well as a valuable painting by Andrea Carlone (1639–97), a *St Joseph with Baby Jesus* on the left-hand altar, there are mementoes of the era of the Risorgimento, including the funerary monument of Alessandro de Stefanis, a local hero who died in 1848, and, in the parish office, a case with flags of subalpine, Ligurian and Lombard peoples. The church is also famous for its *Nativity (presepe)*, which contains figures dating from the 1700s.

❻ Castello D' Albertis

Corso Dogali 18. **Map** 2 E1. **Tel** 010 272 38 20/34 64. 🚌 39, 40. **Open** Apr–Sep: 10am–6pm Tue–Fri, 10am– 7pm Sat & Sun; Oct–Mar: 10am–5pm Tue–Fri, 10am–6pm Sat & Sun. 🅿️ 🆆 **museidigenova.it**

This fortress, built in just six years, from 1886 to 1892, occupies a striking position on the bastion of Montegalletto, not far from the city centre. The man behind the building was the captain Enrico Alberto D'Albertis, a curious figure who was a courageous explorer and navigator. He was passionate about the project and employed a group of four architects, under the leadership of Alfredo D'Andrade, the great exponent of the Neo-Gothic revival of that time.

One of the most emblematic symbols of revivalism in Genoa, Castello D'Albertis stands out for the forcefulness of the complex: from its mighty 16th-century base to its battlemented towers; the terracotta cladding echoes a style used in similar Genoese Romanesque monuments.

The captain bequeathed the building to the town council in 1932, together with the ethnographic collections that are now on display in the **Museo Etnografico** that now occupies the castle. Among items left by the captain are several sundials (made by D'Albertis himself), nautical instruments and geographical publications, as well as arms from that era. The museum also received a donation of finds from the American Committee of Catholic Missions in 1892. This included Native American costumes, crafts and jewellery and terracotta pieces, masks, stone sculptures and vases dating from the Mayan and Aztec civilizations. Other acquisitions include objects from South-East Asia, Oceania and New Guinea.

The impressive Castello D'Albertis

⑨ Parco Durazzo Pallavicini

The man responsible for transforming the gardens of the Villa Durazzo Pallavicini was Michele Canzio, set designer at Genoa's Teatro Carlo Felice *(see p59)*. Between 1837 and 1846 he created a splendid English-style garden, following the romantic fashion of the time. He was commissioned by Marchese Ignazio Alessandro Pallavicini, who inherited the villa from his aunt Clelia Pallavicini Durazzo. She was passionate about plants and had begun a botanic garden here in the late 18th century. Today, more than 100 varieties of exotic species, including tropical carnivorous plants, are grown here. The park covers around 11 ha (27 acres).

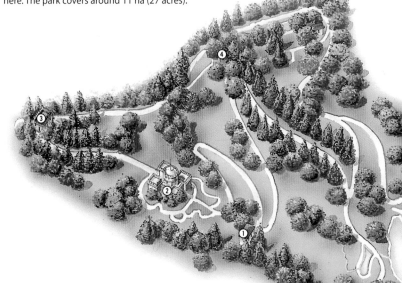

KEY

① **Swiss chalet**

② **The 14th-century castle** stands on the top of the hill, well concealed among trees. Squarely constructed around a circular, battlemented tower, the castle was conceived as the house of an imaginary lord of the time. The interior features fresco and stucco decoration, as do most of the other buildings in the park. The castle, sadly, is not open to the public.

③ **Mausoleum of the captain**

④ **Cappelletta della Madonna**

⑤ **The Triumphal Arch** bears an inscription in Latin which invites the onlooker to forget city life and become immersed in the appreciation of nature. The reliefs and statues were by Gian Battista Cevasco.

⑥ **Coffee house**

⑦ **Turkish kiosk**

Frieze on the Temple of Flora

The Park as a Stage Set

As a set designer, it is perhaps not surprising that Michele Canzio saw the park as a stage for a historical fairy tale, whose story unwinds en route through the grounds and evokes musings on the mystery of existence. The narrative, typical of a romantic melodrama, consists of a prologue and three acts of four scenes each. The prologue is made up of the Gothic Avenue and the Classic Avenue, while the first act, Return to Nature, develops through the hermitage, a pleasure garden, the old lake and the spring. The second act, representing the Recovery of History, passes from the shrine of the Madonna to the Swiss chalet and on to the captain's castle and the tombs and mausoleum of the captain. The third and final act, Purification, takes in the grottoes, the big lake, a statue of Flora (the goddess of flowers) and her charming temple, with a small square ("remembrance") surrounded by cypresses and a stream.

The Chinese Pagoda
The pagoda roof is adorned with little bells and sculpted dragons. This fun and exotic construction, one of the most charming in the entire park, is built on the lake and can be reached across a double iron bridge.

Temple of Flora
This feminine, octagonal building could not be dedicated to anyone other than a goddess, the ancient protectress of the plant kingdom. Located just south of the lake, and surrounded by box hedges, the temple is a sign of the renewed interest in the Classical Greek and Roman periods that was so influential in the 19th century.

★ Temple of Diana
This circular Ionic-style temple, dedicated to the Graeco-Roman goddess of hunting, stands in a wonderful position at the centre of the lake. A statue of Diana, the work of Gian Battista Cevasco, poses elegantly beneath the dome, while four tritons stand guard in the water around the temple.

Paving at the Santuario della Madonnetta

❼ Santuario della Madonnetta

Salita della Madonnetta, 5. **Map** 2 F1.
Tel 010 272 53 08. 🚋 Zecca–Righi
funicular. 🚌 33. **Open** 9am–noon,
3:30–6pm daily.

Lying at the end of a *creuza*,
one of Liguria's distinctive steep
narrow streets, paved with brick,
this sanctuary is one of the highlights along the Circonvallazione
a Monte.

The complex Baroque
building was erected in 1696 for
the Augustine Order. The delightful area paved with black and
white pebbles outside dates
from the 18th century. On one
side a niche contains a marble
sculpture of a *Pietà* by
Domenico Parodi.

The interior is also charming,
with a light-filled central chamber
in the form of an irregular
octagon linked to the presbytery
by two side staircases.

Another ramp leads beneath
the presbytery down to the so-
called "scurolo", an underground
chamber on whose altar
stands a revered statue of the
Madonnetta (17th century),

from which the sanctuary
takes its name; it is the
work of Giovanni Romano.
In the chapel alongside is
a wooden *Pietà* (1733), by
Anton Maria Maragliano.

The sanctuary's crypt
houses some of Genoa's
best-loved nativity scenes
(presepi), of particular
interest because of their
faithful reproduction of parts of
the old city centre. The wooden
figures were carved mainly in
the 17th and 18th centuries,
including some by Maragliano
and others by the Gagini, a
hugely talented family of
sculptors originally from
Lombardy.

In the sacristy visitors can see
an interesting rendition of the
Annunciation (1490), attributed
to Ludovico Brea, a native of
Nice who was active in Liguria
from around 1475 to 1520
(see p163).

❽ San Bartolomeo degli Armeni

Piazza San Bartolomeo degli Armeni 2.
Map 6 F1. **Tel** 010 839 24 96.
🚌 33. **Open** 7:30–11:30am,
4–6:30pm daily.

This church was founded
in 1308 by Basilian monks
(followers of St Basil)
and then passed to the
Barnabites, who rebuilt
it in 1775 and are the
current occupants.
The church is almost
completely enclosed by

a 19th-century building, but
still has its bell tower, dating
from 1300.

San Bartolomeo owes its
fame to the fact that it is home
to the relic of Santo Volto (Holy
Face), a piece of linen with an
image of the face of Jesus Christ.
People also call it "Santo
Sudario", or "Mandillo" (handker-
chief in the local dialect). This
relic was given to Leonardo
Montaldo, doge of Genoa, in
1362 by the Constantinople
emperor Giovanni V Paleologo,
in return for military assistance.
The doge, in turn, gave the relic
to the Basilian monks. Much
of the decoration inside the
church relates to the tradition
of the relic.

The Santo Volto itself is set
against a background of gold
and silver filigree (a masterpiece
of Byzantine goldsmithery),
with ten embossed tiles
describing the origins of the
portrait and later episodes
in its history. The most
valuable work of art is the

Madonna and Saints in San Bartolomeo, 1415

The Nativity Scenes Tradition

Nativity scene at the Santuario della Madonnetta

The spread of the cult of the nativity scene *(presepe)*
may date back to the Jesuits, who were particularly
active in Genoa in the first half of the 17th century.
Although the tradition was not as strong here as in
Naples, it was nonetheless very popular. During the
17th and 18th centuries, aristocratic houses assembled
presepi but kept them in private family chapels. The
scenes were eventually made public and bourgeois
families of the late 19th century and early 20th century
became accustomed to making special visits to the
presepi at Christmas. Today, it is possible to follow the
19th-century custom all year round. Several churches
still display nativity scenes, including the Madonnetta and Oregina sanctuaries. Typical figures, usually
carved from wood, sometimes made of coloured wax or plaster, included those of a young, smiling peasant
girl, an old peasant woman with a grotesque expression, and a lame beggar *(lo zoppo)*; the latter became a
famous symbol of poverty and need.

triptych on the high altar, *Madonna and Saints*, by Turino Vanni (1415).

❾ City Walls and Fortresses

Parco Urbano della Mura. 🚆 Genova–Casella line. 🚌 40, 64. 🚡 Zecca–Righi funicular (terminus). ⬛ organized by Cooperativa DAFNE (010 247 39 25).

Genoa's defensive walls have been rebuilt or moved several times over the centuries. Traces remain of the 1155 and 1536 walls, but the impressive 13-km (8-mile) triangle of walls that still encloses the city dates from the 1600s. These fortifications, which became known as La Nuova Mura ("the new wall"), were designed in part by Bartolomeo Bianco, and became one of the city's outstanding features.

Major alterations had to be made to the walls in the 1800s, after attacks by Austrian troops made clear their inadequacy; most of the forts along their length date from this period.

The best way to explore the old walls is to drive along the scenic Strada delle Mura, which begins at Piazza Manin, north of the Centro Storico, and follows the line of what remains of the 17th-century walls (and which also defines the boundaries of the Parco Urbano delle Mura). Piazza Manin itself is home to the fanciful **Castello Mackenzie** (1896–1906), the work of Gino

Coppedè, which embraces medieval, Renaissance and even Art Nouveau influences.

Travelling along the line of the walls in an anti-clockwise direction, you reach **Forte Castellaccio**, mentioned in the 13th century but rebuilt in the 16th century by Andrea Doria and again altered in the 1830s; within its ring of bastions is the Torre della Specola, where condemned men were once hanged.

Forte Sperone juts out on the top of Monte Peralto, at the apex of the triangle. Originally 16th-century, the massive citadel you see today was built in 1826–7 by the Houseof Savoy.

Inland from Forte Sperone, off the line of the city walls, lies **Forte Puin** (accessible by train from the Genoa–Casella line), completed in 1828. Its square tower is one of the key landmarks in the Parco Urbano delle Mura. Polygonal **Forte Diamante**, the furthest inland of the forts, is in a high and delightful position. Dating from 1758, it has survived almost intact.

Back along the walls, **Forte Begato** has a rectangular layout, with robust buttresses supporting bastions from which there are fine views.

Forte Tenaglia, which dominates the Valle del Polcevera, was first recorded in the 16th century. Its horn-shaped structure, acquired in the 19th century, was badly damaged in World War II.

The funerary monument to Giuseppe Mazzini at Staglieno

❿ Cimitero di Staglieno

Piazzale Resasco 1. **Tel** 010 870 184. 🚌 12, 14, 34, 48. **Open** 7:30am–5pm daily. **Closed** 1 Jan, Easter Monday, 1 May, 24 Jun, 15 Aug, 8 Dec, 26 Dec. 🔳 **comunegenova.it**

This vast and extraordinary monumental Neo-Classical cemetery on the bank of the River Bisagno, northeast of the city centre, was designed by Carlo Barabino, but he died before the grand project was carried out (1844–51).

Containing a great panoply of grandiose and exuberant monuments to the dead, the cemetery fills an area of 160 ha (395 acres), hence the shuttle bus which ferries people around.

In a dominant position, on the side of the hill, stands the circular Cappella dei Suffragi, adorned with statues by Cevasco, sculptor of the statues in the Parco Durazzo Pallavicini *(see pp88–9)*. Other works of note include the colossal 19th-century marble statue of *Faith* by Santo Varni, and, probably the best-known monument at Staglieno, the tomb of Giuseppe Mazzini, the great philosopher of the Risorgimento. Also buried here, in the Protestant section, is the wife of Lord Byron, Constance Mary Lloyd.

Two wooded areas – the broad Boschetto Regolare and an area of winding paths known as the Boschetto Irregolare – enhance the atmosphere of the place.

Aerial view of Forte Diamante, along the line of the old city walls

⓫ San Siro di Struppa

Via di Creto 64. **Tel** 010 809 000.
🚌 12, 14. **Open** summer: 8am–8pm
daily; winter: 8am–6:30pm. ♿

This abbey church sits in an isolated position among pretty gardens and rows of vines in the district of Struppa, the most north-easterly part of Genoa. Mentioned in 13th-century documents, it was built around 1000 and named after the bishop of Genoa, San Siro, who was born here in the 4th century. From the late 16th century onwards, the church was tampered with periodically, by the end of which its early Romanesque appearance had greatly suffered. Separate projects to restore the building, carried out in the 1920s and 1960s, have restored San Siro to its original form, including the decorative masonry in grey sandstone and the pavement of black and white pebbles outside the church.

Wooden statue of San Siro, 1640

The façade, pierced by a rose window, is divided by pilasters into three sections that correspond to the three

Polyptych of San Siro (1516), San Siro di Struppa.

interior aisles. Above is a bell tower, with three-mullioned windows at the top.

Inside, traces of the original fresco decoration are still visible, and the columns in the nave feature interesting capitals. On the wall in the right-hand aisle is an almost jaunty, heavily gilded wooden statue of *San Siro*, dating from 1640 and much restored. The high altar is modern, but visitors should notice that the front part was the architrave of a door from a 16th-century palazzo in Genoa.

The splendid *Polyptych of San Siro* (depicting the saint enthroned, eight scenes from his life and the Virgin and Child) dates from 1516. It is possibly the work of Pier Francesco Sacchi and hangs in the left-hand aisle.

⓬ Albaro

Road Map D3. 🚌

Albaro was one of the towns annexed to the city in 1926. It marks the start of the eastern, Levante zone of Greater Genoa, an almost unbroken succession of settlements rich in both artistic and historical interest, extending as far as Nervi. The scenic Corso d'Italia road hugs the coast along the way.

Since the Middle Ages, Albaro has been a popular spot for Genoa's high nobility to build their country houses. It remains the residential district par excellence of the city. Though now rather over-developed, it boasts a series of beautiful suburban villas. One of these is the 16th-century **Villa Saluzzo Bombrini**, also known as "il Paradiso". Its charming Renaissance garden features in *Trattenimento in un Giardino di Albaro* (1735), the famous painting by Alessandro Magnasco, now in Palazzo Bianco (*see p75*).

Villa Saluzzo Mongiardino, dating from the early 18th century, played host to the English poet Lord Byron in 1823. **Villa Giustinani Cambiaso** (1548) is the work of the great Renaissance architect Galeazzo Alessi, and was highly influential at the time. Set in an elevated position, surrounded by extensive grounds, it now houses

The Casella Train

The Casella train crossing a viaduct

🚉 Genova–Casella: Via alla Stazione per Casella 15, Genova. **Tel** 010 837 321. 🚌 33.
ⓦ **ferroviagenovacasella.it**

First opened in 1929, the Genova–Casella line is one of the few narrow-gauge railway tracks remaining in Italy. It takes around 55 minutes to make the 24-km (15-mile) journey from Piazza Manin in Genoa to the Apennine hinterland. The route passes through forests, over viaducts and through tunnels and reaches its highest point (458 m/1,503 ft) at Crocetta, the ancient border of the Genoese Republic; Casella, at 410 m (1,345 ft), is the head of the line. This mountain railway follows a steep gradient and is known as the "tre valli", after three valleys, the Val Bisagno, Val Polcevera and Valle Scrivia. The small stations along the way (Trensasco, Campi, Pino, Torrazza, Sardorella, Vicomorasso and Sant'Olcese) are starting points for walking and biking trails (bikes can be hired at the stations), and have trattorias eager to feed hungry travellers. You can choose to travel either in a modern or period carriage; either way, you should book.

Museo Giannettino Luxoro, Nervi

the university's faculty of engineering. Inside are decorative reliefs which are reminiscent of Classicism and Roman Mannerism. Two frescoes by the Bergamo artist Gian Battista Castello and Luca Cambiaso embellish the upstairs loggia.

⓭ Boccadasse

Road Map D3. 🚌

At the start of the Riviera di Levante, but still within Greater Genoa, Boccadasse is a fishing village which has managed to retain its picturesque charm. The houses, their façades painted in lively colours, are tightly packed around the small harbour. This is one of the most popular destinations for the Genoese, who come for day trips, especially at the weekends. It has also become very popular with tourists, for whom Boccadasse has the air of a place where time has stood still.

⓮ Nervi

Road Map D3. 🚆 🚌 🌐 **nervi.ge.it**

Nervi was, from the second half of the 19th century, a major holiday destination for the European aristocracy, especially the English. These days it is better known for its international dance festival, held in the summer.

The town's seaside location, gardens and art are the main attractions. A path called the Passeggiata Anita Garibaldi, created for Marchese Gaetano Gropallo in the 19th century, offers one of the most beautiful panoramas in Italy, with views along Nervi's own rocky shore and, beyond, the entire Riviera

Portrait of Miss Bell, by Boldini, Raccolte Frugone

di Levante as far as Monte di Portofino. The 2-km (1-mile) path passes the 16th-century Torre Gropallo, which was later modified by the Marchese in Neo-Medieval style.

In the town, the gardens of three villas have been combined to form a single park, planted with exotic or typically Mediterranean species and extending over 9 ha (22 acres). The first of these, Villa Gropallo, houses the town library, while Villa Serra contains the **Galleria d'Arte Moderna**, a gallery with a fine gathering of Ligurian paintings from the last two centuries. Villa Grimaldi Fassio houses the **Raccolte Frugone**, with mainly figurative works from the 19th and 20th centuries.

The **Museo Giannettino Luxoro** has three paintings by Alessandro Magnasco, but is best known for its decorative arts, including ceramics, clocks and nativity scene figures.

🏛 **Galleria d'Arte Moderna**
Villa Serra, Via Capolungo 3. **Tel** 010 372 60 25. **Open** 10am–7pm Tue–Sun. ♿

🏛 **Raccolte Frugone**
Villa Grimaldi Fassio, Via Capolungo 9. **Tel** 010 322 396. **Open** 9am–7pm Tue–Fri, 10am–7pm Sat & Sun. ♿

🏛 **Museo Giannettino Luxoro**
Villa Luxoro, Via Mafalda di Savoia 3. **Tel** 010 322 673. **Open** 9am–1pm Tue–Fr, 10am–1pm Sat. 📷 🚫 without permission. 📷
🌐 **museidigenova.it**

The picturesque fishing village of Boccadasse

GENOA STREET FINDER

The attractions described in the Genoa section of this guide, as well as the city's restaurants and hotels (listed in the Travellers' Needs section), all carry a map reference, which refers to the six maps in this Street Finder. The page grid below shows which parts of Genoa are covered by these maps. A complete index of the names of streets and squares marked on the maps can be found on the following pages. In addition, the maps show other sights and useful institutions (including ones not mentioned in this guide), including, police stations, hospitals, bus stations and railway termini, sports grounds, public parks, and the principal places of worship in the Ligurian capital. The medieval part of Genoa is made up of an intricate web of narrow streets and alleys, and therefore maps 5 and 6 feature an enlarged map of the Centro Storico, in order to help visitors orientate themselves within this complicated labyrinth.

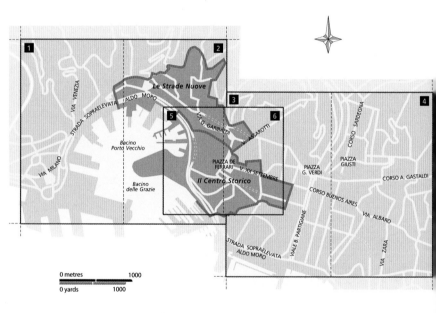

| 0 metres | 1000 |
| 0 yards | 1000 |

Scale of Maps 1-2 and 3-4

| 0 metres | 250 |
| 0 yards | 250 |

Scale of Maps 5-6

| 0 metres | 150 |
| 0 yards | 150 |

Key to Street Finder

- Major sight
- Places of interest
- Other buildings
- **FS** Railway station
- Bus terminus
- Funicular station
- **M** Metro station
- Ferry terminal

- **i** Tourist information
- Hospital with casualty unit
- Police station
- Church
- Synagogue
- Pedestrian street
- Railway line
- Funicular railway

Street Finder Index

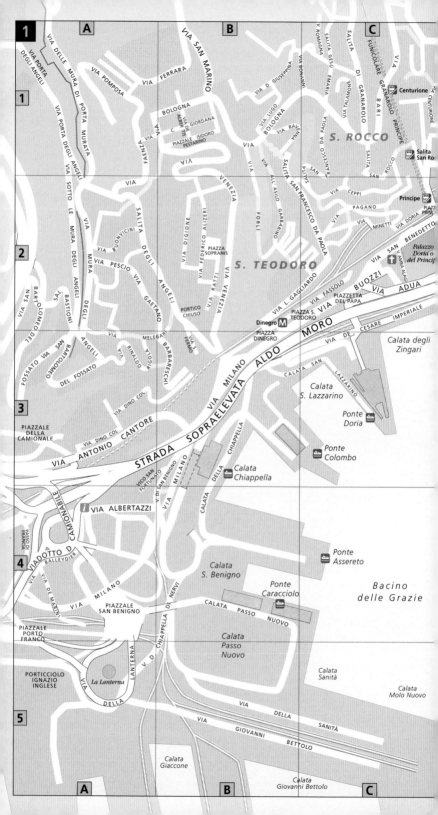

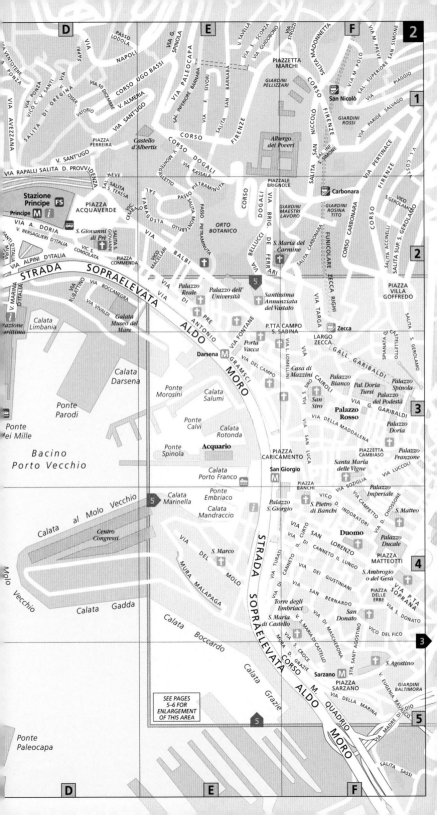

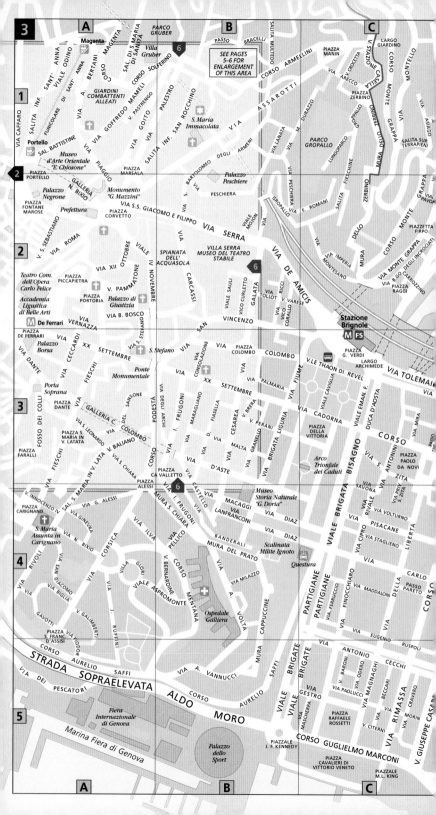

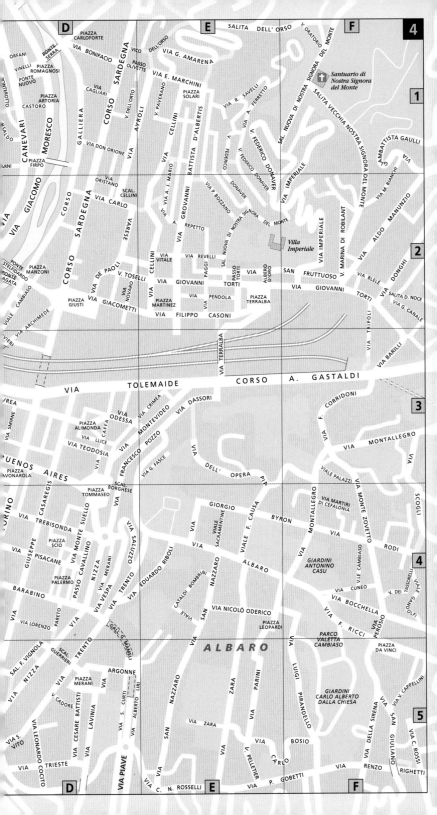

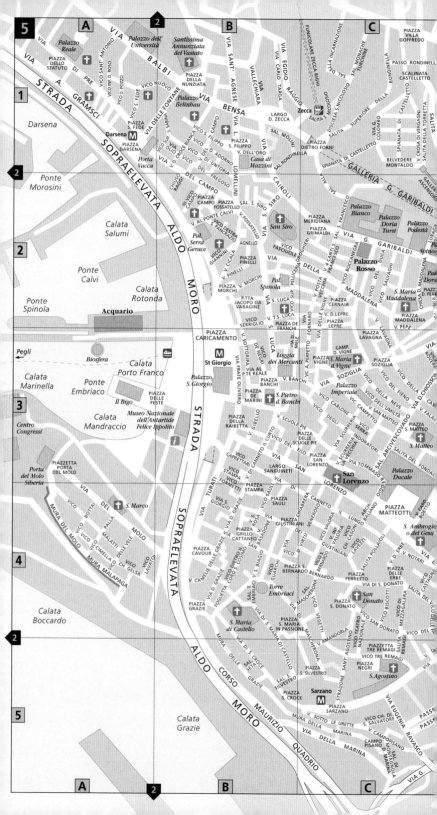

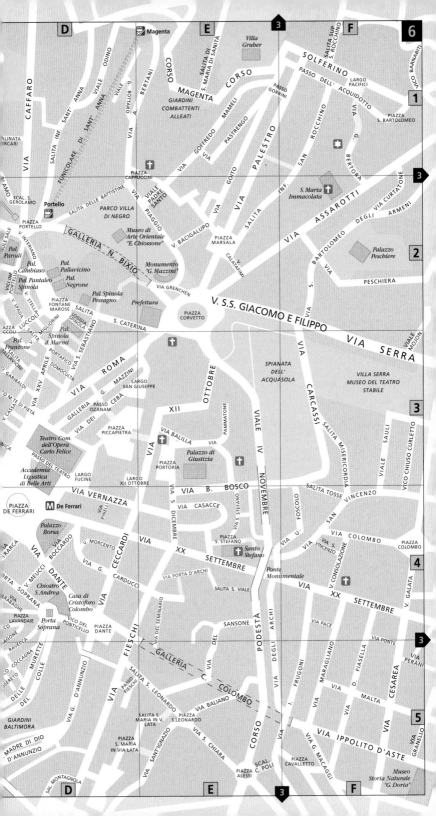

THE ITALIAN RIVIERA AREA BY AREA

The Italian Riviera at a Glance

Liguria may be one of the smallest regions in Italy but it still has plenty to offer. As well as dramatic landscapes, both along the coast and in the mountains behind, the region has a rich cultural history. Genoa, the Ligurian capital, lies midway along the coast. To the east of the city lies the Riviera di Levante (which includes La Spezia, a provincial capital), bordering the regions of Tuscany and Emilia-Romagna. To the west is the Riviera di Ponente, which meets the border with France, and has two more provincial capitals, Savona and Imperia. Liguria's long, rocky coast is often superbly picturesque, particularly in the Cinque Terre and the headland of Portofino, both on the Riviera di Levante. Punctuating the shores are seaside resorts which are buzzing with life in summer, as well as towns of historic interest such as Albenga and Bordighera. The often forested and mountainous hinterland (the so-called *entroterra*) is also home to some fascinating medieval towns, such as Pieve di Teco, Pigna and Dolceacqua.

Albenga *(see pp152–5)* shelters within its historic centre some of the oldest and most significant monuments in the region, such as the cathedral of San Michele *(above)* and the Early Christian baptistry.

The town of Cervo *(see p157)* clings to a peak and is overlooked by the lovely parish church of San Giovanni Battista (1686–1734). This fine example of Ligurian Baroque has a great concave façade embellished with stuccoes.

Cairo Montenotte

Varazze

Riviera Di Ponente
(See pp133–75)

Savona

Finale Ligure

Albenga

Triora

Cervo

Imperia

San Remo

Ventimiglia

The Casino *(see p168)* in San Remo is an example of the Art Nouveau style so popular in the heyday of this wonderful and old-fashioned seaside resort. San Remo is also known for its Festival of Italian Song.

◄ A cluster of colourful houses in Vernazza, Cinque Terre

The town of Portofino *(see pp114–15)* is packed with tall, narrow, pastel-coloured houses gathered around a small harbour. This is one of the most appealing sites in the entire region, on one of Italy's most famous stretches of coastline.

Luni *(see p131)*, close to the border with Tuscany, is an important archaeological site with a large Roman amphitheatre. It is also the source of these prehistoric statue-stelae.

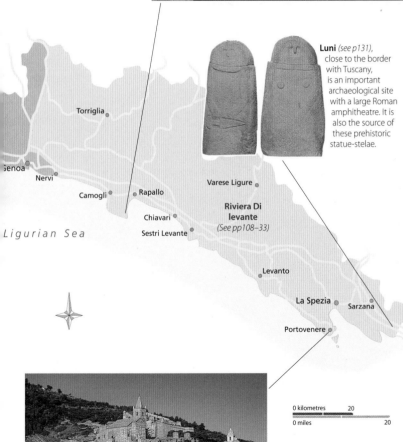

Torriglia

Genoa
Nervi
Camogli Rapallo
Chiavari
Sestri Levante

Varese Ligure

Riviera Di levante
(See pp108–33)

Ligurian Sea

Levanto

La Spezia Sarzana

Portovenere

0 kilometres   20

0 miles   20

The church of San Pietro *(see p124)* at Portovenere stands on a rocky promontory overlooking the sea. The striped church dates from the 6th century.

THE RIVIERA DI LEVANTE

Thoughts turn, inevitably, when considering this part of the world, to the great poets who have lauded it, including the romantic poets Percy Bysshe Shelley and Lord Byron; there is even a gulf named in their honour. These poets and other writers have celebrated the enchantment of the Riviera di Levante, the gentleness of the climate, the colourful flowers and the beautiful coves.

This stunningly beautiful area genuinely deserves their praise. The often beautifully positioned coastal resorts and villages are truly delightful, the result of the combined efforts of man and nature. The contrast between the sea and the steep mountains immediately behind adds to the fascination, which only increases as you head inland, into the jagged valleys and ravines where villages cling to hilltops.

The Riviera di Levante is home to a number of chic resorts – including Portofino, Santa Margherita Ligure and Rapallo – once the haunt of European, and particularly English aristocrats, but now frequented mainly by Italians. Tourism has thrived in this area since the 1800s, though this formidable success has meant the arrival of mass tourism and, with it, inevitably, over- development in some areas and periods of overcrowding (both

on the beaches and the roads). But what may seem like high-season chaos to some, is liveliness and fun to others. Largely in response to the effects of increased development, including pollution and erosion, nature reserves, national parks and other protected areas have been founded both along the coast (such as the Cinque Terre) and inland, and are a vital contribution to the conservation of this precious landscape.

The way of life in the interior is a world away from the bustling scene on the coast. Steep valleys, formed by the rivers Magra, Vara and Aveto, cut deep into the landscape and are carpeted with dense forest. There is a serious problem of population decline in some areas (a problem common to all parts of the Italian Apennines), but village communities do survive in the hinterland, dependent mostly on agriculture.

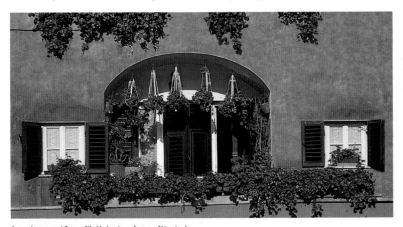

Green shutters and flower-filled balconies, a feature of Ligurian houses

◀ Boats in the harbour of the pretty medieval village of Camogli

Exploring the Riviera di Levante

This slim tongue of land starts just south of Genoa and runs as far as the easterly region of Lunigiana. Dotted along the coast are famous beaches and pretty resorts, from Camogli, Rapallo and Portofino in the west to Portovenere in the east. The inland mountains and valleys are less visited, but shelter attractive towns of both historical and architectural interest, such as Varese Ligure and Sarzana, and the archeological ruins at Luni; walks through chestnut woods reveal the contrast with the exuberant Mediterranean flora of the coast. Important monuments in the region include the forts of Sarzana, the churches of San Salvatore dei Fieschi and Sant'Andrea di Borzone and the abbey of San Fruttuoso, examples of the magnificent Romanesque and Gothic architecture which developed in the 3rd and 4th centuries in the region.

A typical tall house in the medieval town of Tellaro

Sights at a Glance

For map symbols *see back flap*

Fishing boats at Manarola, one of the villages in the Cinque Terre

The seafront at La Spezia, the easternmost city on the Riviera di Levante

KEY

===== Motorway

===== Main road

===== Minor road

━○━ Railway

===== Regional border

△ Summit

Getting Around

The main communication routes in the Riviera di Levante are the A12 (the motorway linking Livorno with Genoa) and the A15, linking Parma to La Spezia. Running the length of the coast is the Via Aurelia (Strada Statale 1). Numerous roads link the coast to the hinterland, often travelling through spectacular landscapes. The Genoa–Livorno railway line provides train links, with regional and local train services connecting all towns and villages, with the important exception of Portofino. Efficient coach services ensure daily links between all the towns on the coast and those inland. In high season, there are also ferry services running between the key centres along the coast between Portofino and La Spezia, including the Cinque Terre, as well as to the most popular offshore islands.

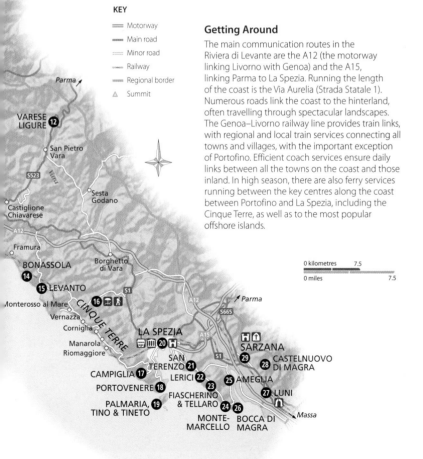

Typically painted façades in the charming fishing village of Bogliasco

❶ Bogliasco

Genoa. **Road Map** D4. 🏠 4,600.
🚊 🚌 ℹ️ Via Aurelia 106, 010
347 04 29. 🎭 Festa Patronale della
Madonna del Carmine (Jul).
🌐 prolocobogliasco.it

On the aptly named Golfo di Paradiso east of Genoa, Bogliasco is an elegant residential and tourist town with a few small beaches. It retains the look of a traditional fishing village, though, with painted houses arranged prettily around the mouth of the River Bogliasco (crossed by a medieval bridge known as the Ponte Romano).

The town is dominated by the 1,000-year-old **Castello**, a defensive tower built by the Republic of Genoa. To the west, high up on a cliff, is the 18th-century parish church, with a terrace of black and white pebbles in front. The **Oratory of Santa Chiara** (15th century) is also of note. Inside are several traditional, highly ornate, processional crosses, among them one by Maragliano (1713).

❷ Torriglia

Genoa. **Road Map** D3. 🏠 2,300.
🚊 Genoa. 🚌 ℹ️ Ente Parco
d'Antola:, Via Nostra Signora della
Provvidenza 3, 010 944 931.
🎭 Presepe di Pentema (Dec–Jan).
🌐 parcoantola.it

This small summer holiday resort is distinguished by its position among the forested Antola mountains. In the Roman period it was a significant commercial centre, located as it was at an important crossroads on the main route between Genoa and Emilia-Romagna.

The town is overlooked by the imposing ruins of a medieval **castle**. Built by the Malaspina family, it was later occupied by the Fieschi family and, from the second half of the 16th century, by the Doria dynasty.

Environs
Two pleasant trips can be made from Torriglia. The first is to **Pentema**, about 6 km (4 miles) north of the town along a winding road. Having crossed a totally unspoilt landscape of hills and mountains covered in dense forest, you reach one of the loveliest villages inland from the Riviera di Levante. Pentema consists of a handful of houses scattered on a sun-facing hill, with a church at the top. The houses, set on terraces, are identical, all very simple and with chalet-style roofs. The village streets are still paved with river stones, or simply earth.

Absolute silence seems to reign at the wonderfully peaceful **Lago del Brugneto**, some 8 km (5 miles) east of Torriglia. An artificial basin created as a reservoir for Genoa, the lake lies within the **Parco Regionale del Monte Antola** and is entirely surrounded by hills and mountains. A scenic walking trail snakes around the shores of the lake: some 13 km (8 miles) long, the walk takes about six hours to complete.

❸ Camogli

Genoa. **Road Map** D4. 🏠 5,900. 🚊
🚌 ℹ️ Via XX Settembre 33, 0185 771
066. 🎭 Sagra del Pesce (second Sun
in May; 0185 729 01). 🌐 camogli.it

An old fishing and seafaring village on the Golfo di Paradiso, Camogli is named after the women (*moglie*) who ran the town while their husbands were at sea. It has an enchanting medieval heart, with tall, narrow houses (some are over six storeys high) crowded around the harbour and along the maze of alleys and steps behind.

A small promontory, known as the "Isola" (island) because it was once separated from the mainland, is home to the **Basilica di Santa Maria Assunta**, founded in the 12th century but much modified. It has a Neo-Classical façade and a 17th-century pebbled courtyard. The interior is richly decorated: the vault in the central nave has a fresco by Francesco Semino and Nicolò Barabino, and the high altar has a sculpture of the Virgin Mary by Bernardo Schiaffino (18th century). On a cliff overlooking the sea stands **Castel Dragone**, medieval but much altered.

The **Museo Marinaro Gio Bono Ferrari**, at the end of the seafront, documents a glorious period in Camogli's history that seems almost unthinkable today: namely, the 18th and 19th centuries, when Camogli supplied a fleet of some 3,000 merchant ships under contract to the major European states;

The seafront at Camogli with the "Isola" in the background

The seafront at Santa Margherita Ligure

they even fought with Napoleon. Camogli's fishing fleet today is tiny by comparison.

The museum contains models of ships, navigational instruments and also paintings of ships (often by the ships' owners), which served as ex votos. The cloister next to the sanctuary of **Nostra Signora del Boschetto**, just outside Camogli, is also full of sailors' ex votos.

If you are in the area in May, don't miss the famous Sagra del Pesce, when vast numbers of fish are cooked in a giant frying pan (*see p32*).

🏛 Museo Gio Bono Ferrari
Via GB Ferrari, 41. **Tel** 0185 729 049.
Open 9am–noon Mon, Thu & Fri;
9am–noon, 3–6pm Wed, Sat, Sun & hols (4–7pm Jun–Sep).

❹ Portofino Peninsula

See pp114–17.

❺ Santa Margherita Ligure

Genoa. **Road Map** E4. 🏔 10,800.
FS 🚌 **ℹ** Via XXV Aprile 2/B, 0185 287 485. 🎎 Nostra Signora della Rosa (Jul). **W** turismoinliguria.it

Built along an inlet on the Golfo del Tigullio, Santa Margherita is a lively resort with a beautiful harbour and grand hotels and villas. The lavish rococo church of Santa Margherita d'Antiochia gave the town its name.

Santa Margherita emerged in its own right only in the 19th century, when it was created out of the two villages of Pescino and Corte. It soon became a popular destination among the (mainly British) holidaying elite.

The hill between the two old villages has been transformed into the public **Parco di Villa Durazzo**. The villa at the top, begun in the mid-16th century, still has its original furnishings as well as an art collection. The large Italian-style garden offers lovely views of the city and the sea.

At the foot of the hill, in the district known as Corte, is the 17th-century church of the Cappuccini, with a 15th-century wooden cross.

❻ Rapallo

Genoa. **Road Map** E4. 🏔 29,300.
FS 🚌 **ℹ** Lungomare Vittorio Veneto 7, 0185 230 346. 🎎 Mostra Internazionale dei Cartoonists (Nov–Dec); Festa della Madonna di Montallegro (Jul).
W turismoinliguria.it

Rapallo enjoys a gorgeous position on the Golfo del Tigullio and is perhaps the best-known resort along the Riviera di Levante. It has a large marina, swimming pool, sailing, tennis and riding schools, as well as an 18-hole golf course.

The climate was a big draw for aristocrats from the 19th century, as can be seen from the Art Nouveau cafés and hotels lining **Lungomare Vittorio Veneto**. Max Beerbohm (1872–1956), the English wit and critic, was a resident for many years. In the centre, the parallel streets Via Venezia, Via Mazzini and Via Marsala define the medieval "borgo murato" (walled village), so-named because of the way the buildings are closely packed together. Historic monuments include the old parish church of Santo Stefano (mostly 17th century) and the adjacent 15th-century civic tower, and the medieval Ponte di Annibale (Hannibal's bridge), with a single-span arch of 15 m (49 ft).

From Piazza Pastene, on the seafront, you can reach the **Castello**, built in 1551 on a cliff to defend the settlement against pirate raids. There is also a highly enjoyable funicular ride up to the **Santuario di Montallegro** (16th century), from where there are superb views of the coast and sea.

Villa Tigullio is home to the **Museo del Merletto**, a museum of lace with more than 1,400 pieces from the 16th to 19th centuries. Among these are lace clothing, lace for furnishing, and several 18–19th century pillows. There is also a collection of designs.

Environs
Just east of Rapallo, **Zoagli** is a small resort which still feels like a fishing village despite being bombed in World War II.

🏛 Museo del Merletto
Villa Tigullio, Parco Casale. **Tel** 0185 633 05. **Open** 3–6pm Tue, Wed, Fri & Sat; 10–11:30am Thu & Sun. 🎟

The castle at Rapallo, a defensive structure dating from 1551

❹ Portofino Peninsula

This headland extends for around 3 km (2 miles) out to sea and separates the Paradiso and Tigullio gulfs. The southern part, hot and dry, has high cliffs that enclose gorgeous inlets hidden in the Mediterranean maquis; on the northern side, woods of chestnut trees dominate. The small area is extraordinarily rich botanically, and its favourable position has drawn human settlements since antiquity: *Portus Delphini* (the bay was, and still is, known for its large dolphin population) was an important settlement in the Roman era. Today, the peninsula is dotted with impossibly picturesque hamlets and villages, including the world-famous port and celebrity mecca of Portofino. There are also magnificent walks to be done, as well as all kinds of maritime sports, including some great diving.

A splendid view of the rocky coast close to Portofino

↑ Camogli
(see p112)

San Fruttuoso

Cristo degli Abissi
This bronze statue by Guido Galletti was lowered into the sea at San Fruttuoso in 1954, a symbol of the attachment of the Ligurian people to the sea. Every year, on the last Sunday in July, garlands of flowers are given to the statue in memory of those who have lost their lives at sea. Divers pay homage to the statue at all times of the year.

KEY

① **Punta di Portofino** can be reached on foot. Beyond the 16th-century Fortezza di San Giorgio, known as "Castle Brown", is the lighthouse and the Madonnina del Capo statue.

② **Fortezza di San Giorgio**

★ **San Fruttuoso**
A symbol of the Italian heritage and conservation organization FAI, to which it has belonged since 1983, San Fruttuoso is a delightful village with houses grouped around a Benedictine abbey, built by the Doria family in the 1200s. It is dominated by the church's octagonal bell tower. Alongside is the cloister and mausoleum of the Doria family. San Fruttuoso is accessible only by boat or on foot: it is 30 minutes by boat from Camogli, for example, or 75 minutes' walk from Portofino.

Paraggi

In Paraggi, a short distance from Portofino, multicoloured houses are gathered around a small sandy cove, with terraces rising up the mountain behind. Nowadays, the once-flourishing trades of fishing and olive-pressing have given way to tourism. The views from here are beautiful.

VISITORS' CHECKLIST

Practical Information
Genoa. **Road Map** D4. 590.
Via Roma 35, 0185 269 024.
Abbey of San Fruttuoso: **Tel** 0185 772 703. **Open** Mar, Apr & Oct: 10am–3:45pm daily; May–Sep: 10am–5:45pm daily; Jan, Feb, Nov & Dec: 10am–3:45pm Tue–Sun (Opening timings vary depending on the weather). **Closed** 25 Dec.

Transport
Santa Margherita Ligure.
Santa Margherita Ligure to Portofino. boats around the Golfo del Tigullio and to Cinque Terre (Apr–Sep); 0185 284 670.

Santa Margherita Ligure *(see p113)*

Paraggi

Key

— Boat Routes

Portofino

2

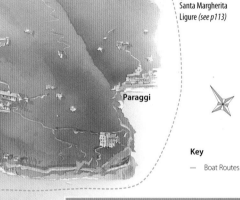

★ Portofino

The town, with its lovely harbour and rows of coloured houses facing the piazzetta, is best viewed from the headland opposite. The cove is sheltered both by its position and by the mountain range, which rises to a height of 600m (1,970 ft) and forms a 3-km (2-mile) long cliff behind the town. While small, the port still has space for 300 mooring berths.

1

0 kilometres 50

0 miles 50

Colourful houses in the quaint village of Portofino on the Ligurian coast ▶

⑦ Chiavari

Genoa. **Road Map** E4. 🚗 28,200.
🚆 🚌 ℹ Corso Assarotti 1, 0185
325 198. 🎉 Festa Patronale di
Nostra Signora dell'Orto (2 Jul).
W turismoinliguria.it

One of the principal cities in
Liguria, Chiavari stands on an
alluvial plan on the eastern
shores of the Golfo del Tigullio
and on the west bank of the
Entella torrent. Called Clavarium,
("key to the valleys") by the
Romans, the town was once
known for its old crafts, particularly
ship-building, chair-making and
macramé. Nowadays, tourism is
the most important source of
income. The marina has space
for some 450 boats.

The ruins of a necropolis,
dating from the 8th–7th
centuries BC, now held in the
local archaeological museum,
demonstrate that the area was
inhabited by the Liguri Tigulli
people in the pre-Roman era.
The fortified town of Chiavari
dates from 1178, when the
Genoese expanded into the
Riviera di Levante in their
struggle to counter the power
of the Fieschi family (arch
rivals of the Doria dynasty).

The heart of Chiavari is
Piazza Mazzini, around which
the arcaded streets of the old
city are laid out. One of these,
Via dei Martiri della Liberazione,
is a straight alleyway known
as a *"carruggiu dritu"*; it was
occupied by the bourgeoisie
from the 14th century. This

The abbey of Sant'Andrea di Borzone, in a stunning position

street, Via Rivarola and Via
Ravaschieri have porticoes
made of the local slate.

The cathedral, **Nostra
Signora dell'Orto**, has 17th-
century origins but many
alterations were carried out in
the 19th–20th centuries. The
interior, richly decorated with
gilded stucco and marble
inlay, contains works by Orazio
De Ferrari and Anton Maria
Maragliano. The parish church
of San Giovanni Battista was
founded in 1182 but was
rebuilt in 1624.

In the outskirts, at Bacezza,
is the 15th-century **Santuario
della Madonna delle Grazie**,
from where there is a lovely
view stretching from Porto-fino
to Sestri Levante. Inside is a
16th-century cycle of frescoes
by Teramo Piaggio and
Luca Cambiaso.

⑧ Abbazia di Sant'Andrea di Borzone

Via Abbazia 63, Borzonasca. **Road
Map** E3. 🚆 Chiavari. 🚌 **Tel** 0185 342
503. **Open** until sunset daily. ♿

The lovely abbey of Sant'Andrea
di Borzone can be reached along
a winding road that runs
eastwards from the centre of
Borzonasca, an inland town
some 16 km (10 miles)
from Chiavari.

Standing in splendid isolation,
Sant'Andrea is one of the oldest
Benedictine settlements in Italy.

It was founded in the 12th
century by the monks of San
Colombano in Bobbio (in Emilia-
Romagna) and donated in 1184
to the Benedictines of Marseille,
who reclaimed the land and
used it for cultivation. The monks
undertook a programme of
terracing and irrigation: even
today, despite the fact that the
woods have begun to encroach,
the remains of dry stone walls
can still be seen along the
paths. The abbey was rebuilt in
the 13th century, at the behest
of the Fieschi counts, but has
managed to retain its original
Romanesque look.

The church, with a square
bell tower, is built of brick and
stone. It has a single nave and a
semicircular apse, and a cornice
of terracotta arches. Several
cloister columns survive from
the old monastery. In the
presbytery is a polyptych dating
from 1484, by an unknown
Genoese artist, and a slate
tabernacle from 1513.

⑨ Santo Stefano d'Aveto

Genoa. **Road Map** E3. 🚗 1,250.
🚌 ℹ Piazza del Popolo 6, 0185 880
46. 🎉 Cantamaggio (2 May).
W provincia.genova.it and
W parks.it

Situated in an almost Alpine-
looking hollow, dominated by
Monte Maggiorasca, Santo
Stefano is both a summer and
a winter holiday resort. It is a
popular centre for cross-country

The old centre of Chiavari, with its
characteristic arcaded streets

skiing. In summer, you can enjoy the simple pleasure of strolling around the pretty historic centre, with its winding alleys and small squares.

Close to the village are the isolated, imposing ruins of **Castello Malaspina**, built by the local nobles in the 12th century, and subsequently passed to the Fieschi and Doria families.

The Val d'Aveto was formed by the Aveto torrent, which carves out an upland plain southwest of the town, where pastures are enclosed by mountains covered in forests of silver fir, Norway spruce, and beech and ash trees. Much of this is now part of the **Parco Naturale Regionale dell'Aveto.**

From Santo Stefano, you can reach Monte Aiona, the tallest peak in the park at 1,700 m (5,576 ft), along trails that show off the beauty of this wild, unspoilt area. Note that the western slopes form part of the **Riserva Naturale delle Agoraie** and are open only to those doing scientific research.

Another area of interest is the great forest of Le Lame, where there are marshes and small lakes of glacial origin. The icy cold water has perfectly preserved some 2,500-year-old fir trunks, which can be seen lying on the bottom of Lago degli Abeti.

Impressive Basilica di San Salvatore dei Fieschi, Lavagna

⑩ Lavagna

Genoa. **Road Map** E4. 🚗 12,900. 🚉
ℹ️ Piazza della Libertà 48/A, 0185 395 070. 🎉 Torta dei Fieschi (7–14 Aug).
🌐 **turismoinliguria.it**

The town of Lavagna lies across the Entella from Chiavari, to which it is linked by several bridges, including the fine medieval Ponte della Maddalena.

In the Middle Ages this coastal town was a stronghold of the local Fieschi counts. Historically, its prosperity has been due largely to the local slate quarries. Nowadays, the town depends more on its beach and marina, which has space for more than 1,500 yachts. The town's medieval heart developed inland from the sea, from what

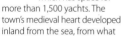

Logo of the Parco Naturale dell'Aveto

is now Via Nuova Italia. Historic monuments include the church of **Santo Stefano**, dating from the 10th century, but rebuilt in 1653, when a Baroque staircase and asymmetrical bell towers were added; the imposing 17th-century Palazzo Franzone, now the town hall; and the church of **Santa Giulia di Centaura** (1654), reached along a scenic road from Viale Mazzini and with panoramic views along the coast.

Environs

A short drive or 30 minutes' walk inland from Lavagna lies the village of San Salvatore di Cogorno, from where you can reach the **Basilica di San Salvatore dei Fieschi**, one of the most important Romanesque-Gothic monuments in Liguria. It was commissioned in 1245 by Ottobono Fieschi, the future Pope Hadrian V and nephew of Pope Innocent IV (another Fieschi), who made it a basilica in 1252. The building lies in a particularly lovely setting, on the top of a hill covered in olive groves, and surrounded by ancient buildings, among them the ruined 13th-century Palazzo dei Conti Fieschi.

The church is dominated by a powerful square tower which rises over the crossing. It has cornices of blind arches and four-mullioned windows, and is crowned with a tall spire with four pinnacles. The upper façade features alternating bands of marble and slate, and a large rose window. The marble and slate striped bands are repeated inside the rather austere interior, and slate is used elsewhere, too, in the form of tiles in the transept and presbytery.

🏛️ **Basilica di San Salvatore dei Fieschi**
Piazza Innocenzo IV, San Salvatore di Cogorno. **Tel** 0185 380245.
Open 8am–noon, 1:30–6pm daily (7pm in summer).

The Slate Road

For information on the Via dell'Ardesia: GAL Fontanabuona e Sviluppo, Via Chiapparino 26, Cicagna. **Tel** 0185 971 091 🌐 **fontanabuona.com**

From the black stripes of San Salvatore dei Fieschi to the roofs of numerous houses, slate is a characteristic element of many buildings in the Riviera di Levante. It is still quarried in the hinterland behind Chiavari (not far, in fact, from the town of Lavagna, the Italian for blackboard). To visit the quarries, take the SS225 road from Chiavari to the Fontanabuona valley. There are six itineraries to follow as part of the so-called Via dell'Ardesia ("slate road"). You can visit a slate quarry at Isolana di Orero, and there is a slate museum at nearby Cicagna, 20 km (12 miles) from Lavagna.

Sculpture in slate

Fishing boats on the Baia del Silenzio at Sestri Levante

⓫ Sestri Levante

Genoa. **Road Map** E4. 🏛 19,000.
🚉 🚌 *i* Piazza Sant'Antonio 10,
0185 457 011. 🎭 Premio Letterario
per la Fiaba Hans Christian Andersen
(end May). **w** turismoinliguria.it

At the far western point of the
Golfo del Tigullio, Sestri Levante
is one of the liveliest resorts on
the coast. The resort clusters
around a rocky peninsula known
as the "Isola". In the heart of the
old town, the most interesting
monuments are the **Basilica
of Santa Maria di Nazareth**
by Giovan Battista Carlone
(1604–16); the **Palazzo Durazzo
Pallavicini** (17th century), which
is now the town hall; and the
lovely Romanesque church of **San
Nicolò dell'Isola** (12th century).

Of much greater appeal
altogether, however, is the
wonderful Grand Hotel dei
Castelli, at the tip of the peninsula. Built in the 1920s on the
site of an old castle, the hotel
has a magnificent park overlooking two bays: the sandy
Baia delle Favole, named
after Hans Christian Andersen,
who stayed here in 1833 (*favole*
means fairy tales), is now rather
built up; but the smaller and
more secluded **Baia del Silenzio**,
framed by multicoloured
houses and dotted with fishing
boats, is utterly charming.

Also in the grounds is the
tower where Marconi carried
out some of his radio experi-
ments in 1934. Back in the old
town, the **Galleria Rizzi** has

paintings, sculptures, ceramics
and furniture collected by the
local Rizzi family. The paintings
include works by Giovanni
Andrea De Ferrari and
Alessandro Magnasco.

🏛 **Galleria Rizzi**
Via dei Cappuccini 4. **Tel** 0185 413 00.
Open Apr–Oct: 10:30am–1pm Sun;
May–Sep: 4–7pm Wed (mid-Jun–Sep:
9:30–11:30pm Fri, Sat). 🎭

⓬ Varese Ligure

La Spezia. **Road Map** E4. 🏛 2,500.
🚌 from Sestri Levante. *i* Via Portici
19, 0187 842 094 (in high season).
w comune.vareseligure.sp.it

This pretty, inland summer
resort was, for centuries, an
important market town and
stopping place on the route
north to Parma, in Emilia-
Romagna. After the decline in
traffic across the mountains
in the 19th century, the town
acquired the rural role it still
has today. Agriculture is the
main trade in this region.

Varese Ligure was a
possession of the Fieschi family,
who obtained it in fief from
Emperor Frederick I (Barbarossa)
in 1161. They built the rather
splendid 15th-century castle.
This stands in a piazza which
was once the market square,
around which the so-called
Borgo Rotondo was built: almost
perfectly circular, with a continuous screen of buildings, this
ring of shops and houses around
the market was an ingenious
defensive idea dreamt up by the
Fieschis. Charming to look at,

the multicoloured façades
are supported by arches and
porticoes. The 16th-century
Borgo Nuovo, which grew up
alongside, features aristocratic
palazzi dating from the 16th to
19th centuries, a long, affluent
period for the town.

Nearby, crossed by a medieval
bridge, is the River Crovana. This
is one of the tributaries of the
Vara, whose valley, the **Val di
Vara**, extends for more than
60 km (37 miles) and has a
varied landscape, among the
best preserved in the region.
The upper reaches of the river
flow through wonderful
mountain scenery, among
woods of beech and chestnut,
interspersed by meadows
where cows and horses graze;
elsewhere there are scenic
stretches where the river is
confined between rocks.
Towards the coast the valley
widens and the river flows
through the Parco Naturale
Regionale di Montemarcello-
Magra (see p130).

⓭ Moneglia

Genova. **Road Map** E4. 🏛 2,700.
🚉 🚌 *i* Corso Longhi 32, 0185
490 576. 🎭 Mostra-Mercato dell'Olio
d'Oliva (Easter Mon).
w prolocomoneglia.it

The town once known as
Monilia faces a small gulf which
interrupts the high, jagged
cliff extending between Sestri
Levante and Deiva Marina.
Moneglia is a typical fishing
town, with picturesque *carruggi*
and slate roofs, and a thoroughly

View of the unusual Borgo Rotondo in Varese Ligure

The beach at Moneglia in summer, crowded with tourists

gentle pace. Long years of loyalty to the Republic of Genoa have left many traces: among them, the **Fortezza Monleone**, dating from 1173, and the 16th- century **Castello di Villafranca**, on the slopes above the town centre.

The striped parish church of **Santa Croce** (1726) has a *Last Supper* by Luca Cambiaso, the great 16th-century artist who was born in Moneglia. Inside, there are also two links from the chain that once closed the gates of Pisa, trophies from the battle of Meloria (*see p43*), in which the Monegliese helped Genoa to defeat Pisa.

There is lots of scope for swimming at Moneglia, especially beneath the cliffs, and you can go on lovely walks through the maquis west towards Punta Baffe and Punta Manara, or through hillside villages and scenic vineyards towards the Bracco mountain pass.

⑭ Bonassola

La Spezia. **Road Map** E4. 🚇 1,000.
🚊 🚌 🛈 Via Fratelli Rezzano, 0187 813 500. 🎪 Madonna del Rosario (first weekend in Oct).
🔲 **prolocobonassola.it**

Built around a cove, in a splendid spot, Bonassola was selected by the Genoese in the 13th century as the site

for a defensive naval base. These days, Bonassola has no marina, but it is not difficult to land small boats here. The town also has a wide beach, mostly pebbles, and the sea bed is varied and suited to dives of medium difficulty.

Sights of interest include the parish church of **Santa Caterina** (16th century), with sumptuous Baroque decoration and numerous ex votos, evidence of the busy seafaring lives of the inhabitants.

The tiny church of **Madonna della Punta**, built on a cliff jutting out over the sea to the west of the village, is the focus of a popular sunset walk.

Several old villages in the vicinity are worth exploring, either on foot or by car. One path, following a route through vineyards and olive groves, takes walkers the 9 km (6 miles) to **Montaretto**, known for its production (albeit limited) of good white wine.

Santa Croce bell tower, Moneglia

⑮ Levanto

La Spezia. **Road Map** E4. 🚇 5,800.
🚊 🛈 Piazza Mazzini, 0187 808 125.
🎪 Festa del Mare (24–25 Jul).
🔲 **levanto.com**

Over the years, Levanto has been a centre for trade, agriculture and, most recently, tourism: it has a long and lovely beach. The small town is divided into Borgo Antico,

the medieval district around the church of Sant'Andrea and the hill of San Giacomo, and the Borgo Nuovo, which grew up in the 15th century on the nearby plain. In the medieval district is the lovely Loggia del Comune (13th century), the Casa Restani, with a 13th–14th-century portico, a castle (privately owned) and a stretch of the old town walls, dating from 1265.

The principal monument is the parish church of **Sant' Andrea**, a lovely example of Ligurian Gothic. The façade is striped with white marble and local serpentine (a softish green stone), with a finely carved rose window. Serpentine is also used in the capitals of the columns in the nave. Works of art inside include two canvases from a polyptych by Carlo Braccesco (1495) depicting *Saints Augustine and Jerome* and *Saints Blaise and Pantaleon*. In the ex-oratory of the church is a **Museo Permanente della Cultura Materiale**, which reconstructs various aspects of the rural and seafaring life of the Riviera di Levante.

Among vestiges of Levanto's more recent past are several important palazzi (often with pretty painted façades) dating from the 17th and 18th centuries, when many Genoese noble families chose to build their summer residences here: **Palazzo Vannoni**, facing on to Piazza Cavour, is the most important one.

🏛 **Museo Permanente della Cultura Materiale**
Piazzetta Massola 4. **Tel** 0187 817 776. **Open** Jul & Aug: 9–11pm Tue–Sun; at other times by request.

Striped white marble façade of Sant'Andrea in Levanto

⓰ The Cinque Terre

Translucent sea and cliffs plunging into the water; towns clinging to rocky slopes, and terraces dug into the contours of the mountains directly behind the coast. These are the Cinque Terre (Five Lands), today a national park encompassing some 20 km (12 miles) of coast and the immediate hinterland. A UNESCO World Heritage site, this is a place where the relationship between man and the environment is preserved in miraculous equilibrium. The five small towns on the coast that give the area its name are Monterosso al Mare, Vernazza, Corniglia, Manarola and Riomaggiore. The coastal paths are great for both walking and horse riding *(see p201)*, and you can go diving, too. Access is primarily by foot, boat or train (rather than car), and note that accommodation gets very booked up in high season.

Lontani andremo e serberemo un'eco della tua voce, come si ricorda del sole l'erba grigia nelle corti scurite, tra le case.

① **Monterosso al Mare**
For Italians, the words of writer Eugenio Montale (1896–1981), who holidayed here as a child, capture the atmosphere of Monterosso. Alongside the old town is the popular tourist area of Fegina, with a sandy beach.

Levanto

Pignone

Pignone

S.Antonia Semaforo

0 kilometres   1

0 miles   1

② **The Terraces**
The steep-sided landscape of the Cinque Terre is an extraordinary example of an architectural landscape. The terraces sculpted out of the mountain slopes have been used primarily to cultivate olives and vines (from which the highly coveted Sciacchetrà fortified wine – see p187 – is made).

③ **Vernazza**
With its colourful houses clustered around an inlet, Vernazza is the only town in the Cinque Terre to have a harbour; this is known to have been in use in antiquity. The port has made Vernazza the richest village in the area, while the combination of the surroundings and architectural grace also make it the prettiest place in the Cinque Terre.

For hotels and restaurants in this region see pp181–2 and pp191–4

④ Corniglia
This town, built high on a ridge, 100 m (320 ft) above a beautiful and sheltered beach, was called Cornelia by the Romans. The beach has a history almost totally separate from that of the town above, which has always been an agricultural centre. The local vineyards produce limited quantities of white Cinque Terre and Sciacchetrà wine.

VISITORS' CHECKLIST

Practical Information
La Spezia.
Road Map E–F4. 🛈 **Tel** 0187 812 523 (Corniglia station); 0187 760 511 (Manarola station); 0187 817 059 (Monterosso al Mare station); 0187 920 633 (Riomaggiore station); 0187 812 533 (Vernazza station). 🎫 Compulsory Carta Cinque Terre gives access to transport, paths and maps. 🆆 parconazionale5terre.it

Transport
🆵🆂

⑤ Manarola
Clinging to a cliff overlooking the sea, the village of Manarola makes a striking sight with its compact, coloured houses. The headquarters of Le Cinque Terre National Park are located here.

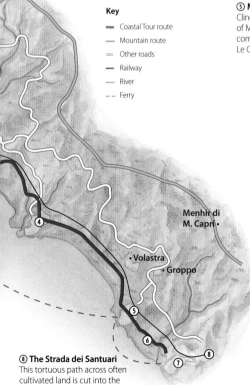

Key
- ▬ Coastal Tour route
- ── Mountain route
- ══ Other roads
- ▬ Railway
- ── River
- ‒ ‒ Ferry

Menhir di M. Capri •

• Volastra
• Groppo

⑥ Via dell'Amore
Constructed in the 1920s, the Via dell'Amore (Path of Love) traces a route from Manarola to Riomaggiore. The path, cut into the steep cliffs, is just a 20-minute easy walk, but is scenic, thrilling and justifiably renowned.

⑧ The Strada dei Santuari
This tortuous path across often cultivated land is cut into the mountainside and links the five coastal towns. It can be covered on foot, by bicycle or on horseback, and offers superlative views.

⑦ Riomaggiore
Riomaggiore has two rows of tall narrow houses and lots of seafood restaurants. You can go diving off nearby Punta di Montenero.

The church in the pretty medieval village of Campiglia

⑰ Campiglia

La Spezia. **Road Map** F5. 🔼 150.
🚉 La Spezia. 🚌 from La Spezia.
ℹ️ IAT Cinque Terre, 0187 770 900.
🌐 **campiglia.net** and
🌐 **tramontidicampiglia.it**

This rural village, founded in the Middle Ages and occupying a precipitous position near the coast only a short distance from La Spezia, is fascinating and magical.

Campiglia was built on an old mule road along the ridge between Portovenere and Levanto, and it is still a great starting point for walks. The most beautiful, and hardest, walk is along CAI (Italian Alpine Club) path no. 11. This takes visitors through the spectacular terrain of the **Tramonti**, a continuation of the Cinque Terre with terraces of vines, until you descend a steep flight of 2,000 steps, as far as the small beach of Punta del Persico: the landscape open to the sea is genuinely breathtaking.

⑱ Portovenere

La Spezia. **Road Map** F5. 🔼 4,600.
🚉 La Spezia. 🚌 ℹ️ Piazza Bastreri 7, 0187 790 691. 🎭 Festa della Madonna Bianca (17 Aug).
🌐 **portovenere.it** and
🌐 **prolocoportovenere.it**

Portus Veneris (the port of Venus) was fêted for its beauty as far back as Roman times. Nowadays, its beauty and cachet even rival those of Portofino.

Lying at the base of the rocky cliff that fringes the western side of the Golfo della Spezia, Portovenere looks like a typical fortified fishing village, with rows of gaily painted houses on the slope down to the harbour. Behind is a maze of narrow alleys and vaulted staircases, populated by Portovenere's famous cats.

At the tip of the headland is the striped church of **San Pietro**, built in 1277 in honour of the patron saint of fishermen. It incorporates elements of a 6th-century, early Christian church and has a small Romanesque loggia, open to the sea.

Also worth visiting is **San Lorenzo**, a short walk up an alley from the harbour. This beautiful Romanesque church was built in the 12th century, but reworked in the Gothic and Renaissance eras. It has a wonderfully rustic font inside.

Further up the alley (it's a steep climb), visitors will reach the 16th-century **castello**. Built by the Genoese, this is a grandiose example of military architecture, and also offers fantastic views. It is linked to the town by a line of walls with square towers. The remains of various medieval fortifications are still visible around Portovenere.

Le Grazie, along the winding route north from Portovenere to La Spezia, is another place of great beauty. Monte Muzzerone nearby is hugely popular among free-climbers. The village itself is home to the church of Santa Maria delle Grazie (15th century) and the 16th-century monastery of the Olivetans. By the inlet of Varignano, nearby, is a ruined **Roman villa** (2nd to 1st centuries BC), with a mosaic pavement and a small museum, known as the **Antiquarium**.

🏰 **Castello**
Tel 0187 791 106. **Open** 10:30am–5:30pm daily. **Closed** during events & in winter. 🅿️

🏛️ **Antiquarium del Varignano**
Le Grazie. **Tel** 0187 790 307.
Open on request.

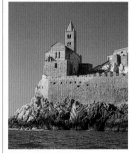

The church of San Pietro at Portovenere, overlooking the sea

⑲ Palmaria, Tino and Tinetto

La Spezia. **Road Map** F5. 🚤 from La Spezia or Portovenere for Isola Palmaria, 0187 732 987. ℹ️ IAT Portovenere, 0187 790 691.

Liguria's only archipelago once formed part of the headland of Portovenere.

The largest island, **Isola Palmaria**, is divided from the mainland by just a narrow channel. It is covered in dense vegetation on one side, and has steep cliffs and caves on the other. In the past, Portor marble, a valuable black stone used in

The harbour at Portovenere, with its characteristic painted houses

The island of Palmaria, the largest in the Ligurian archipelago

some buildings in Portovenere, was quarried here, which has partially disfigured the island. Palmaria is a popular among the locals, who come for day trips, but the island's appeal can't compete with that of the mainland.

The much smaller islands of Tino and Tinetto are in a military zone. Access to **Tino** is allowed only on the 13th of September, for the Festa di San Venerio. There is a ruined 11th-century abbey, built on the site of a chapel where the hermit saint lived in solitude. The island light-house guides ships into the gulf.

Tinetto is an inhospitable rock, but the rich diversity of the sea beds make this a popular diving area. The ruins of two religious buildings on the island confirm the earliest known Christian presence in the area (5th century).

⑳ La Spezia

See pp128–9.

㉑ San Terenzo

La Spezia. **Road Map** F5. 🚊 La Spezia. 🚌 *i* Lerici, 0187 967 346.

San Terenzo lies on the northern side of the Golfo della Spezia, overlooking the pretty bay of Lerici. Once a small group of fishermen's houses clustered on the shore, San Terenzo was a favourite among certain 19th- century poets, including Percy Bysshe Shelley. (Casa Magni, the last home Shelley shared with his wife Mary, is nearby.) Today, sadly, the village is suffering from the effects of mass tourism. Sights to visit include a castle on a rocky promontory nearby; the

church of Santa Maria Assunta; and Villa Marigola, with lovely gardens.

㉒ Lerici

La Spezia. **Road Map** F5. 🚊 12,000. 🚉 La Spezia. 🚌 *i* Via Biaggini 6, 0187 967 346. 🎉 Festa di Sant' Erasmo (Jul).

In the Middle Ages Lerici was a major port, and enjoyed both commercial and strategic importance. Today, it is a popular tourist town, but one that manages to still feel like

a working community with a strong identity.

The old centre is dominated by the **Castello**, the most important example of military architecture in the region. Built by the Pisans in the 13th century to counter a Genoese fort at Portovenere, it was taken by Genoa shortly afterwards; they enlarged it in the 15th century. It is still in a remarkably good state, with its pentagonal tower and massive walls. There is an archaeological museum inside.

Below the castle is the lovely (and sandy) Baia di Maralunga, good for a swim.

🏰 Castello and Museo

Piazza San Giorgio. **Tel** 0187 969 042. **Open** mid–Oct–mid–Mar: 10:30am–12:30pm Tue–Fri; 10:30am–12:30pm, 2:30–5:30pm Sat, Sun, public hols; mid–Mar–Jun, Sep–mid–Oct: 10:30am–1pm, 2:30–6pm Tue–Sun; Jul–Aug: 10:30am–12:30pm, 6:30pm–midnight Tue–Sun. **Closed** Mon. 🅿

The port of Lerici, dominated by an imposing castle

The Gulf of Poets

It was the Italian playwright Sem Benelli who first described the Gulf of Lerici as the "Gulf of Poets" in 1919. It is an evocative and romantic epithet, and not inaccurate given the personalities who came here in the 19th and 20th centuries: including Percy Bysshe Shelley (who drowned at sea en route to La Spezia from Livorno, in 1822, and was cremated at Viareggio) and his wife Mary (author of *Frankenstein*), Lord Byron, DH Lawrence and Virginia Woolf. The gulf still has strong appeal today and attracts artists and intellectuals, mainly Italians. As a consequence a "cultural park" has been established, called the Parco Culturale Golfo dei Poeti, joining similar parks dedicated to Eugenio Montale, in the Cinque Terre, and in the Val di Magra and Terra di Luni. For more information contact the tourist office APT Cinque Terre-Golfo dei Poeti in La Spezia *(see p207)*.

Shelley

The unmistakably picturesque Cinque Terre ▶

⑳ La Spezia

The port of La Spezia has been important since antiquity as a trading centre for produce from all over the world, especially spices (*la spezia* means spice in Italian). In the 13th century, the Fieschi family transformed what had been a fishing village into a fortress surrounded by walls. The city expanded and a second defensive ring was built in the 1600s. This city was lauded by poets in the 19th century, and attracted generations of European travellers, drawn by La Spezia's elegance and attractive position on the gulf. The city, and its role, changed radically after 1861, when the Savoy government began construction of a naval base. Today, traces of the distant past are tucked away amid the sprawling metropolis. The naval base and port are still thriving.

🏛 Arsenale Militare and Museo Navale

Viale Amendola 1.
Tel 0187 784 693. **Open** 8am–6:45pm Mon–Sat, 8am–1pm Sun. **Closed** 1 Jan, 15 Aug, 8, 24–26 Dec. 🅿️ 🅿️ ✉️ no flash. 🔲 **turismoprovincia.laspezia.it**

In exile on St Helena, Napoleon, tracing a portrait of the Italian peninsula, wrote of La Spezia that "it is the most beautiful port in the universe; its defence by land and by sea is easy… maritime institutions would be sheltered here". It was not Napoleon, however, who transferred the naval base from Genoa to La Spezia, but the Savoy government under Camillo Cavour.

Construction of the colossal site began in 1861. The city inevitably expanded as a result of the building of the base, and from 1861 to 1881 the number of inhabitants tripled. Badly damaged by bombing in World War II and further damaged by German troops, who occupied the site between 1943 and 1945, the base was reconstructed with meticulous care.

Today the structure illustrates how the designer, colonel Domenico Chiodo, responded carefully to the practical requirements: the workshops are located close to the entrance for the convenience of the workers, the general warehouse and offices

are placed at the centre of the entire complex, and so on. The predominant style is Neo-Classical. It is possible to visit parts of the base, including the old workshops, sailmakers' yards, masonry docks and the swing bridge.

The **Museo Tecnico Navale della Marina Militare** is one of Italy's oldest and most important naval museums. The core of its collection dates back to the 16th century, and was started by Emanuele Filiberto of Savoy, who gathered mementoes from the Battle of Lepanto (1571). Models help to illustrate the history of the port; there is also a fine collection of anchors (around 120 different ones) and a good display of 28 figureheads from old sailing ships.

Figurehead, Museo Navale

🏛 Museo Amedeo Lia

Via Prione 234. **Tel** 0187 731 100. **Open** 10am–6pm Tue–Sun. **Closed** 1 Jan, 15 Aug, 25 Dec. 🅿️ 🅿️ 🅿️ 🅿️ 🔲 **http://museolia.spezianet.it**

This excellent and award-winning museum, opened in 1996, is based around the works donated by Amedeo Lia and his family. It is housed in part of the ancient church and monastery of the monks of San Francesco da Paola, restored for the purpose. The museum includes paintings and miniatures, medieval ivory, Limoges enamels, medals and numerous archaeological finds from excavations around the Mediterranean basin.

Paintings are the collection's most significant element: indeed, the 13th- and 14th-century paintings form one of the finest private collections in Europe.

Besides fine works by Paolo di Giovanni Fei, Pietro Lorenzetti, Sassetta and Lippo di Benivieni, there are two 16th-century highlights: a presumed *Self Portrait* (1520) by Pontormo, painted, unusually, using tempera on terracotta, and a *Portrait of a Gentleman* (1510) by Titian.

The 17th-century paintings by followers of Caravaggio are also worth seeking out, as are the Venetian views by Canaletto, Bellotto, Marieschi and Guardi. There are also bronzes from the 16th and 17th centuries.

Self Portrait by Pontormo, Museo Amedeo Lia

🏰 Castello di San Giorgio

Via XXVII Marzo. **Tel** 0187 751 142. **Open** see Museo Archeologico.

The oldest architectural vestige of centuries past, the Castello di San Giorgio occupies a commanding position overlooking the city. The imposing fortification was commissioned by the Fieschi family in the 13th century, though what you see today dates from a reconstruction that took place in the 14th century, and from defence work carried out in the 17th century. Following major restoration work, the castle is now home to the Museo Civico Archeologico.

Castello di San Giorgio, home to the Museo Archeologico

🏛 Museo Civico Archeologico Ubaldo Formentini

Castello di San Giorgio, Via XXVII Marzo. **Tel** 0187 751 142.
Open 9:30am–12:30pm Mon, 5–8pm daily; winter: 9:30am–12:30pm, 2–5pm. **Closed** Tue (except hols), 1 Jan, 24, 25 Dec. 🦽 ♿ 🎧 📷
🌐 castagna.it/sangiorgio

This museum was established in the 19th century as a home for the many archaeological finds and fossils discovered in the city environs, mainly as a result of excavation work carried out

when the naval base was being built.

Some of these finds provide evidence of the first human settlements in the Lunigiana area: coins and ceramics dating from the prehistoric, Etruscan and Roman eras are among the objects found near the ancient city of Luni (*see p131*). Also of interest are paleolithic finds from the Grotta dei Colombi on the island of Palmaria.

The most significant section of the museum is, however, the collection of statue-stelae, sculptures in sandstone dating from the Bronze and Iron ages, depicting in stylized form warriors grasping weapons and figures of women. Although typical art of the Lunigiana, their function and significance are unclear.

🏛 Chiesa di Santa Maria dell'Assunta

Piazza Beverini.
Open 9:30–11am, 3–5:30pm daily.

This 14th-century church has been modified more than once. Its appearance today, with its black and white façade, owes much to reconstruction after

VISITORS' CHECKLIST

Practical Information
Road Map F4. 🔼 97,000.
🛈 Viale Mazzini 47,
0187 770 900. 🚗 San Giuseppe (19 Mar); Festa del Mare con Palio del Golfo (first Sun in Aug).
🌐 comune.sp.it
🌐 http://turismocultura.
spezianet.it

Transport
🚆 🚌

the war. It contains a *Coronation of the Virgin*, a glazed terracotta relief by Andrea Della Robbia and a *Martyrdom of St Bartholomew* (16th century) by Luca Cambiaso.

🏛 Pieve di San Venerio

This charming Parish church dates from the 11th century, although excavations carried out in the last century have revealed much earlier, even Roman, origins. The façade is decorated with a two-mullioned window and is flanked by a bell tower. The interior has two aisles, the older of which ends, unusually, in two apses.

Statue-stele at the Museo Archeologico

La Spezia Town Centre

① Arsenale Militare and Museo Navale
② Museo Amedeo Lia
③ Castello di San Giorgio
④ Museo Civico Archeologico Ubaldo Formentini
⑤ Chiesa di Santa Maria dell'Assunta

Ligurian Sea

| 0 metres | 500 |
| 0 yards | 500 |

For map symbols *see back flap*

A picturesque alley in the small fishing village of Tellaro

❷❸ Fiascherino and Tellaro

La Spezia. **Road Map** F5. 🏔 800.
🚆 La Spezia. 🚌 ℹ️ Lerici, 0187 967 346. 🎭 Natale Subacqueo (24 Dec).
🌐 **tellaro.net**

These two pretty fishing villages of painted houses lie next to each other, just south of Lerici. Both face small bays, with verdant hills behind.

Tiny **Fiascherino** has a lovely beach, and the cliffs conceal enchanting coves accessible only by boat. The writer DH Lawrence lived in the village from 1913–14.

Thanks to its position on the cliffs high above the sea, medieval **Tellaro** has preserved its original features almost intact, though the instability of the rock itself has caused some damage. The oldest part is built on a promontory that marks the furthermost limit of the Riviera di Levante: the tall houses here had to be built on different levels in order to accommodate the terrain. The village's extremely narrow streets are linked by flights of steps and tunnels. The Baroque church of San Giorgio overlooks the sea, while the Oratory of In Selàa has a lovely courtyard, which also faces the water.

❷❹ Montemarcello

La Spezia. **Road Map** F5. 🏔 4,600.
🚆 La Spezia. 🚌 ℹ️ Via Nuova 48, 0187 691 071 (seasonal). Parco N R Montemarcello-Magra; Via Paci Agostino 2, Sarzana, 0187 600 324.
🌐 **parcomagra.it**

This town on the eastern fringes of the Golfo della Spezia offers fantastic views, both west towards the gulf and east towards the Versilia coast.

Montemarcello doesn't share the structure common to hilltowns: lacking the traditional concentric arrangement, it is instead laid out on a square network, echoing the layout of the original Roman military camp, or *castrum*. The houses in the oldest part, still partially enclosed by the remains of the town walls, are painted in the bright colours usually seen in coastal towns, an anomaly in a mountain village. Indeed, the street layout and the architectural style of the houses give Montemarcello a particular and unusual atmosphere, more akin to an elegant holiday resort than a rural village. As such, it has become a discreet haven for Italian intellectuals and artists – a situation that has, in effect, saved Montemarcello from attempts at major development.

Logo of the Parco di Montemarcello

The landscape around the town is delightful: this is the southern tract of the **Parco Naturale Regionale Montemarcello-Magra**, Liguria's only river park, which offers great opportunities for walks, with several marked walking trails. The park extends from the summit of the eastern headland of the Golfo della Spezia as far as the plain of the river Magra. In the southern stretches, near Bocca di Magra, the vegetation and the wildlife are typically Mediterranean, while in the northern part of the park cultivated fields and wetlands alternate.

❷❺ Ameglia

La Spezia. **Road Map** F5. 🏔 4,500.
🚆 Sarzana, Santo Stefano Magra.
🚌 ℹ️ Via della Mura 7, 0187 691 071. 🎭 Carnevale Amegliese (Feb).
🌐 **comune.ameglia.sp.it**

Although it is not far from the mouth of the river Magra, Ameglia still has the look of a hill town. Tall, narrow houses are packed together around a hilltop where a castle once stood. Its ruins include a round tower and parts of the original walls; the main part was replaced in the Renaissance period by the Palazzo del Podestà, later the Palazzo Comunale (town hall).

From the summit, alleys extend in concentric circles, broken up by small squares, several of which have a view of the Carrara marble mountains. The piazza in front of the church of Santi Vincenzo e Anastasio is lovely, with views over the lower Lunigiana and the Apuan Alps. The church has a 16th-century marble door.

❷❻ Bocca di Magra

La Spezia. **Road Map** F5. 🏔 4,300.
🚆 Sarzana, Santo Stefano Magra.
🚌 ℹ️ Via Fabbricotti, 0187 608 037.

Originally a fishing village at the mouth *(bocca)* of the river Magra, this town manages to keep a grip on its heritage, despite its role as a tourist resort. In addition to numerous holiday

A glimpse of Montemarcello, known for its excellent views

The ancient Roman amphitheatre at Luni

homes, there is a small beach, a spa and a well-equipped marina.

The coast here is very different from that of the Cinque Terre and the Golfo della Spezia: it is near here that the low-lying, sandy stretch, known as the Versilia coast, begins.

The appeal of Bocca di Magra, which stems largely from its combined seaside and riverside location, was not lost on writers, poets and other demanding holidaymakers, who were attracted to Bocca in the first half of the 20th century, just as they were to other towns in the area.

Nearby are the remains of a **Roman villa** dating from the 1st century AD. It is built on sloping terraces on the cliff, in a panoramic position above the mouth of the river.

㉗ Luni

Via Luni 37, Ortonovo (La Spezia). **Road Map** F5. Tel 0187 668 11. Site and museum: **Open** 8:30am–7:30pm Tue–Sun. **Closed** 25 Dec, 1 Jan, 1 May.

The Roman colony of *Portus Lunae* was founded in 177 BC in an effort to counter the native Ligurians. Its role as an important port grew as Luni became a major channel for the shipping of marble from the nearby Apuan Alps (known as Luni marble) to all corners of the Roman empire.

Luni's prosperity faltered during the early centuries of the Middle Ages, due to the tailing-off of the marble trade, with full-blown decline accompanying the silting-up of the harbour. (The coast is now 2 km/1 mile away.) In 1204, the bishopric was moved to nearby Sarzana, and soon, all that was left of Luni was its name, which had also given the surrounding area its title, the Lunigiana.

The archaeological site at Luni is the most important in northern Italy. Surrounded by walls, the city was built to a perfectly regular layout, with the public buildings equally neatly placed. A great temple and several prestigious houses stood near the huge, marble-paved Forum. Nearby was the Capitolium, a temple dedicated to Jove, Juno and Minerva, encircled by a marble-edged basin and with a flight of steps in front. Remains of these buildings are still visible.

Nearby was the Casa dei Mosaici, with an atrium in Corinthian style surrounded by rooms with mosaic floors; some of these 3rd–4th century AD mosaics survive. The vast Casa degli Affreschi was built around a garden and had numerous rooms with fine floors and frescoes. Inside the walls there are also the ruins of the Early Christian basilica of Santa Maria, including the remains of three early Romanesque apses and the base of a bell tower.

Outside the walls is the amphitheatre, built in the Antonine era (1st–2nd centuries AD) and the scene of bloody gladiatorial fights. The lower section of stepped seats, as well as part of a covered portico, survives. The complex system of steps and corridors that led to the seating is still visible.

On the site of the Forum is an **archaeological museum**, with displays of Imperial-era marble statues, busts, fragments of frescoes, jewellery, tools, stamps and ceramics.

㉘ Castelnuovo di Magra

La Spezia. **Road Map** F5. 8,000. Sarzana, Santo Stefano Magra. Via Aurelia 241, 0187 693 306. Corteo Storico "A Pace de Dante" (end Aug).

It seems probable that the origins of this inland town coincided with the decline of nearby Luni and the abandonment of the port by its inhabitants.

Castelnuovo, built on a hilltop in view of the mouth of the River Magra, is spread out attractively along a ridge, with the church at one end and the bishop's palace (a 13th-century castle) at the other. Linking these two landmarks is Via Dante, lined with handsome palazzi with elegant façades. Sections of the old town walls and two 15th-century towers are still visible.

The church at one end of Via Dante is **Santa Maria Maddalena**, built in the late 16th century but with a 19th-century façade. The marble columns inside are thought to have come from Santa Maria Assunta at Luni. Inside is a *Calvary* by Brueghel the Younger.

Between Castelnuovo and Luni, up a very winding road, is **Nicola**, a pretty medieval hilltop village centred around the church of Santi Filippo e Giacomo.

Nicola, a lovely hilltop village near Castelnuovo

㉙ Sarzana

This lively agricultural and commercial centre has a splendid historic centre which has remained almost intact, despite being bombed during the war. Built by the River Magra and on the Via Francigena, the main land route between Rome and northern Europe, Sarzana was of strategic importance both under the Romans and in the Middle Ages. It is no surprise that such a desirable town was fought over at length by its most powerful neighbours, including Pisa and Florence, until in 1572 the town became a stable possession (and the easternmost outpost) of the Republic of Genoa. A sophisticated town, Sarzana has a famous antiques market and great shops.

Church of Sant'Andrea
This ancient Romanesque church has a sober stone façade with an unusual 16th-century door decorated with caryatids.

PIAZZA MATTEOTTI

VIA MASCARD

VIA BONAPARTE

VIA FIASELLA

VIA MAZZINI

VIA ROSSI

PIAZZA CALANDRI

VIA DEI GIARDINI

PIAZZA NICOLÒ

Piazza Matteotti, with its distinctively tapered corner

★ Cathedral
The cathedral of Santa Maria Assunta, begun in 1204 after the transfer of the bishopric from Luni to Sarzana, was completed in the 15th century and modified in the 17th century. The 14th-century door, the finely carved marble rose window and the bell tower are all enchanting. Inside are two marble altarpieces (mid-1400s) by Leonardo Riccomanni.

La Fortezza di Sarzanello

Just north of Sarzana, the Fortress of Sarzanello rises on a hill in an excellent strategic position from which to control the lower Lunigiana. Built for Castruccio Castracani, a lord of Lucca, in around 1322, it was altered in later centuries, including in 1493, when it was restored by the Florentines. The fortress is built on a triangular plan and has three cylindrical corner towers. Access is over a bridge, which straddles a deep moat.

VISITORS' CHECKLIST

Practical Information
La Spezia.
Road Map F4–5.
🚗 20,000. 🛈 Piazza San Giorgio, 0187 620 419.
🎪 "Soffitta in Strada", crafts and antiques market (first 3 weeks of Aug).
🔲 aptcinqueterre.sp.it

Transport
FS 🚌

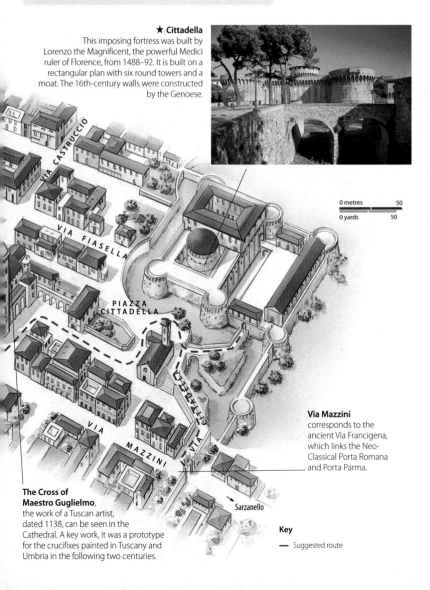

★ Cittadella

This imposing fortress was built by Lorenzo the Magnificent, the powerful Medici ruler of Florence, from 1488–92. It is built on a rectangular plan with six round towers and a moat. The 16th-century walls were constructed by the Genoese.

0 metres 50
0 yards 50

VIA CASTRUCCIO

VIA FIASELLA

PIAZZA CITTADELLA

VIA MAZZINI

Via Mazzini
corresponds to the ancient Via Francigena, which links the Neo-Classical Porta Romana and Porta Parma.

The Cross of Maestro Guglielmo, the work of a Tuscan artist, dated 1138, can be seen in the Cathedral. A key work, it was a prototype for the crucifixes painted in Tuscany and Umbria in the following two centuries.

Sarzanello

Key

— Suggested route

THE RIVIERA DI PONENTE

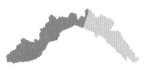

With the capital city of Genoa at one end and Ventimiglia, on the border with France, at the other, the Riviera di Ponente extends for around 150 km (93 miles). There is spectacular scenery in the interior, and the coast is so green and lush that it is divided, fittingly, into the Riviera delle Palme (of palm trees) and the Riviera dei Fiori (of flowers).

Any visitor to this area cannot fail to appreciate the mild climate of the coast, which has been exploited in the past for the cultivation of citrus fruits and is now used in the growing of cut flowers and house plants, adapting customs as well as the landscape in the creation of a new industry.

Liguria is now one of the most important flower-growing areas in the world. It is no coincidence that San Remo, one of the main towns along this coast, is known as the "città dei fiori", or city of flowers. Olives are the other major crop, particularly around Imperia.

Like the Riviera di Levante, the Riviera di Ponente became a favourite holiday destination among the European aristocracy, particularly the British and the Russians, from the late 19th century. Hotels and Art Nouveau villas are still in evidence almost everywhere.

The western part of Liguria also has a rich history, evoked by numerous atmospheric towns and villages. You need head only a short distance inland to discover fascinating medieval towns which are in stark contrast to the touristy coastal towns. Traces of the Romans can also be found both on the coast and in the interior, such as the five Roman bridges in the Parco del Finalese (in whose limestone caves paleolithic utensils and burial tombs have been found), or the excavations of Albintimilium, ancient Ventimiglia.

In between excursions, as well as spending time on the beach or swimming in the sea, visitors can relax and breathe fresh clean air in one of the region's parks: such as the Parco Naturale del Monte Beigua, above Savona, with trees and plants of tremendous variety and numerous animal species.

Triora, in the hinterland behind Imperia, also known as the "village of witches"

◄ The parish church of San Tommaso in Dolcedo

Exploring the Riviera di Ponente

The two provincial capitals on the Riviera di Ponente are Savona and Imperia. San Remo, with its grand Art Nouveau architecture, is the main holiday resort. New developments have spoilt the coast closest to Genoa, but there are many interesting places to visit elsewhere along the coast: these range from Noli, with its church of San Paragorio, one of the key monuments of Ligurian Romanesque, and Albenga, with its well-preserved historic centre and its Early Christian baptistry, to the splendid English gardens at Hanbury Botanical Gardens, close to the French border, and the nearby caves at Balzi Rossi, a fascinating prehistoric site. In the hinterland, the delightful medieval village of Dolceacqua is especially worth a visit, as is Triora, famous for a witch trial held here at the end of the 16th century. The luxuriant vegetation and mild climate make this part of the Ligurian coast a pleasure to explore.

Exotic plants in the interesting Hanbury Botanical Gardens

Sights at a Glance

0 kilometres 10

0 miles 10

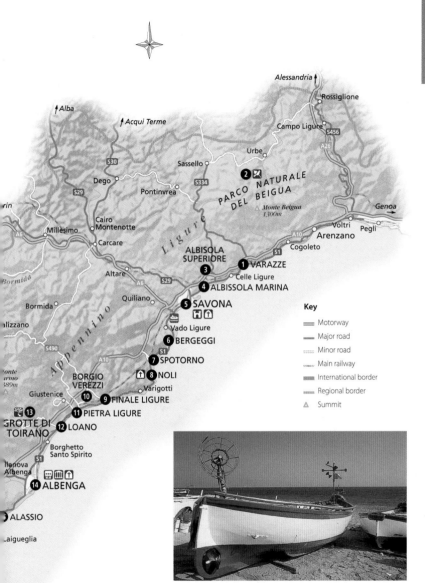

Fishing boats on the beach at Noli

Getting Around

The main communication routes along the Riviera di Ponente are the A10, the motorway between Genoa and Ventimiglia, and the SS1, or Via Aurelia (once a Roman road), which runs parallel to the motorway at sea level, passing by all the main towns. The roads leading into the interior are narrow and twisting, although they do pass through very beautiful countryside. The A6, the motorway from Savona to Turin, gives access to Altare, Carcare and other towns located inland from the Riviera delle Palme. Regional, inter-regional and intercity trains connect Genoa and Ventimiglia (with up to 15 trains a day). It is also possible to get around using coaches, particularly if heading inland; the provincial coach companies operate a good network of services.

For hotels and restaurants in this region see pp182–3 and pp194–7

❶ Varazze

Savona. **Road Map** C3. 🏔 14,000.
🚉 🚌 ℹ️ Corso Matteotti 56, 019
935 043. 🎭 Processione e Corteo
Storico di Santa Caterina da Siena
(30 Apr); Festa del Mare (early Aug).
ⓦ turismo.provincia.savona.it

At the eastern end of the
Riviera di Ponente, Varazze
is a major seaside resort,
complete with a beach and
palm-shaded promenade.

The town's name derives
from the Roman name of
Varagine ("trees"), though it
was later known as *Ad Navalia*
("At the shipyards"). Both names
were appropriate since much
of the local wood was used for
boat-building. The town was
the birthplace of Jacopo da
Varagine, a famous 13th-century
friar and writer, and later a saint.

In the old centre, sights of
interest include the church
of **Sant'Ambrogio**, dating from
1535. Remaining from an earlier
14th-century construction is an
imposing brick bell tower in the
Lombard style, complete with a
spire. The Neo-Renaissance
façade, in Finale stone, was built
in 1916. The courtyard is paved
in beach pebbles, laid out in a
pretty geometrical design. The
façade of an earlier, Romanesque
church dedicated to Sant'
Ambrogio has been incorporated, curiously, into the **town
walls**, an impressive work
dating from the 12th century.

Built in 1419, but much
modified since, the church
of **San Domenico** is famous
as the home of the silver urn
containing the remains of
Jacopo da Varagine. There is

The Romanesque church of Sant'Ambrogio
at Varazze

also a polyptych
(16th century) depicting
*Blessed Jacopo and other
saints*, by Simone da
Pavia, and a 12th-
century fresco, probably
of the Sienese school,
with a *Madonna delle
Grazie*. A cannon ball,
fired from a French ship
in 1746, is embedded in
the church façade.

From San Domenico
visitors can go on a
lovely seafront walk
along disused railway
tracks; various paths en
route cut inland up to
Monte Beigua.

Environs
Celle Ligure, 3 km
(2 miles) west of Varazze,
is a small fishing village with
twisting *carruggi* (narrow streets)
and a wall of hills behind. The
tradition of painting the houses
bright colours began so that
sailors could make them out
while still at sea.

The **Deserto di
Varazze**, 9 km
(6 miles) inland
from Celle Ligure,
is another lovely
spot. It is a simple
17th-century
hermitage
associated with
the barefoot
Carmelite friars, surrounded
by a dense wood.

❷ Parco Naturale del Beigua

Genoa/Savona. **Road Map** C3. 🚉
🚌 ℹ️ Ente Parco del Beigua: Via G
Marconi 165, Arenzano, 010 859 03 00.
ⓦ parks.it

This densely forested park
covers an area of 17,000 ha
(42,000 acres) and runs from
the border with Piemonte down
to the coast, east of Varazze.
It is the biggest of the region's
three national parks and takes
its name from Monte Beigua
(1,300 m/4,265 ft), which is
accessible by road. The grassy
plain at the mountain summit
provides a platform for
wonderful views stretching

The seafront at Varazze

Scented daphne, symbol of the
Parco del Beigua

for miles in all directions,
and is a starting point for
numerous walks.

The park's rocky heart is typically
composed of ophiolites, also
known as "green rocks"
(mainly serpentine) –
metamorphic rocks
deriving from
changes which
occurred in the
original igneous
rock. Prehistoric
axes found in
this area are on
display, along
with other
prehistoric utensils, at the
Museo Civico Archeologico
in Pegli, near Genoa *(see p86)*.
Prehistoric as well as more
recent graffiti have also been
discovered in Monte Beigua.

The flora and fauna in the
park are extremely varied. In
terms of the plant life, there are
vast numbers of beeches, and
the Alpine aster *(Aster alpinus)* is
also common; drosera *(Drosera
rotundifolia)*, an insect-eating
carnivorous plant, can be found
in the wetland area known as
the Riserva del Laione. And
there is the scented daphne
(Daphne cneorum), too, whose
characteristic pink flowers have
been chosen as the symbol of
the park. The wildlife is varied,
too, and includes foxes, badgers,
weasels, wild boar and roe deer.
Two endemic species of

amphibian – *Salamandrina terdigitata* and *Triturus vulgaris meridionalis* – have also been seen, here at their westernmost limit. From the southern slopes you can also see migratory birds in spring.

The park headquarters is in Sassello, a pretty town on the park's western fringes.

❸ Albisola Superiore

Savona. **Road Map** C3. 🏛 12,000. 🚉 🚌 ℹ️ IAT Albissola Marina, Piazza Lam, Albissola Marina, 019 400 25 25. 🖥 turismo.provincia.savona.it

Known to the Romans as Alba Docilia, Albisola consists, in fact, of two parts: Albissola Marina, on the coast, and Albisola Superiore, a short way inland. The different spelling of Albisola perhaps indicates the towns' wish to reinforce their separation, but since the 15th century they have both enjoyed fame for their ceramics, made from the local clay and typically decorated in blue and white.

Albisola's ancient heritage can be seen in traces of a vast Roman **villa**, occupied from the 1st to 5th centuries AD. The parish church of **San Nicolò** was reconstructed in 1600 in the shadow of the castle, now in ruins. The Baroque wooden

The remains of an Imperial-era Roman villa at Albisola Superiore

statues inside were carved by Maragliano and Schiaffino. A 17th-century oratory stands alongside.

Within a large park, adorned with fountains and statuary, stands **Villa Gavotti**, built in 1739–53 for the last doge of Genoa, Francesco Maria Della Rovere, replacing a 15th-century building. The sumptuous interior contains stuccoes by the Lombard school and local ceramics. The villa is home to the **Museo della Ceramica Manlio Trucco**, which is devoted to ceramics from the 16th century onwards. Displays include work by artists from Albisola and elsewhere in Liguria, as well as tools of the trade.

Ceramic plate from Albisola

🏛 Museo della Ceramica Manlio Trucco

Corso Ferrari 193. Tel 019 48 22 95. **Open** 8:30am–12:30pm Wed–Fri, 8:30am–12:30pm, 5:30–7:30pm Sat.

❹ Albissola Marina

Savona. **Road Map** C3. 🏛 5,600. 🚉 🚌 ℹ️ IAT Albissola Marina, Piazza Lam, 019 400 25 25. 🎨 Mostre Nazionali di Ceramica d'Arte (biennial, next in 2016). 🖥 turismo.provincia.savona.it

Separated from Albisola Superiore since 1615, this coastal town is also known as Borgo Basso (or "lower town"). Like its neighbour, Albissola Marina has prospered historically thanks to its ceramics industry, but it is also now a well-known seaside resort.

Of interest in the old town is the **Forte di Sant'Antonio**, known as the Castello, built in 1563 against a Saracen invasion, and **Piazza della Concordia**, attractively paved with concentric circles of black and white pebbles, in front of the parish church.

The unmissable sight is the handsome 18th-century **Villa Faraggiana** (named after its last owner, who gave it to the town in 1961), formerly Palazzo Durazzo. The lavishly furnished interior includes some lovely local majolica tiles, while the delightful gardens feature grottoes and statuary, including nymphs and sculptures of the god Bacchus and goddess Diana.

On **Lungomare degli Artisti**, the mosaic paving dating from 1963 was created with works by contemporary painters and sculptors, among them the artists Lucio Fontana and Aligi Sassu.

🏛 Villa Faraggiana

Via Salomoni 117–119. **Tel** 019 480 622. **Open** 15 Mar–15 Oct: 3–7pm daily. **Closed** occasional Sat & Sun for private functions. 🅿️ 🖥 villafaraggiana.it

The 18th-century Villa Faraggiana at Albissola Marina

❺ Savona

One's first impression of Savona tends to be of a sprawling and industrial port. Yet this thriving, untouristy city has a lovely historic centre. Savona (the name derives from the Ligurian tribe of the Sabates) is the largest town on the Riviera di Ponente, and a provincial capital. Its history has always been linked with that of Genoa: the rivalry between the two has existed since ancient times, when, during Hannibal's Punic wars, Savona sided with Carthage, and Genoa with Rome. The port (destroyed by the Genoese in 1528) was rebuilt only in the 1800s. It was heavily bombed in World War II. There is lots to see here. The Fortezza del Priamàr, a symbol of the city, is now a vast museum complex; you can stroll around the medieval centre and port; or explore the arcades and the Art Nouveau palazzi in Via Paleocapa, jewels of 19th-century architecture.

The imposing bulk of the Fortezza del Priamàr

🏛 Il Priamàr

Corso Mazzini (access from Ponte di San Giorgio). **Tel** 019 8310 325. **Open** summer: 9am–midnight; winter: 9am–6:30pm daily. Pinacoteca Civica: Palazzo Gavotti, Piazza Chabrol. **Tel** 019 811 520. **Open** 8:30am–1:30pm Mon, 8:30am–1pm Wed & Fri, 2–7pm Tue & Thu, 8:30am–1pm, 8:30–11:30pm Sat (winter: 3:30–6pm), 10am–1:30pm Sun. 📷 ♿ Civico Museo Storico-Archeologico: **Tel** 019 822 708. **Open** Sep–Jun: 10am–12:30pm, 3–5pm Wed–Fri, 10:30am–3pm Sat–Mon; Jun–Sep: 10:30am–3pm daily.

The Roman writer Livy records the building of an early fortress here. Today's fort was erected on the site of the first Savona settlement (destroyed by the Romans following the war against Hannibal) in the 16th century, in a bid by Genoa to establish its hold over the port. It wasn't completed until 1680. During the 19th century, the Priamàr (derived from *pietra sul mare*, or "stone above the sea") was used as a prison: Giuseppe

Mazzini, a key figure in the Risorgimento, was imprisoned here in 1830–31. Now restored, the Priamàr houses two of Liguria's most important museums, but it is also well worth a visit as a work of military architecture.

The entrance is across the San Giorgio bridge. To the left is the keep, from which visitors can reach, via ramps and embankments, the Bastione dell'Angelo, the Bastione di San Carlo and the so-called Cavallo Superiore, from which there are stunning views over the city.

Palazzo Gavotti (also known as Palazzo della Loggia), between the Angelo and San Carlo bastions, was built in the middle of the 16th century on medieval foundations, and modified in the 19th century.

The building houses two interesting museums. The most important one is the **Pinacoteca Civica**; spread over 22 rooms on the second and third floors,

it is dedicated to works by Ligurian artists from the Middle Ages to the 20th century. Highlights on the third floor include *Crucifixions* by Donato de' Bardi and Giovanni Mazone, who were active in the 14th and 15th centuries. There is also a lovely polyptych (a part of which is in the Paris Louvre) by Mazone entitled *Christ on the Cross between the Marys and St John the Baptist* (1460s).

Many other painters from the 17th and 18th centuries, who were working in both Genoa and Savona, are represented, including Fiasella, Robatto, Guidobono, Brusco, Agostino and Bozzano. Among the contemporary art on display, Eso Peluzzi's works from the 1920s stand out.

The third floor also houses a collection of ceramics ranging from the 12th to the 20th centuries. Among the items on display are a particularly fine majolica jar decorated with historical scenes, ornamental vases and a 172-piece collection of apothecary jars created for a hospital that used to be located on this very site around the 16th century.

The second floor is taken up by the art collection of the late Italian president Sandro Pertini. It includes around 90 works by modern artists, such as Arnaldo and Giò Pomodoro, De Chirico, Guttuso, Manzù, Morandi, Sassu and Sironi. Some of the works, including those of Henry Moore and Joan Miró, bear a dedication.

Also on the third floor are the four rooms of the Foundation Museum of Contemporary Art Milena Milani, with works by

Beautiful peacocks adorn the façade of the Palazzo Pavoni on Via Paleocapa

Crucifixion by Donato de' Bardi,
an early painting on canvas

the likes of Magritte, Mirò,
Picasso and Man Ray.

On the first floor of the
palazzo is the **Civico Museo
Storico-Archeologico**. The
focus of the exhibits here is the
original Savonese settlement,
with finds gathered mostly from
other (Roman or pre-Roman)
collections, as well as items
discovered in the city environs.
Ceramics, amphorae and
funerary objects from the Bronze
and Iron ages are on display,
along with medieval weaving
tools, ornamental objects and

eating and drinking vessels.
Well worth seeking out are the
superb Arab- and Byzantine-
influenced ceramics and the
multicoloured and Savona
majolica (typically coloured
blue and white).

There are also cooking pots
and metal, bone and glass
objects from local excavations,
as well as a 5–6th-century
burial ground.

🏛 Torre del Brandale
Piazza del Brandale.
The old port is one of the
most attractive parts of the
city, not so much for the
mass of boats that moor here
but for the backdrop of
medieval towers.

Dating from the 12th
century, the Torre del
Brandadlei is one of the
most interesting of
Savona's old towers.
It owes its name to
the flagstaff on top,
commonly known
as the "brandale".

Inside, traces of
frescoes from the
same era can be seen,
while on the façade

The Torre del Brandale

there is a ceramic relief, entitled
Apparition: first carved in
1513, what you see today
dates from the 1960s.

The tower's great bell is
known to the Savonesi as
"*a campanassa*" – a name
used by a local history
association which has its
head-quarters in the
adjacent Palazzo
degli Anziani,
formerly the seat of
the podestà. Built in
the 14th century, its
façade dates from
the 1600s.

Savona Town Centre

① Il Priamàr
② Torre del Brandale
③ Piazza Salineri
④ Torre di Leon Pancaldo
⑤ Chiesa di Sant'Andrea
⑥ Palazzo Della Rovere
⑦ Oratorio del
    Cristo Risorto
⑧ Cattedrale di Nostra
    Signora Assunta
⑨ Nostra Signora
    di Castello

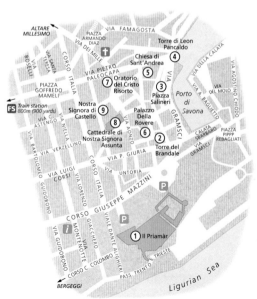

0 metres   300

0 yards   300

🏛 Piazza Salineri

The heart of mercantile trading in the Middle Ages, thanks to its position by the sea, this lovely square still has traces of its former splendour, especially in the streets opening on to it: Via Orefici and Via Quarda Superiore.

Two interesting towers rise up above the piazza: the Ghibellina (dated 1200) and the tower of the Aliberti (1100). Nearby stands the dilapidated 16th-century Palazzo Martinengo, which bears a curious conundrum. Five proverbs have been muddled up to create a word game, and the onlooker is invited to reconstruct the sayings.

🏛 Torre di Leon Pancaldo
Piazza Leon Pancaldo.

This small tower at one end of the harbour (by the cruise ship terminal) is the last remnant of the 14th-century walls. It is dedicated to the Savona-born navigator who accompanied Magellan on his voyages to the Americas, and who died on the Rio della Plata in 1537.

The tower features an effigy of the *Madonna della Misericordia*, patron saint of the city, dated 1662. Beneath it is a verse by the local poet Gabriello Chiabrera, dedicated to the Madonna: "In mare irato/In subita procella/ Invoco Te/Nostra benigna stella", unusual because the words are the same in both Italian and

The Torre di Leon Pancaldo, known as the "Torretta"

Fishing boats in the harbour, with the Torre del Brandale behind

Latin. In English it reads:"In this raging sea, this sudden storm, I beseech thee, oh guiding star."

🏛 Chiesa di Sant'Andrea
Via Paleocapa. **Tel** 019 851 952.
Open 8:30am–noon daily.

The lovely arcaded Via Paleocapa, Savona's main shopping street, runs inland from the Torre di Leon Pancaldo. Notice the lovely Palazzo dei Pavoni at no. 3, designed by Alessandro Martinengo.

A short distance along the street, a broad flight of steps leads up to the church of Sant'Andrea. This was built at the beginning of the 18th century as the Jesuit church of Sant'Ignazio, on the site of a medieval church. It has an elegant façade, while inside there is an *Immaculate Conception* (1749) by Ratti and a *Madonna* (1500s) by Defendente Ferrari. In the sacristy is an icon of *St Nicholas* from Constantinople, and a *Madonna della Misericordia* (1800s), sculpted by Antonio Brilla.

🏛 Oratorio del Cristo Risorto
Via Paleocapa. **Tel** 019 838 63 06. **Open** 4–7pm Mon–Sat; 8:30am– noon Sun.

Further along Via Paleocapa, this oratory was reconstructed in the early 17th century as part of an existing convent of Augustinian nuns, the Santissima Annunziata. The façade is typical of many Baroque buildings in the region, which have richly painted architectural decoration instead of more sculptural motifs. The interior, where chapels face onto a single room with a barrel vault, is charming. Liberally adorning the place are 18th-century trompe l'oeil frescoes and stuccoes, which create a wonderfully illusionistic background.

Traditionally, the high altar is attributed to Francesco Parodi, but he may have been responsible only for the design; in the presbytery, the powerful statue of *Christ Arisen* (Cristo Risorto), to whom the oratory is dedicated, is by an unknown artist. The organ dates from 1757, and there are also some fine 15th-century carved choir stalls.

Maragliano's *Annunciation* (1722), the *Addolorata* (1795) by Filippo Martinengo and the *Deposition* (1866) by Antonio Brilla are three processional floats for which the oratory is famous. (Many churches in Savona have floats featuring scenes from the Passion which go onto the streets on Good Friday.)

🏛 Palazzo Della Rovere
Via Pia 28.

The ancient Via Pia, which begins near the oratory, is one of the most charming streets in the old city. Hemmed in and full of shops of every description, itsmedieval layout has lost none of its original fascination.

At the far end of Via Pia, at no. 28, is Palazzo Della Rovere, now the police headquarters. This fine palace, begun in 1495, was designed by Giuliano da Sangallo (one of the architects of St Peter's in Rome) for Cardinal Giuliano Della Rovere, later Pope Julius II. It became the property of the Spinola family and then, in 1673, was acquired by the Order of the Poor Clares. The nuns covered up the magnificent interior decoration with plaster and renamed it Palazzo Santa Chiara. (At one stage it was the Napoleonic prefecture).

With its façade divided into three storeys with pilasters, its two-tone marble cladding, and its vast courtyard, this palazzo is a clear example of Tuscan architecture, a rarity in the region. Only a very few of the splendid original frescoes are now visible inside.

Statue of the *Assumption* on the cathedral

🏛 Cattedrale di Nostra Signora Assunta

Piazza del Duomo.
Museo del Tesoro della Cattedrale:
Tel 019 813 003. **Open** 10am–noon, 4–5:30pm Sat.

This church was built in the late 16th century to replace the old cathedral of Santa Maria del Castello, which had been demolished (along with other buildings) to make space for the Priamàr fortress. Many of the contents of the old building were transferred to the new, including the splendid baptismal font, made from a beautifully carved Byzantine capital, and a late 15th-century marble *Crucifixion;* both are found in the central nave, behind the façade.

The imposing marble façade dates from the late 19th century and features, above the central door, an *Assumption* by the Carrara artist, Cibei (1706–84). Inside, the three aisles are divided by imposing columns and flanked by chapels.

The frescoes in the central nave, like those of the presbytery and the transept, were produced between 1847 and 1951; the walls and the cupola (dated 1840) were decorated between 1891 and 1893. In the presbytery is a masterpiece by Albertino Piazza, *Enthroned Madonna with Child and saints Peter and Paul,* and *Presentation of Mary at the Temple,* a marble relief dating from the 16th century.

Also in the presbytery stand the splendid wooden choir stalls, dated 1515. Commissioned and financed by the Republic of Savona and Cardinal Giuliano Della Rovere for the first cathedral, they were removed from their original setting and then remodelled for the new semicircular apse.

In one of the chapels in the left-hand aisle is a notable fresco of the *Madonna della Colonna (early 15th century),* originally on a column in the Franciscan monastery on whose site the current cathedral was constructed. Also of note is the pulpit of the Evangelists (1522).

To the left of the presbytery there is access to the **Museo del Tesoro della Cattedrale**, a treasury museum with works from different sources. The core of the collection dates from the first half of the 14th century. Other works include a polyptych, *Assumption and Saints,* by Ludovico Brea (1495), a *Madonna and saints* by Tuccio d'Andria (1487), and an *Adoration of the Magi* (early 16th century) by the Master of Hoogstraeten.

In the cloister alongside the church are 21 marble statues of saints. At the far end is Savona's own **Cappella Sistina**, built in 1481 for another Della Rovere pope, Sixtus IV (for whom the Sistine Chapel in the Vatican was built), as a resting place for his parents. The interior of the chapel was transformed in the 18th century, when rococo decoration in the form of multicoloured stucco was introduced. The marble tomb of Sixtus IV's parents (1483) is on the left-hand side.

🏛 Nostra Signora di Castello

Corso Italia. **Tel** 019 804 892.
Open Sun am, for Mass.

This small oratory is almost hidden from view on Corso Italia, a long street of elegant shops which, along with Via Paleocapa, was the most important road built during the expansion of Savona in the 19th century. It houses one of the finest paintings in the city – a late 15th-century polyptych of the *Madonna and Saints,* by the Lombard artist Vincenzo Foppa, completed by Ludovico Brea (one of Liguria's most active painters at that time).

The oratory also contains what is claimed to be the world's tallest processional float, a *Deposition* built by Filippo Martinengo in 1795.

Adoration of the Magi by the Master of Hoogstraeten, Museo del Tesoro

The Ponte della Gaietta at Millesimo

Environs

Heading inland from Savona the first place of interest, about 14 km (9 miles) from the coast, is **Altare** in the Apennines. This town has been famous for the production of glass since at least the 11th century (before Murano glass from Venice came onto the scene.) The **Museo del Vetro e dell'Arte Vetraria** houses both antique and modern examples, as well as objects from the local school of engraved glass, and documents and books related to the subject, some as much as 800 years old. The displays include some splendid vases in blue crystal decorated in pure gold.

Also in the town is the church of the Annunziata (late 15th century), with a bell tower belonging to an earlier Roman building, and the late 17th-century Baroque church of Sant'Eugenio, whose façade is flanked by two bell towers. On the nearby hill of Cadibona is the Forte Napoleonico della Bocchetta, built in the late 18th century.

Nine km (6 miles) beyond Altare, on the left bank of the River Bormida di Spigno, lies **Cairo Montenotte**, important historically because Austro-Piemontese troops were defeated here by Napoleon Bonaparte in 1796.

Within the town, a large tower, called the Torrione, and the ogival Porta Soprana are all that remain of the original circle of 14th-century walls. On the hill overlooking the village are the ruins of an old castle, also dating from the 14th century and belonging originally to the Del Carretto family, local lords during the Middle Ages. The parish church of San

Lorenzo, with a tall bell tower, dates from 1630–40, though it was modified later. Local gastronomic specialities are fruit-flavoured amaretti and black truffles, best tasted with a glass of the local Dolcetto wine. **Millesimo**, 27 km (17 miles) from Savona, is a charming hill town and the main centre in the upper Valle Bormida. It retains well-preserved traces of the late Middle Ages. The ruined castle (1206), on the edge of the town, dominates from on high, and once belonged to the Del Carretto family; the castle, like the town, later passed to the Spanish, and eventually ended up in the hands of the House of Savoy.

The central **Piazza Italia**, much of it arcaded, is very pretty; the so-called **Torre**, now the town hall, dates from around 1300 and was a Del Carretto residence.

The most striking monument in the town is the **Ponte della Gaietta**, whose simple design, complete with watch tower, dates from the 12th to 13th centuries.

🏛 **Museo del Vetro e dell'Arte Vetraria**
Villa Rosa, Piazza Consolato 4, Altare. **Open** 4–7pm Tue–Fri & Sun, 3–7pm Sat.
🔳 museodelvetro.org

🜔 Bergeggi

Savona. **Road Map** C4. 🅰 1,200.
🇫🇸 🚌 ℹ Pro Loco, Via Aurelia 1, 019 859 777 (seasonal).
🔳 turismo.provincia.savona.it

This small but busy coastal resort lies in a lovely spot on the slopes of Monte Sant'Elena. Records of a settlement on this site date back to Roman times. Its strategic position and its defences enabled the town to fend off Saracen raids in the 10th and 11th centuries. In 1385, Bergeggi became the seat of a colony of deportees set up by the Republic of Genoa, which governed the town at that time.

The town is distinctive for its houses with roof terraces overlooking the sea, and famous for its Claudio restaurant, which serves some of the best (and dearest) seafood on the entire Riviera. Traces of the Middle Ages can be seen in two look-out towers, the **Torri di Avvistamento**, at the top of the town; the parish church of **San Martino** dates from the early 18th century.

The ruins of two ancient churches, a monastery and a tower can be seen on the nearby island of **Bergeggi**, an important religious centre in the Middle Ages. Now uninhabited, and also a nature reserve, the island is covered in thick vegetation. The entrance to a cave, 37 m (121 ft) long and 17 m (23 ft) wide, is

Coat of arms on the Porta Soprana, Cairo Montenotte

Bergeggi rooftops, with Bergeggi island in the background

The arching beach overlooked by the resort of Spotorno

visible at sea level. There are boats to Bergeggi from Savona and Finale Ligure in high season.

❼ Spotorno

Savona. **Road Map** C4. 🏘 4,300. FS 🚌 ℹ️ Piazza Matteotti 6, 019 741 50 08. 🎉 Festival del Vento (end Mar–early Apr); Rassegna Nazionale di Musica Etnica (Jul & Aug). 🌐 **comune.spotorno.it**

Despite the growth of tourism in this part of the region, which has transformed Spotorno into a large resort, the historic nucleus of this town has not lost the appearance of a Ligurian fishing village, with buildings scattered along the waterfront. There is also a good beach that is popular with locals and tourists.

Once the possession of the bishops of Savona, and later of the Del Carretto family,

The castle on Monte Ursino at Noli, with its tall central tower

Spotorno was destroyed by neighbouring Noli in 1227.

At the centre of the old town, focused around Via Mazzini and Via Garibaldi, rises the 17th-century parish church of the **Assunta**. Inside, the chapels feature frescoes by artists such as Andrea and Gregorio De Ferrari, Domenico Piola and Giovanni Agostino Ratti.

There is more to see at the **Oratorio della Santissima Annunziata**, which contains works by the Genoese school (17th century) and a wooden sculpture by Maragliano (18th century), as well as curious maritime ex votos. Above the town are the ruins of the 14th-century **castello**.

❽ Noli

Savona. **Road Map** C4. 🏘 2,900. ℹ️ Corso Italia 8, 019 749 90 03. 🎉 Regatta Storica dei Rioni (first or second Sun in Sep). 🌐 **inforiviera.it**

This is one of the best preserved medieval towns in the entire region. Its good fortune began in 1097, when it assisted in the first Crusade, thereby setting itself up to become a maritime power. In the early 13th century Noli allied itself with Genoa, and fought at her side against Pisa and Venice.

In the old town, the narrow alleys with suspended arches between the houses are reminiscent of the Centro Storico in Genoa. Several of the once-numerous medieval towers survive. On Corso Italia, Noli's

main street, look out for the 13th-century Torre Comunale and, next door, the **Palazzo Comunale** (15th century); the loggia that forms part of this palace recalls the arcades that once lined the Corso Italia.

The **Cattedrale di San Pietro** is medieval beneath its Baroque shell. Inside, the apse contains a *Madonna enthroned with Child, angels and saints*, a polyptych by the school of Ludovico Brea (late 1400s). Also of note is the altar, which incorporates a Roman sarcophagus. The key monument in Noli is, however, the church of **San Paragorio**, one of the finest examples of Romanesque in Liguria, originally built in the 11th century and beautifully restored in the late 19th. Blind arches and pilasters decorate the façade, adorned with exotic majolica. On the left are several Gothic tombs in Finale stone.

Inside, the church has three aisles with semicircular apses, also Romanesque. Highlights include a vast wooden cross (Romanesque), a 12th-century bishop's cathedra in wood, fragments of 14th-century frescoes, and a marble pulpit.

On the slopes of Monte Ursino rise the ruins of a 12th-century **castello**. Battlemented walls connect the castle to the town below.

The wooden cross in the church of San Paragorio

Panoramic view of the town of Borgio Verezzi ▶

❾ Finale Ligure

Savona. **Road Map** C4. ⚑ 13,000.
FS ⚏ ℹ Pro Loco, Via San Pietro 14,
Finale Marina, 019 681 019. ⚑ Festa
dell'Assunta at Finalpia (15–20 Aug);
historic re-enactment of the exploits of
the Marchesi Del Carretto (Aug & Sep).
ⓦ turismo,provincia.savona.it and
ⓦ comunefinaleligure.it

Finale Ligure consists of the
three separate communities
of Pia, Marina and Borgo, united
in 1927 to form one of the
main towns on the Riviera di Ponente.
Finale Marina, the buzzing resort
overlooking pebbly beaches, with
a smattering of smart 16th–18th
century palazzi, is the newest
part, while nearby Finale Pia
and Finalborgo, just inland and
protected from the worst of the
modern development along the
coast, grew up in the Middle Ages.

Finale Pia, across the river Sciusa
from Finale Marina, developed
around the church of **Santa Maria
di Pia**, which is the most important monument in the town and
was first documented in 1170.
The rococo-style façade dates
from the 18th century, and the
interior is also Baroque. The bell
tower is medieval. The grandiose
16th-century Benedictine abbey
next door contains some coloured
terracottas by the Tuscan
Della Robbia school (15th–
16th centuries).

The most interesting of the
three villages is Finalborgo, whose
old centre remains almost intact
within its 15th-century walls.
Elegant houses and palazzi
abound, many now housing
shops, small cafés and restaurants. (Finalborgo is famous for
its basil, so pasta with pesto
is a speciality here and should
not be missed.) The church of
San Biagio dates largely from
the 17th century, but retains
its Gothic bell tower, the symbol
of Finalborgo. Inside is a marble
pulpit by Schiaffino, a fine
example of Genoese Baroque.

The ex-convent of **Santa
Caterina**, founded in 1359, is
home to the **Civico Museo del
Finale**, which exhibits archaeological finds from prehistoric
times to the Middle Ages,
including Roman-era objects.
One of the best examples of

Grotto in the Parco
del Finalese

The Parco del Finalese

Limestone rock with reddish veining is
found in abundance in the hinterland
behind Finale, and forms an amphitheatre
of cliffs that is the focus of the Parco del
Finalese. Some 20 million years old, the cliffs
are riddled with caves in which evidence of
paleolithic life has been found. To reach the
area, take the road to Manie, which runs
inland from Finale Pia. Fans of freeclimbing
will find the upland plain of Le Manie an
absolute paradise. There are traces of
Roman and even pre-Roman roads in this
area. A Roman road, the Via Julia Augusta,
ran through the tiny Val Ponci, just north of Manie, and you can still
see the remains of five Roman bridges, some of which are in
excellent condition.

Ligurian Baroque is the basilica
of **San Giovanni Battista** in Finale
Marina. Its façade is flanked by
two bell towers, and inside
there is a wooden *Crucifixion*
by Maragliano (18th century).

🏛 Civico Museo del Finale
Chiostri di Santa Caterina, Finalborgo.
Tel 019 690 020. **Open** Jul & Aug:
10am–noon, 4–7pm Tue–Sun (to
10pm Wed & Fri); Sep–Jun: 9am–noon,
2:30–5pm Tue–Sun. ⚙

Environs
Varigotti, some 6 km (4 miles)
up the coast towards Noli, is
almost impossibly pretty, with
its colourful houses and a truly
gorgeous setting overlooking
a broad sandy beach. The

fishermen's houses, painted in
all shades of ochre and pink,
are of particular interest since
they date from the 14th-century
settlement founded by the
Del Carretto, a local dynasty
all-powerful in the Middle Ages.

On Capo di Varigotti, you can
see the ruins of the Byzantine-
Lombard fortifications (Varigotti
was originally a Byzantine
settlement, destroyed in the
7th century by the Lombards),
as well as the remains of a
castle built by the Del Carretto.

North of the old town is
the church of San Lorenzo
Vecchio, of medieval origin.
It stands in a dramatic position,
facing a precipice juttingover
the sea.

Typical fishermen's houses on the beach at Varigotti

Piazza Sant'Agostino in Borgio Verezzi

⑩ Borgio Verezzi

Savona. **Road Map** C4. ⚑ 2,200.
FS ⬛ **i** Via Matteotti 158, 019
610 412 (seasonal). 🎭 open-air
and classic theatre seasons (summer;
w festivalverezzi.it
w comuneborgioverezzi.it

This town is formed by the
two distinct centres of Borgio,
on the coast, and Verezzi, on
the slope above. The medieval
heart of Borgio has remained
virtually intact: old cobbled
streets alternate with gardens
and orchards, rising up to the
17th-century parish church of
San Pietro. Near the cemetery
is the pretty medieval church
of **Santo Stefano**, with a bell
tower of decorative brick.
    A winding scenic road leads
up to Verezzi. Of the four groups
of houses that make up the
village, all on different levels, the
best preserved is Piazza, which
still displays some Saracen
influence. At the centre stands
the church of **Sant'Agostino**
(1626). There is a view over the
sea from one side of the pretty
church square.

Environs
Inside the limestone caves
of the nearby **Grotte di
Valdemino** are stalactites so
slim that they vibrate at the
sound of a voice, as well as
magical underground lakes.
Fossils of saber-tooth tigers,
cave bears and elephants
have been discovered here.

🦇 **Grotte di Valdemino**
Via Battorezza. **Tel** 019 610 150. 📷
Jun–Sep: 9:30am, 10:30am, 11:30am,
3:20pm, 4:20pm, 5:20pm; Oct–May:
9:30am, 10:30am, 11:30am, 3pm, 4pm,
5pm. **Closed** 25 Dec, 1 Jan.
📷 with permission.

⑪ Pietra Ligure

Savona. **Road Map** B4.
⚑ 9,400. FS ⬛ **i** Piazza
Martin Liberté 31, 019 629 003.
🎭 Processione di San Nicolò
(8 Jul); Confoëgu (24 Dec).
w turismo.provincia.savona.it

The name of this delightful
beach resort translates as
"Ligurian stone" and derives
from the rocky outcrop to
the northeast of the old town,
where a fortified site stood in
the Byzantine era. The medieval
town grew up around the base
of the **castello**, a Genoese
stronghold that underwent
alterations in the 16th century
and again in later centuries. The
so-called **Borgo Vecchio** was
planned on a regular layout
with five streets running parallel
to the coastline. As you stroll
along these streets today, you
notice how both medieval
houses and 16–17th century
palazzi rub shoulders, an
unusual architectural combination that resulted from a
programme of partial reconstruction in the 16th century.
    The 10th-century **Oratorio
dei Bianchi** stands in Piazza
Vecchia (also known as Piazza
del Mercato). In the bell tower
is the "holy bronze" – according
to local legend, the bell rang in
1525 to announce the end of
the plague. In Piazza XX Settembre,
not far from the sea, stands the
18th-century church of **San
Nicolò di Bari**, its façade flanked
by two bell towers.

Environs
Just inland, high up above Pietra
Ligure, is the village of **Giustenice**,
from where there are superb
views over the coast. This former
Del Carretto stronghold lost its
castle in the 15th century.

⑫ Loano

Savona. **Road Map** B4. ⚑ 11,000.
FS ⬛ **i** Corso Europa 19, 019
676 007. 🎭 Carnevalöa, Liguria's
largest carnival (in summer).
w turismo.provincia.savona.it
and **w** cai.loano.com (for up-to-
date information on walking in the
Loano and Finalese areas).

Ever since Roman times, Loano
has been a desirable place to
live. It has been the property
of, among others, the bishops
of Albenga, the Doria family and
the Republic of Genoa. (It was
also the site of Napoleon's first
victory in Italy.) These days
Loano is an extremely pleasant
town with an extensive beach.
    The most interesting building
is the 16th-century **Palazzo
Comunale**, built for the Doria
family. Its austere appearance
is softened by balconies and
loggias, while a gallery links
it to a watch tower (1602) that
features a beautiful Roman
mosaic pavement.
    In 1603, the Doria family
founded the **Convento di Monte
Carmelo**, in a lovely spot in the
hills above Loano. The complex
includes a church full of Doria
tombs and the Casotto, a
favourite Doria residence.

The medieval castle dominating Pietra Ligure

⓭ Grotte di Toirano

These caves, a real wonder of nature, are among the most beautiful in Italy. They are situated in the karst area of the Val Varatella, between Albenga and Pietra Ligure. Discovered by young researchers and speleologists from Toirano in 1950, these subterranean caves, full of broad caverns, stalactites and stalagmites of all sizes and rare crystal formations, are reminiscent of images of hell. Of prime importance is the beautiful Grotta della Bàsura ("Cave of the Witch" in Ligurian dialect), where traces of Paleolithic man and also the extinct cave bear have been found. The caves are also the habitat of a small crawfish ("Niphargus") while the largest ocellated lizards in Europe can also be seen near the caves. The site, which is about 1.3 km (0.8 miles) in length and can be toured in around 90 minutes, is one of the greatest attractions of the western Riviera.

★ Sala dei Misteri
Traces of prehistoric man are still visible here. The balls of clay hurled at the cave walls were probably concerned with propitiatory rites or hunting ceremonies. The Sala dei Misteri is currently closed to the public.

Sala Morelli
The route within the Grotta della Bàsura starts in this room. A little further ahead is the Torre di Pisa (left), an impressive central stalagmite formed when water ceased to flow on the cave floor.

Entrance

KEY

① **In the Bear Cemetery** visitors can see footprints of *Ursus spelaeus* (cave bear).

② **Grotta della Bàsura**

③ **The Antro di Cibele** offers the extremely rare spectacle of rounded concretions, spherical even, which have been shaped by rhythmical but continuous fluctuations in the water level.

④ **In the Corridoio delle Colonne** evidence of ancient earthquakes can be seen in the fracture lines which split numerous formations in half.

⑤ **Grotta di Santa Lucia Inferiore**

⑥ **Grotta di Santa Lucia Superiore** (open only on 13 Dec for patron saint's day)

⑦ **Grotta del Colombo** (closed to the public)

★ Salotto
Venturing further into the cave system, you reach the area known as the Salotto ("drawing room"). Here, stalactites, stalagmites and wall concretions create a truly fairytale environment, mirrored in the waters of an underground pool, with light playing off the surfaces.

Sala del Pantheon
This cavern contains a stalagmite which reaches the great height of 8m (26 ft) and which, in its vast scale and visual impact, evokes images of Dante's *Inferno*. Aragonite flowers cover it like a light dusting of sugar on a biscuit.

VISITORS' CHECKLIST

Practical Information
Toirano (Savona).
Road Map B4.
Tel 0182 980 62.
ℹ Piazzale Grotte, Toirano.
🔲 **toirano.it**
🔲 **toiranogrotte.it**
Caves and Museo Etnografico Toirano: **Open** Oct–Jun: 9:30am–12:30pm, 2–5pm; Jul, Aug: 9:30am–12:30pm, 2–5:30pm. Night excursions: 9pm Thu (book ahead). 🎫 📷 💻 🅿

Transport
🚌

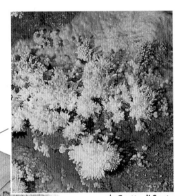

★ Grotta di Santa Lucia Inferiore
This cave shows no human or animal traces but contains beautiful and rare crystallized deposits, including these aragonite flowers.

The Landscape
Toirano is in the high Val Varatella, characterized by steep-sided walls of karst rock. There are lovely views of the landscape from the road leading to the caves.

⑭ Street-by-Street: Albenga

In the province of Savona, Albenga is one of the Riviera di Ponente's most important cities. It owes its fame not only to its historic centre, one of the best-preserved in Liguria, but also to the mildness of its climate and the fertility of the surrounding plain, which has been under cultivation since the Roman era and produces a wide range of fruit and vegetables. The Roman town of *Albingaunum* was founded on the site of a port built by the Ingauni, a Ligurian tribe. For centuries, Albenga's prosperity depended on the River Centa, but its role as a major sea power declined after Genoa asserted itself, and following the silting-up of the port. A long avenue links the old city to the coast, now a short distance away.

Porta Molino
is the largest of the gates in the city walls.

Porta Torlaro
A solid bastion called Il Torracco, once used as a prison, projects from the northwest corner of the city wall. Alongside is 17th-century Porta Torlaro.

Lengueglia Doria Tower and House lie at the end of Via Ricci. The tower dates from the 13th century, while the brickwork house was built in the 15th century.

Via Bernardo Ricci, lined with intact or restored medieval houses, is Albenga's most picturesque long street. In the Roman era it formed part of the main road or *decumanus maximus*, as did its continuation Via Enrico d'Aste.

Loggia dei Quattro Canti
Set at the corner of Via Ricci and Via Medaglie d'Oro, this loggia features one rounded arch and one ogival arch and dates from the transitional period between the Romanesque and Gothic styles. In the Middle Ages, it served to increase visibility and ease the traffic flow at the crossroads.

★ Baptistry
This is the only example of late Roman architecture left intact in Albenga. Built by the general Costanzo in the early 5th century, the baptistry is the foremost Early Christian monument in Liguria.

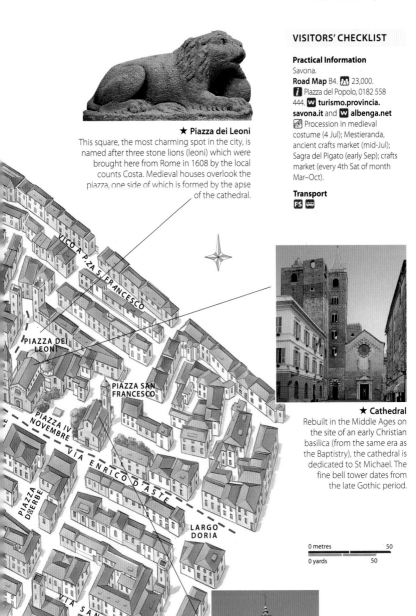

★ Piazza dei Leoni

This square, the most charming spot in the city, is named after three stone lions (leoni) which were brought here from Rome in 1608 by the local counts Costa. Medieval houses overlook the piazza, one side of which is formed by the apse of the cathedral.

VICO A P.ZA S. FRANCESCO

PIAZZA DEI LEONI

PIAZZA SAN FRANCESCO

PIAZZA IV NOVEMBRE

VIA ENRICO D'ASTE

PIAZZA D'ERBE

LARGO DORIA

VIA SANTA EULALIA

★ Cathedral
Rebuilt in the Middle Ages on the site of an early Christian basilica (from the same era as the Baptistry), the cathedral is dedicated to St Michael. The fine bell tower dates from the late Gothic period.

0 metres   50
0 yards   50

Santa Maria in Fontibus
This church on Via Enrico d'Aste has medieval origins but was remodelled in 1600. The façade has a 14th-century stone door.

Key

━ Suggested route

Exploring Albenga

In the old heart of Albenga, with its superb collection of medieval piazzas, palazzi and churches, the streets are set at intersecting right angles, reflecting the grid layout of the *castrum* (or military camp) of the early Roman town. With its plethora of red-brick tower-houses, some still standing proud, some now much reduced, and many now restored, the historic centre of Albenga is utterly delightful. This rare example of a medieval city built on Roman foundations is undoubtedly one of the top places to visit in the whole of Liguria and should not be missed. There are two excellent museums, the Museo Navale Romano and the Civico Museo Ingauno, but a stroll along Via Enrico d'Aste, Via Bernardo Ricci and Via Medaglie d'Oro is sufficient to appreciate the beauty of the place.

Medieval fresco in the loggia of Palazzo Vecchio del Comune

Roman amphorae at the Museo Navale in Palazzo Peloso Cepolla

🏛 Palazzo Peloso Cepolla

Piazza San Michele. Museo Navale Romano: **Tel** 0182 512 15. **Open** winter: 10am–12:30pm, 2:30–6pm Tue–Sun; summer 9.30am–12:30pm, 3:30–7:30pm Tue–Sun. 🅿 📷

Originally made up of several buildings – the medieval part of the palazzo came to light only recently – the Palazzo Peloso Cepolla was unified in a single late Renaissance building in the 17th century. The building is dominated by a Romanesque tower.

The palazzo is home to the **Museo Navale Romano**. Its most important finds include more than 1,000 amphorae, vases and other objects found on board the wreck of a Roman ship which sank off the coast of Albenga in the 1st century BC.

Pharmacy jars from the hospital of Albenga, dating from between 1500 and 1700, are made of the white and blue pottery typical of Savona and Albisola.

🏛 Cathedral of San Michele

Piazza San Michele.
Open 7:30am–8pm daily.

Overlooking Albenga's lovely main square, the cathedral is the old seat of both civil and religious authority. It has been remodelled several times since its construction in the Middle Ages (on the site of an Early Christian church), but remnants of the Romanesque building survive: including blind arches in the lower part of the façade, and elements of the apse. The fine bell tower, rebuilt in the late 14th century, is Gothic, but its base of large stone blocks is Romanesque.

The interior was returned to its simple 13th-century form by restoration work carried out in the 1960s. Highlights inside include a fresco of the *Crucifixion with Saints* (1500), the 19th-century frescoes in the central nave, an enormous 19th-century organ, and the Carolingian crypt.

🏛 Palazzo Vecchio del Comune

Via Nino Lamboglia 1. Civico Museo Ingauno: **Tel** 0182 512 15. **Open** winter: 10am–12:30pm, 2:30–6pm Tue–Sun; summer: 9:30am–12:30pm, 3:30–7:30pm Tue–Sun. 🅿 📷

This building dates from the early 14th century and, with the contemporaneous Torre Comunale, forms a truly impressive medieval complex. The cathedral tower, the Torre Comunale and the tower of the Palazzo Vecchio itself are known as "Preghiera" (prayer), "Governo" (government) and "Giustizia" (justice) respectively.

The side of the palazzo facing Via Ricci has the great Loggia Comunale (1421), built of brick and with sturdy round pillars supporting the heavy arches. On the rear façade, facing the Baptistry, are decorative Ghibelline (swallowtail) battlements and a steep double staircase. At the top of the tower is a big bell known as the *campanone*, cast in 1303. The Palazzo Vecchio del Comune houses the **Civico Museo Ingauno**, with finds from around Albenga, dating from the pre-Roman era to the Middle Ages. Objects include mosaics, tombstones, sculptures and Roman ceramics. Make sure you carry on right to the top floor, from where there is a lovely view of the city.

Decoration on the façade of the cathedral

⬆ Baptistry

Piazza San Michele. **Open** combined ticket with the Museo Ingauno.

Albenga's most important monument is also the only remaining evidence of the Early Christian era in the whole of Liguria. It is thought to have been founded by Constantius, general to the emperor Honorius, in the 5th century. Restoration work done in the 20th century returned the building to its original appearance.

Unusually, the Baptistry takes the form of an irregular decagon outside and a regular octagon inside. There is a niche in each of these eight sides, with columns of Corsican granite topped by Corinthian capitals supporting the arches above. The entrance to the Baptistry is through one of these niches, while others function as windows; two of the latter feature beautiful sandstone transennas. In another niche, part of its original blue and white mosaic decoration is still visible.

On the altar niche is a *Trinity and the apostles*, a 5–6th century mosaic in Byzantine style; in another is a Romanesque fresco of the *Baptism of Christ*. The Baptistry also contains some interesting medieval tombs with Lombard-style reliefs, and at the centre is an octagonal font for total immersion baptisms, with traces of 5th-century frescos.

The cupola dates from the 19th century: its predecessor, possibly the original, was dismantled prior to that, probably in error.

Isola Gallinara

Riserva Naturale Regionale dell'Isola Gallinara. **Tel** 0182 541 351 *(comune di Albenga)*. **W** parks.it

This island lies just off the coast between Albenga and Alassio. Its name derives from the hundreds of wild hens *(galline)* that used to be resident here. It was also once inhabited by hermit monks: St Martin of Tours found refuge here in the 4th century and Benedictine monks later founded an abbey, which was destroyed in the late 15th century; its ruins are still visible. At the top of the island stands the Torre di Vedetta, a tower built by the Republic of Genoa in the 16th century. Isola Gallinara is now a nature reserve and cannot be visited. Boat trips (including for diving) leave from Alassio.

Isola Gallinara

⬆ Palazzo Vescovile

Piazza San Michele.
Museo Diocesano d'Arte Sacra:
Tel 0182 502 88. **Open** 10am–noon, 3–6pm Tue–Sun. 📷

This palazzo, whose principal façade faces the Baptistry, is an assembly of medieval buildings, rebuilt in the 16th century. The oldest wing, to the far right, dates from around 1000, while a 12th-century tower rises from the left-hand corner. On Via Ricci, typically Genoese black and white striped decoration, dating from the 15th century, is still visible.

The Palazzo Vescovile is now home to the **Museo Diocesano d'Arte Sacra**, where visitors can admire precious church furnishings, illuminated manuscripts, Flemish tapestries, silverware and some fine works of art, including *Martyrdom of St Catherine* by Guido Reni, a *Last Supper* by Domenico Piola and an *Annunciation* by Domenico Fiasella, all painted in the 17th century.

Environs

A short distance south of Albenga, interesting archaeological ruins of the Roman town of *Albingaunum* can be seen, including an amphitheatre, aqueduct, various other buildings and a funerary monument known as "il Pilone"; there are also traces of Roman road, thought to have been part of the Via Julia Augusta *(see p148)*.

Around 10 km (6 miles) west of the city, **Villanova d'Albenga** (close to the international airport) is well worth a visit. This fortified settlement, laid out in the 13th century to provide extra protection for Albenga, has a polygonal layout and outer walls reinforced with square towers. The alleys through the town are full of atmosphere and the scent of the abundant flowers that the locals use to adorn their windows and doorways.

The interior of the Baptistry, with the remains of a font at its centre

The famous "Muretto" of Alassio, in front of Caffè Roma

⑮ Alassio

Savona. **Road Map** B4. 🚂 11,300.
🚉 🚌 🛈 Piazza della Libertà 5, 0182
647 027. 🎭 Election of "Miss Muretto"
(late Aug); Premio Alassio Centolibri,
a literature prize (summer).
🌐 comune.alassio.sv.it

A beach of beautifully fine sand, which extends for some 4 km (over 2 miles) and slopes almost imperceptibly down to the sea, makes Alassio the undisputed queen of the Riviera delle Palme. In the 19th century, it became a favourite holiday destination among the English, who came here and built splendid villas with gardens. Many of these, including some Art Nouveau gems, have since been turned into hotels.

Local legend has it that the town's name derives from Adelasia, daughter of Holy Roman Emperor Otto I of Saxony, who came here in the 10th century; (Alassio is still very popular with German visitors). Originally a fishing village, in the Middle Ages it became the property of Albenga and, later, of Genoa. The Roman road Via Aurelia still passes through it.

The typically Ligurian character of Alassio can be seen in the long *carruggio* (narrow street) that runs parallel with the sea, hemmed in by 16th–17th-century houses and modern shops: this is Via XX Settembre, known as the "Budello", and the heart of the town's commercial life. From here, narrow streets known

locally as *esci* fan out, leading to the seafront.

At the corner of Via Dante and Via Cavour, **Caffè Roma** has been a popular meeting place since the 1930s. In the 1950s, the café's owner had the idea of making ceramic tiles out of the autographs of famous visitors to Caffè Roma, to hang on the wall of the garden opposite.

The **Muretto** now bears the signatures of many famous personalities, including Ernest Hemingway, Jean Cocteau and Dario Fo.

Alassio's most signficant monument is the parish church of **Sant'Ambrogio**. Founded in the 1400s, it has a 19th-century façade, an early 16th-century bell tower and a Baroque interior.

Environs

From Alassio, you can go on a lovely (but steep) panoramic walk along the route of an old Roman road, the start of an archaeological walk that runs all the way to Albenga. In 45 minutes you can reach Capo Santa Croce, where a small 13th-century church of the same name overlooks the sea.

At the southern end of the bay of Alassio lies **Laigueglia**, a civilized seaside resort with a well-preserved and picturesque old centre. Of Roman origin, it became an important centre for coral fishing in the 16th century.

Colourful boats near the round tower in Laigueglia

A round tower, known as the **Torrione circolare** (1564), the only bastion remaining of three which once protected Laigueglia from pirates, is the oldest building in the village.

The church of **San Matteo** has two bell towers with bright, majolica-covered cupolas, a delightful example of Ligurian Baroque.

On the ridge between Laigueglia and Andora is **Colla Micheri**, a hamlet whose houses were restored and made into a home by Thor Heyerdahl, the Norwegian navigator and ethnologist famous for his epic journey by raft from Peru to Polynesia in 1958; he died here in 2002.

Santi Giacomo e Filippo church, Andora

⑯ Andora

Savona. **Road Map** B4. 🚂 6,500. 🚉
🚌 🛈 Via Aurelia 122/a, Villa Laura,
0182 681 004. 🎭 Estate Musicale
Andorese, festival of classical music in
church of Santi Giacomo e Filippo (Jul
& Aug). 🌐 comune.andora.sv.it

The last coastal town at the western end of the Riviera delle Palme, Andora groups together several communities, including Marina di Andora on the coast. Founded perhaps by the Phocaeans, from Asia Minor, several centuries BC, Andora later belonged to the Romans, who built a bridge over the River Merula. The ten-arched Ponte Romano visible today dates, in fact, from the Middle Ages. The old Roman road goes up to the ruins of **Andora Castello**, in a lovely spot at the top of the hill.

Built by the Marchesi di Clavesana in around 1000, this fortified complex must have been impressive in its heyday. Through the castle gate is the lovely church of **Santi Giacomo e Filippo**, founded in around 1100 and once part of the castle's defences. Entirely built out of stone from nearby Capo Mele, the church façade is adorned with Gothic cornices and arches. Inside, there are great round columns and octagonal pilasters of bare stone.

Another church within the castle, San Nicolò, is of proto-Romanesque origins.

⑰ Cervo

Imperia. **Road Map** B5. 🚘 1,300. 🚆 🚌 *i* IAT, Piazza Santa Caterina 2, 0183 408 197. 🎼 Festival Internazionale di Musica da Camera, chamber music festival (nine evenings Jul & Aug). **W** rivieradeifiori.org

This village, perched on a hill between Capo Cervo and the mouth of the River Cervo, signals the beginning of the province of Imperia. Once the property of the Del Carretto and then the Doria families, from the 14th century Cervo came under Genoese domination and followed that city's fortunes.

Nowadays, Cervo is an extremely pretty resort, with houses painted in white and pale shades of yellow overlooking a shingle beach. Dominating the village is a 12th-century **castello**, which belonged to the Marchesi di Clavesana and was a control point along the Via Aurelia in the Middle Ages. The site is now occupied by the **Museo Etnografico del Ponente Ligure**, which features reconstructions of life at sea and on land, together with original rooms from a local house.

Facing the sea is the attractive parish church of **San Giovanni Battista**, with its distinctive concave, stucco-embellished façade that features a stag (*cervo* in Italian). Begun in 1686, it is a fine example of Ligurian Baroque. The bell tower and the interior, which is decorated with frescoes and stuccoes, both date from the 18th century.

The latter contains a *St John the Baptist*, a 17th-century work in multicoloured wood by Poggio, and an 18th-century *Crucifixion* attributed to Maragliano.

Also in the town there are several interesting 17th- and 18th-century palazzi. These include **Palazzo Morchio**, now the town hall, and **Palazzo Viale**, which has 18th-century porticoes.

🏛 Museo Etnografico del Ponente Ligure
Piazza Santa Caterina 2. **Tel** 0183 408 197. Open 9am–12:30pm, 3–7pm daily (Jul & Aug: 4:30–10pm).

⑱ Pieve di Teco

Imperia. **Road Map** B4. 🚘 1,450. 🚆 Imperia Oneglia. 🚌 *i* Piazza Brunengo 1, 0183 364 53. 🎼 Mercatino dell'Antiquariato e dell'Artigianato, antiques and craft market (last Sun of month).

Heading inland, almost as far as the border with Piemonte, you reach the busy market town of Pieve di Teco. Founded in 1293, the town belonged, like many others in the area, to the Marchesi di Clavesana and subsequently (from the late 14th century) to Genoa.

The town is known for its handmade walking boots, as well as its small but excellent antiques market held on the last Sunday of the month. Two squares mark either end

The striking arched porticoes on Corso Ponzoni

of the arcaded and typically medieval **Corso Ponzoni**, the heart of the town. On either side, craft workshops alternate with the palazzi of well-to-do families. The oldest part of Pieve di Teco is focused around the 15th-century church of **Santa Maria della Ripa**.

Also of interest is the late 18th-century collegiate church of **San Giovanni Battista**, which contains several important paintings, including a *St Francis de Pauul* attributed to Luca Cambiaso (16th century), and a *Last Supper* by Domenico Piola (17th century).

The 15th-century **Convento degli Agostiniani** has the largest cloister (which is also one of the prettiest) in the whole region.

Not far from the town, a lovely medieval hump-backed bridge straddles the River Arroscia.

The medieval bridge over the Arroscia, close to Pieve di Teco

⑲ Imperia – Oneglia

One of four provincial capitals in Liguria, Imperia lies at the centre of the coastal strip known as the Riviera dei Fiori. It consists of the two centres of Oneglia and Porto Maurizio, united in 1923 by Mussolini. People like to say that he chose the name Imperia out of arrogance, but it derives from the River Impero, which divides the two centres. Historically rivals, the two cities seem to share as little as possible (there are two harbours, two railway stations, even two dialects). Imperia is fascinating because of its split personality.

The name Oneglia probably derives from a plantation of elms *(olmi)*, on which the town was originally built. Oneglia was recorded in documents as far back as 935, when it was destroyed by the Saracens. From the 11th century it was owned by the bishops of Albenga, but they sold it to the Doria family in 1298. (The great admiral, Andrea Doria, was born here in 1466.) The House of Savoy claimed ownership for a time, but Oneglia, along with Porto Maurizio, passed into the hands of the Genoese republic in 1746. The House of Savoy returned in 1814, and made Oneglia the provincial capital. In 1887, an earthquake caused severe damage to the town.

The Port

East of the mouth of the River Impero, the port of Oneglia (Porto di Levante) is dedicated largely to commercial trade, in particular the trade in olive oil (the town has a museum devoted to olive oil); there is also a vast pasta factory on the seafront. The port, whose appearance dates mainly from the Savoy period, is the centre of

activity in Oneglia. In the summer (from mid-June to mid-September), look out for boats offering to take guests out to sea to watch whales and dolphins – a great experience.

🏛 Calata Giovan Battista Cuneo

This characteristic quay building faces the harbour, its traditional arcades perfectly designed to shelter fishmongers, trattorias and fishermen's houses. When the boats of Oneglia's fishing fleet return from their trips out on the open sea, an auction of fresh fish is held here, usually around the middle of the afternoon. The fish trade is vital to the local economy. The local bars and restaurants are always entertaining places to while away the time.

🏛 Collegiata di San Giovanni Battista

Piazza San Giovanni. **Tel** 0183 292 671. **Open** 8am–noon, 3–7pm daily. This church stands in the piazza

of the same name, right at the heart of Oneglia's shopping district. It was built from 1739–62 in late Baroque style, though the façade was finished only in 1838. The fresco decoration inside also dates from the 19th century.

Look out for the marble tabernacle (to the left of the presbytery), which dates from 1516 and is attributed to the Gagini school; various saints are represented here and, in the lunette, *Christ arising from the Tomb*. Also of interest are the wooden choir stalls; the lovely *Madonna del Rosario* (in the first chapel in the left-hand aisle), attributed to the school of the 18th-century sculptor Maragliano; and *St Clare drives out the Saracens* (1681), a moving work painted by Gregorio De Ferrari, a native of Porto Maurizio, though he spent much of his time in Genoa.

The Madonna del Rosario

🏛 Chiesa di San Biagio

Piazza Ulisse Calvi. **Tel** 0183 292 747. **Open** 7–11:30am, 4–6pm daily. This church, dated 1740, has a sober façade and a Baroque bell tower. The spacious, light-filled interior is shaped, curiously, in an oval and ends in a choir.

The church contains various works of art, among them a *Gloria di San Biagio* (Glory of St Blaise) by Bocciardo, visible in the apse, and a wooden *Crucifixion* by the school of Maragliano on the right-hand altar.

🏛 Via Bonfante

From Piazza San Giovanni, the pedestrian street of Via San Giovanni leads north to Via Bonfante, Oneglia's main shopping street. This is a wonderful place for a stroll, and for soaking up the atmosphere of the town. Beneath Via Bonfante's 19th-century arcades visitors can find all manner of art galleries and shops (including several designer boutiques), as well as cafés that manage to tempt even the hardiest passers-by inside.

The multicoloured, arcaded houses of Calata Giovan Battista Cuneo

For hotels and restaurants in this region see pp182–3 and pp194–7

Piazza Dante, at the heart of Oneglia

Piazza Dante

At the end of Via Bonfante is the central Piazza Dante. This is the real heart of Oneglia, also known locally as the "Piazza della Fontana" (square of the fountain).

A busy crossroads, the piazza is surrounded by neo-medieval palazzi: among the most interesting of these is the ex-**Palazzo Comunale**, at no. 4, built in the 1890s in an eclectic mix of styles.

Museo dell'Olivo

Via Garessio 11. **Tel** 0183 295 762. **Open** 9am–12:30pm, 3–6pm Mon–Sat. museodellolivo.com

Housed in an old olive oil mill, the Museo dell'Olivo was opened by the Fratelli Carli, owners of just one of the many local producers of olive oil that compete for market share in the region.

One part of the museum traces the history of olive cultivation, starting with the Roman period, when the oil was used more for medical and cosmetic purposes than as a food; little bottles, used to store oil as perfume or medicine, are on display. There is also a reconstruction of the hold of a Roman ship, which shows how amphorae full of olive oil were stacked ready for transportation. The main section, complete with audio-visual aids, is dedicated to explaining the production of olive oil: on display are all sorts of mills, presses, machines for filtering oil, and containers for storing and for transporting it.

The visit concludes with a visit to an oil mill that is still being used by the Fratelli Carli company.

Reconstruction of the hold in a Roman ship with its cargo of oil

Oneglia Town Centre

① The Port
② Calata Giovan Battista Cuneo
③ Collegiata di San Giovanni Battista
④ Chiesa di San Biagio
⑤ Via Bonfante
⑥ Piazza Dante
⑦ Museo dell'Olivo

0 metres   300
0 yards   300

Imperia – Porto Maurizio

While Oneglia represents the more modern, commercial side of Imperia, Porto Maurizio is its old heart, with its long porticoes, 16th-century bastions and Baroque churches. The quarter of Parasio, the medieval part of town with narrow alleys in typically Ligurian style, is focused around the cathedral. The two most important museums in Imperia are also found here. Porto Maurizio has two coastal districts, known as Borgo Foce and Borgo Marino.

The second town forming the city of Imperia has a history that is very similar to, and yet different from, that of Oneglia. Porto Maurizio, on the west side of the mouth of the River Impero, has kept more traces of its earlier history than Oneglia, which developed primarily in the 18th and 19th centuries. Indeed, its Centro Storico, largely a monument to the Genoese golden age, remains almost intact.

The interior of Porto Maurizio's Duomo

Porto Maurizio fell into Genoese hands in 1797, and in 1805 was annexed, along with Genoa, to France during the Napoleonic era. Restored to the Ligurian Republic in 1814, it was united for the first time with Oneglia as part of the Kingdom of Sardinia, and in 1860 was absorbed into the Kingdom of Piemonte, under whose rule it remained until union with Oneglia in 1923.

The Port

Also known as the Porto di Ponente (to distinguish it from Oneglia's Porto di Levante), the port is protected by two piers. With its floating landing stages, the harbour is reserved for holiday yachts and contrasts sharply with Oneglia's commercial port.

🏛 Duomo

Piazza del Duomo.
Tel 0183 61901. **Open** 7:35–11:45am, 2:45–6:45pm daily.

As you take in the majestic bulk of the Duomo di San Maurizio, it should come as no surprise that this is the largest church in Liguria. It was built between 1781 and 1838 by Gaetano Cantoni in Neo-Classical style to replace the old parish church of San Maurizio, which had been demolished.

The impressive façade features eight Doric columns, culminating in a drum flanked by two solid bell towers, which form a portico. A lantern crowns the great cupola. Beneath the portico are statues that once belonged to the old parish church.

The impressive interior, built on a Greek cross plan, contains a rich array of 19th- century canvases and Neo-Classical-style frescoes, the work of painters mostly from Liguria and Piemonte. Highlights among these include a *Predica di San Francesco Saverio*, attributed to De Ferrari.

In the third chapel on the left, there is a fine wooden cross by the school of Maragliano, while the second chapel on the right contains a statue of the *Madonna della Misericordia*, (1618), which also came from the demolished San Maurizio.

🏛 Pinacoteca Civica

Piazza del Duomo. **Tel** 0183 60847.
Open 4–7pm Wed & Sat (also 9–11pm in Jul & Aug).

Also on Piazza del Duomo is the entrance to the Pinacoteca Civica, the municipal art gallery. On display here are collections derived from legacies and various donations, but exhibitions of local work are held here, too.

Works by Barabino, Rayper, Frascheri and Semino, among others, form part of the Rebaudi collection, which includes 19th-century Ligurian and Genoese works.

🏛 Museo Navale Internazionale del Ponente Ligure

Piazza del Duomo 11. **Tel** 0183 651 541. **Open** summer: 9am–11pm Wed & Sat; winter: 3:30–7:30pm Wed, 4:30–7:30pm Sat.

Imperia's naval museum is one of the most interesting institutions in the city, unmissable for anyone with an interest in seafaring, though the exhibition space is somewhat cramped.

The museum is subdivided into various sections and includes dioramas and models of ships. Most visitors enjoy the section that deals with life on board ship the most. There are also displays of various documents and other mementoes relating to the seafaring tradition along the Riviera di Ponente.

🚪 Parasio

The old palace of the Genoese governor was known in the local dialect as "Paraxu" (the Ligurian for Palatium, as in Palatine Hill, in Rome); translated into Italian, this became Parasio, the name now given

Model of a diving suit, Museo Navale

Parasio, the old city, set above Porto Maurizio

to Porto Maurizio's medieval district. The governor's palace was built on the top of the hill, in Piazza Chiesa Vecchia, now at the heart of the medieval district and only a short walk from the Piazza del Duomo, along Via Acquarone.

After a long period of real neglect and decline, Parasio has in recent years been the subject of an ambitious restoration project, financed mainly by foreign investors.

Visitors cannot truly claim to have seen Imperia unless they have strolled around and climbed these charming and steep streets, lined with handsome palaces and churches, including the convent of Santa Chiara and

the Oratorio di San Leonardo. In Via Acquarone, look out for striking **Palazzo Pagliari** (1300–1400), with an entrance portico with ogival arches.

🔒 Oratorio di San Leonardo

Via Santa Caterina.
Tel 018362783. **Open** 9am–noon, 3–7pm. **Closed** first Mon of the month.

In the southern part of Parasio, looking out towards the sea, this oratory (1600) is dedicated to Imperia's official patron saint. Inside is a lovely work, *Our Lady of Sorrows and souls in Purgatory*, by Gregorio De Ferrari (1647–1726).

St Leonard (1676–1751) was born in the house standing next to the oratory.

🔒 Convento di Santa Chiara

Via Santa Chiara 9. Tel 0183 62762.
Church: **Closed** 7am–noon, 3:30–7pm Mon–Sat (from 9am Sun & hols).

The principal reason to visit these buildings, which date from 1300 (modified in the 18th century), is to see the splendid arcade behind the convent, from which there is a fantastic view of the sea, and which is used to stage classical concerts in summer.

Inside the church are two lovely works of art: a *San Domenico Soriano and Madonna,* the work of Domenico Fiasella, and a *Madonna with Child and Santa Caterina da Bologna* by Sebastiano Conca.

🔒 Chiesa di San Pietro

Salita San Pietro. **Tel** 0183 60356.
Open 6pm Sat for mass.

This Parasio church stands on the same level as a loggia overlooking the sea. Founded in 1100, it was built on the ruins of the old town walls. A medieval lookout tower forms the base of the round bell tower.

The façade, dating from 1789, is lively, with paired columns supporting three arches. Inside, a pictorial cycle on the *Life of St Peter* is attributed to Tommaso and Maurizio Carrega (late 1700s).

Porto Maurizio Town Centre

① The Port
② Duomo
③ Pinacoteca Civica
④ Museo Navale Internazionale del Ponente Ligure
⑤ Parasio
⑥ Oratorio di San Leonardo
⑦ Convento di Santa Chiara
⑧ Chiesa di San Pietro

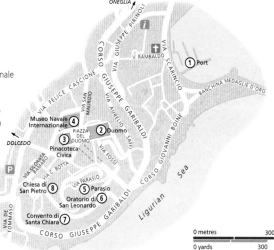

0 metres 300
0 yards 300

For map symbols *see back flap*

The church of the Assunta, Triora

⑳ Dolcedo

Imperia. **Road Map** B4–5. 🏘 1,200.
🚆 Imperia. 🚌 ℹ Comune, 0183
280 004. 🎉 La Mongolfiera,
traditional country festival (1st
Sun, Sep), organic market (3rd
Sun of month).

Situated in the hinterland
behind Porto Maurizio, in
the Prino valley, is Dolcedo a
mountain village with stone-
paved mule tracks and water-
mills along the banks of the
river, evidence of an olive oil
tradition dating back to the
1100s; the local olive groves
are among the most famous
in the region.

There are no less than five
bridges across the river. The
oldest, known as **Ponte Grande**,
was built in 1292 by the Knights
of St John.

The parish church of **San
Tommaso** overlooks a small
piazza, paved in the Ligurian
style in black and white pebbles.
This Baroque jewel was built
in 1738.

㉑ Triora

Imperia. **Road Map** A4. 🏘 500.
🚆 San Remo. 🚌 ℹ Pro Loco, Corso
Italia 7, 0184 944 77. 🎉 Processione
del Monte (2nd Sun after Easter), Festa
della Madonna della Misericordia (1st
Sun in Jul). 🌐 comune.triora.im.it

The old medieval village of
Triora, an outpost of the
Republic of Genoa, lies near
the head of the Valle Argentina.
With the Ligurian Alps rising
up behind, this is a truly
enchanting place. Also known
as the "paese delle streghe"

(village of witches), Triora
is famous above all for
the witchcraft trials, held
here between 1587 and
1589. The unique and
popular **Museo Etnografico
e della Stregoneria** is
devoted to the story of
these trials.

The centre of Triora still
preserves much evidence
of the village's medieval
origins, with little alleys,
narrow streets and houses
huddled together around
small squares. Of seven
original gates, the only survivor
is **Porta Soprana**, with a
rounded arch. Nearby is the
Fontana Soprana, the oldest
fountain in the town.

The one sight not to miss
is the collegiate church of
the **Assunta**. It was originally
Romanesque-Gothic and still
retains the old bell tower and
main door, though the façade
is Neo-Classical. Inside (reduced
to a single aisle in 1770) there
are several notable works of
art, including several by Luca
Cambiaso; but chief among them
is an exquisite painting on a gold
background of the *Baptism of
Christ* (1397), by the Sienese artist
Taddeo di Bartolo. It is the oldest
known painting of its type in the
Riviera di Ponente.

There is also a delightful
church, of **San Bernardino**,
just outside Triora; its interior
is virtually smothered in 15th-
century frescoes.

🏛 Museo Etnografico e
della Stregoneria
Corso Italia 1. **Tel** 0184 944 77.
Open winter 2:30–6pm daily (from
10:30am–noon Sat & Sun); summer
10:30am–noon, 3–6:30 pm daily. 🖼

Environs
About 10 km (6 miles) beyond
Triora, just a stone's throw from
the French border, is the tiny
village of **Realdo**. It is set in a
stunning position, teetering on
a rocky cliff at 1,065 m (3,500 ft)
above sea level, with some of
Liguria's highest peaks as a
backdrop. The houses have a
distinctly Alpine look and the
few inhabitants speak in
old Provençal.

㉒ Taggia

Imperia. **Road Map** A5. 🏘 14,000.
🚆 🚌 ℹ Via Boselli, Arma di Taggia,
0184 437 33. 🎉 Corteo Storico dei
Rioni (4th Sun in Feb); Festa della
Maddalena (3rd Sun in Jul); antiques
market (last weekend of month).
🌐 **rivieradeifiori.org** and
🌐 **taggia.it**

Lying close to the mouth of
the Valle Argentina is Taggia,
whose 16th-century walls
conceal a fascinating medieval
village. One of the most
impressive sights is the **medieval
bridge** across the Argentina,
with 16 arches of which two
are Romanesque.

Via Soleri, the heart of
the old centre, is flanked by
porticoes with black stone
arches and many fine old
buildings. The Baroque parish
church of **Santi Giacomo e
Filippo** is certainly lovely, but
Taggia's most important
monument is the **Convento
di San Domenico**. Built between
1460 and 1490, it is considered
to have the best collection of
works by the Liguria-Nice
school. Its masterpieces include
five works by the French artist
Ludovico Brea.

It is worth popping down to
Arma di Taggia, the small resort
a 10-minute drive along the
coast. It has a lovely beach,
as well as several hotels
and restaurants.

🏛 Convento di San Domenico
Piazza Beato Cristoforo. **Tel** 0184 476
254. **Open** 9am–noon, 3–6pm
Mon–Sat. 🖼

The arcaded Via Soleri in Taggia, with its
black stone arches

Ludovico Brea

Of the many foreign artists working in Liguria, and in particular on the Riviera di Ponente, between the mid-15th century and the mid-16th century, Ludovico Brea (1443–c.1523) is the best documented. Born in Nice, Brea became a painter in his native city and was probably influenced by the artistic trends emanating from Avignon. Cultural exchange, encouraged by trade between Liguria and the South of France – a depot for goods from northern Europe – was lively at that time, and it was not unusual for Flemish paintings, or the artists themselves, to find themselves in the Ligurian area. Thus, Ludovico Brea was able to learn from and be influenced by works from different schools of painting and absorb a variety of cultural elements. Of northern European styles, he was particularly interested in Flemish art, but was also fascinated by the miniatures found in medieval manuscripts. Brea was extremely adept at understanding the taste of his Ligurian patrons, a skill that enabled him to work in Italy for many years. After producing some early work in his native city, Brea transferred to Liguria. Traces of his various moves and of his life in general at that time are scant, and generalizations about his artistic influences are usually made by looking at his later work. While in Liguria, you may also come across the work of Ludovico's brother, Antonio, and his son, Francesco.

The Artist at Work

Ludovico Brea did most of his work in three Ligurian cities: in Genoa, where his works can be seen in the gallery of Palazzo Bianco (a St Peter and Crucifixion) and in the church of Santa Maria di Castello (Conversion of St Paul and Coronation of the Virgin); in Savona, where there are works in the oratory of Nostra Signora di Castello (Madonna and Saints), in the Cathedral treasury (Assunta and Saints, detail shown left) and in the Pinacoteca Civica (Christ on the Cross between the Madonna and St John the Evangelist); and in Taggia, with works in the Convento di San Domenico and the adjacent museum. All three paintings illustrated below can be seen in Taggia.

The Baptism of Christ (1495) is a polyptych in San Domenico, in Taggia, in the chapel on the left of the presbytery, and is the only work complete with its frame and predella.

The Madonna del Rosario, which dates from 1513 and is also in San Domenico in Taggia, features a landscape background of some depth. A lightening sky looms in the background.

The polyptych dedicated to Santa Caterina da Siena (1488), has an astonishing gold background, against which the figures emerge in an almost surreal fashion.

㉓ Tour of the Armea and Crosia Valleys

This itinerary follows a route which can be covered easily in a day. It takes the visitor to some of the most picturesque villages in the far west of the Riviera del Ponente, on the slopes of the hinterland behind the strip between San Remo and Bordighera. Interesting though the coastal towns are, this part of the Ligurian interior also has a great deal to offer visitors. Here you will find ancient towns and villages which grew up along the old salt routes, often very close to the border with France. Set among green hills which rise rapidly to become mountains, many of these ancient centres have managed to preserve their old appearance and atmosphere, despite the passing of time.

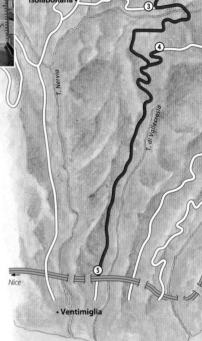

Pigna

R. Bonda

Isolabonana

T. Nervia

T. di Vallecrosia

Nice

Ventimiglia

Bordighera

③ Apricale
At the heart of this medieval village, set in a panoramic position, is Piazza Vittorio Emanuele, with the parish church of the Purificazione di Maria, the Oratory of San Bartolomeo and some castle ruins. Apricale (from *apricus*, which means "facing towards the sun") is also known as the "artists' village", because of the modern murals painted on the façades of the old houses.

④ Perinaldo
At the top of Val Crosia, this village was the birthplace of Italy's greatest astronomer, Gian Domenico Cassini (1625–1712), discoverer of asteroids and moons and famous for his work for Louis XIV; a museum in the Palazzo del Comune is dedicated to him. The parish church of San Nicolò dates from 1495.

⑤ Vallecrosia Alta
Set among fields of flowers and vineyards which produce Rossese, one of Liguria's most prized wines, this town is the older twin of the modern seaside village of Vallecrosia, just west of Bordighera. In the medieval quarter is the church of San Rocco. Nearby, at Garibbe, there is an unexpected Museum of Song and Sound Reproduction.

② Baiardo

This small town lies at the end of a winding road, at 900 m (2,745 ft) above sea level, just beyond the Ghimbegna pass. It is overlooked by the picturesque ruins of the church of San Nicolò, which collapsed during the earthquake which shook the town in 1887 (killing hundreds of people in the process). There are splendid views of the Maritime Alps from the terrace behind the church.

Tips for Drivers

Imperia. **Road Map** A4–5.
Length of tour: 50 km (31 miles).
Time needed: one day.
ℹ Ceriana comune, Corso Italia 141, 0184 551 017. Baiardo comune, Via Roma, 0184 673 054. Apricale IAT, Via Roma 1, 0184 208 641 (seasonal). Perinaldo IAT, Via Arco di Trionfo 2, 0184 672 095. Vallecrosia Alta comune, Via Orazio Raimondo 71, 0184 255 22 11.
Vallecrosia Alta: "U cantun de l'antigu", antiques and crafts market (2nd Sun of month).

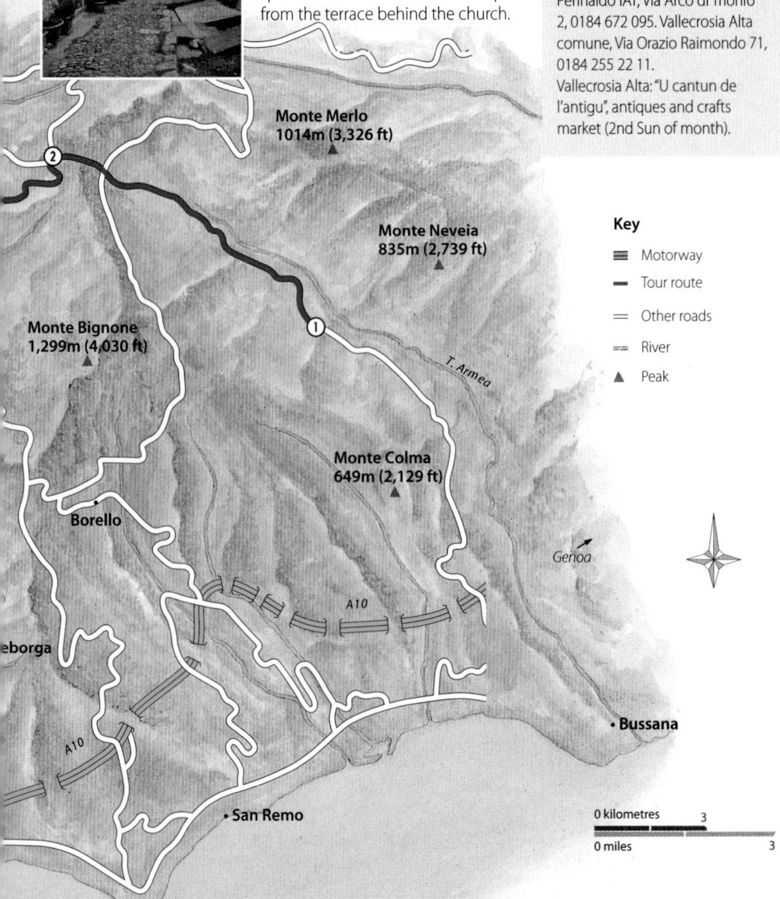

Monte Merlo
1014m (3,326 ft) ▲

Monte Neveia
835m (2,739 ft) ▲

Monte Bignone
1,299m (4,030 ft) ▲

① T. Armea

Monte Colma
649m (2,129 ft) ▲

Borello

Genoa

A10

eborga

A10

• **Bussana**

• San Remo

Key

≡ Motorway
— Tour route
= Other roads
⁓ River
▲ Peak

0 kilometres   3
0 miles   3

① Ceriana

This pretty mountain-top village lies in the Valle Armea, 12 km (7 miles) north of San Remo. Built in the Middle Ages on the site of a Roman villa, Ceriana's old centre is still encircled by perfectly preserved walls. Walking around the narrow streets and alleys, you can enjoy unexpected glimpses of the surrounding countryside.

❷❹ San Remo

Imperia. **Road Map** A5. 🚉 59,000.
🚆 🚌 🛈 IAT Riviera dei Fiori, Largo
Nuvoloni 1, 0184 590 59. 🎭 Festival
della Canzone Italiana (late Feb or
early Mar); Milano–San Remo cycle
race (Sat closest to19 Mar); Rally di San
Remo (early Oct). 🅦 **rivieradeifiori.
org** and 🅦 **comunedisanremo.it**

Defined, in the eyes of many
Italians, by its thriving flower
industry and its Festival of Italian
Song, San Remo is also one of
the Italian Riviera's best-known
and most atmospheric resorts.

The city is divided into three
distinct areas: Corso Matteotti
and around (the heart of the
shopping district), La Pigna (the
old town), and the west end of
the seafront, which was the heart
of the resort during its heyday.

Tourism, mainly English,
boomed in San Remo from the
mid-1800s to the early 1900s, a
period of great expansion when
all manner of grand hotels and
villas were built, including
various Art Nouveau palazzi.
There is no better Belle Epoque
monument than the splendid
and still-thriving **Casinò
Municipale**, built by Eugenio
Ferret in 1904–06.

Another unmistakable San
Remo landmark, with its onion
domes, is the **Russian Orthodox
Church**, built in the 1920s.
The Russians were almost as
passionate about San Remo as
the English, and the seafront

Corso Imperatrice
was named in honour
of Maria Alexandrovna,
wife of Czar Alexander II
and a frequent visitor to
San Remo. This seafront
boulevard is a favourite
place to stroll, and
provides a wonderful
taste of the old
aristocratic resort.

Beyond **Lungomare
Vittorio Emanuele II**
and **Lungomare Italo
Calvino**, where the streets
are broken up by lawns, the
road continues to the modern
marina, Portosole, and the
old, or town, port.

At the end of Corso Trento e
Trieste, beyond the **Giardini
Ormond**, stands **Villa Nobel**,
where the famous Swedish
scientist lived and where
he also died in 1896.

The other part of San
Remo that no one
should miss is its
medieval "città
vecchia", fortified in
the 11th century in
order to keep out
the Saracens. The
area is known as **La
Pigna**, or pine cone,
because of its layout:
the maze of alleys,
steps, arches and
covered walkways
spread out in concentric circles
from the top of the hill.
The main monuments, including
the cathedral and the
Oratorio dell'Immacolata
Concezione (1563), are
found in the central
Piazza San Siro. The
Cathedral of San Siro,
founded in the 12th
century, has two fine side
doors featuring bas-reliefs
in the lunette: the one on
the left, which dates from
the 12th century, represents
the *Agnello pasquale*, or
paschal lamb. Inside, there
are three aisles and three
apses, extended in 1600.
There are good works
of art including a 15th-
century *Crucifixion*.

At the top of La Pigna
is the sumptuous
Santuario di Nostra

San Remo's famous casino

Signora della Costa,
remodelled in the 1630s.
There is a fine pebble mosaic
outside and four statues by
Maragliano on the high altar.

As well as shops, there are
some interesting palazzi on
Corso Matteotti. One of these
is Palazzo Borea d'Olmo, a
curious mix of Mannerism
and Baroque. As the
Museo Civico, it houses
a mix of archaeological
finds, Garibaldian relics
and 18th- and 19th-
century paintings.
Finally, for an
insight into the
local flower trade,
visit San Remo's
famous wholesale flower
market, which lies
just east of the
city centre in the
Armea valley.

Statue of Spring, on the San
Remo seafront

🏛 **Museo Civico**
Corso Matteotti 143.
Tel 0184 531 942. **Open** 9am–7pm
Tue–Sat. ♿

Environs
About 10 km (6 miles) east
of San Remo is the suburb of
Bussana Nuova and, beyond,
Bussana Vecchia, one of the
most charming spots on the
Riviera di Ponente.

Destroyed by the 1887
earthquake, which left only
the bell tower of the Baroque
church of **Sacro Cuore** intact,
Bussana Vecchia was partially
restored in the 1960s, when
an artists' colony moved in.
They opened up studios and
crafts workshops, but took
care to change the original
appearance of the village as
little as possible.

The harbour at San Remo

◀ View of the medieval village of Dolceacqua

⑳ Pigna

Imperia. **Road Map** A4. ⚐ 1,015.
Ⓕ Ventimiglia. 🚌 *i* Comune,
Piazza Umberto I, 0184 241 016.

Situated in the foothills of the
Maritime Alps in the Alta Val
Nervia, some 40 km (25 miles)
north of San Remo, Pigna is a
fascinating place; its form is
reminiscent of the eponymous
district in San Remo. Strolling
around the narrow streets,
known as *chibi*, you can under-
stand how the medieval town
was built, with the houses
grouped defensively on
concentric streets.

Among a number of fine
churches, the most important
is the church of **San Michele**,
founded in 1450. A splendid
white marble rose window,
perhaps the work of Giovanni
Gagini from the early 1500s,
adorns the façade. Inside, the
Polyptych of St Michael is a
monumental work by the
Piemontese artist
Canavesio (1500s),
in which the
influence of the
Brea brothers *(see
p163)* is evident.
Also by
Canavesio are
the frescoes
portraying *The
Passion of Christ*
housed in the small

The rose window at San
Michele, Pigna

church of **San Bernardo**, within
the cemetery. Other places of
interest are the ruins of the
church of **San Tommaso**, and
Piazza Castello, with lovely
views over the village of
Castel Vittorio.

㉖ Dolceacqua

See pp170–71.

㉗ Bordighera

Imperia. **Road Map** A5. ⚐ 11,300.
Ⓕ 🚌 *i* Via Vittorio Emanuele II
172–174, 0184 262 322. 🎭 Bordighera
Città dell'Umorismo, a festival of
humour (late Apr–early May); Sagra
del Pesce (mid-Jul); Berlecata Sasso
(early Aug). 🌐 **visitrivieradeifiori.it**

A famous painting by Monet
called *A View of Bordighera* is
evidence of the historic fame
of this sunny and lively resort.
As was the case elsewhere on
the Riviera, Bordighera was
particularly popular with the
British. Here, too, you find Art
Nouveau palazzi (many conver-
ted into hotels or apartments),
and a popular seafront boulevard – the **Lungomare Argentina**,
with Capo Sant'Ampelio at the
far end. The beach is good and
often busy, and there are palm
trees wherever you look.

The **Biblioteca Museo
Clarence Bicknell**
was founded by
one of Bordighera's
many British visitors,
a vicar, botanist
and archaeologist.
Bicknell's library-
cum-museum
houses Roman
funerary objects and,
more interestingly,
casts of rock drawings and a
vast photographic archive of
ancient graffiti from the nearby
Vallée des Merveilles in France.
There is a handful of sights of
historic interest. By the sea, on
Capo Sant'Ampelio, is the

Romanesque church of
Sant'Ampelio, with an
11th-century crypt; it stands
on the spot where Ampelio
(a hermit who later became
a saint), once lived.

In the historical center, look
out for the 17th-century church
of **Santa Maria Maddalena**,
with a fine early 16th-century
marble sculpture on the high
altar, attributed to the workshop
of Domenico Parodi. In nearby
Piazza De Amicis there is a
marble fountain (1783) featuring
a statue of Magiargiè, a slave to
the Spanish Moors who died
in Bordighera.

For a quiet but interesting
interlude, go to the **Giardino
Esotico Pallanca**, which has
more than 3,000 species of
cacti and succulents.

🏛 **Biblioteca Museo
Clarence Bicknell**
Via Bicknell 3. **Tel** 0184 263 694.
Open 8:30am–1pm, 1:30–4:45pm
Mon, 9am–1pm Tue–Thu.
Closed public hols.

🌿 **Giardino Esotico Pallanca**
Via Madonna della Ruota 1. **Tel** 0184
266 347. **Open** winter: 9am–5pm
daily; summer: 9am–12:30pm, 2:30–
7pm daily. 🚫 🌐 **pallanca.it**

Plaque welcoming people to
Seborga, near Bordighera

Environs

In a lofty position about 12 km
(7 miles) north of Bordighera is
the ancient village of **Seborga**,
which, along with its 350 inhabitants, enjoys the unexpected
title of "principality". Thanks to an
historical anomaly, the town was
able to elect its own sovereign,
Giorgio I, in 1963, and pass a
constitution, which was renewed
in 1995. They have their own
currency, the *luigino* (Seborga's
first mint was set up by
Benedictine monks in 1660), and
print their own stamps, and cars
carry SB on their licence plates.

Cactus in the tropical garden of Pallanca at Bordighera

㉖ Dolceacqua

By a quirk of fate, this delightful medieval village is, despite its name (which means "fresh water"), home to one of the most prized and famous red wines in Italy, Rossese, a favourite with Napoleon and Pope Julius III. Overlooked by the imposing but not overbearing mass of the ruined Castello dei Doria, the village spreads out on the slopes of the mountain and is reminiscent of one of Liguria's traditional *presepi* (nativity scenes) when seen from above. The River Nervia divides Dolceacqua into two. On one side is the older part, known as Borgo, while the newer district on the right is called Terra. The artist Claude Monet, who loved this area, painted the castle and described the old bridge which links the two quarters as a "jewel of lightness".

View of Dolceacqua
The picturesque medieval village has narrow alleyways and tall houses.

★ Ponte Vecchio
This light and elegant bridge has a single ogee arch with an impressive span of 33 m (110 ft). Built in the 15th century, the bridge links the two quarters of Terra and Borgo, separated by the River Nervia.

KEY

① **Palazzo Doria** is where the Doria family settled in the 18th century after their castle became uninhabitable. An old passageway still links the palazzo to the church of Sant'Antonio, a route that was reserved for the Doria family alone.

② **The bell tower** of Sant'Antonio Abate forms part of the village's encircling walls.

③ **Church of San Giorgio** is located across the river from the old village (at the end of the bridge south of this illustration). The 13th-century church of San Giorgio has the remains of a Romanesque bell tower, and a ceiling with interesting painted beams. In the crypt is a Doria family tomb.

Monument to the "Gombo"
This modern work is dedicated to Pier Vicenzo Mela, a local man who was the first to use an olive press *(gombo)* to extract oil, in the 1700s.

★ Castello dei Doria
Built to defend the town in 1100 and bought by the Doria in 1270, this castle gradually acquired the look of a noble palazzo. It was damaged in 1754 but was dealt its final blow by the earthquake in 1887.

VISITORS' CHECKLIST

Practical Information
Imperia.
Road Map A5. ⚄ 2,000.
ℹ Via Barberis Colomba 3, 0184 206 666. 📷 Procession of San Sebastiano (Sun closest to 20 Jan); Festa Patronale dell'Assunta (15 Aug); Festa della "Michetta" (16 Aug).
Ⓦ **dolceacqua.it**

Transport
FS Ventimiglia. 🚌

The church of Sant'Antonio Abate
Dolceacqua's parish church has in front of it a broad square paved with pebbles, in the Ligurian tradition. The church dates from 1400, but was altered in the Baroque era. Inside there is a lovely polyptych painted by Ludovico Brea.

View of the apse of the Cattedrale dell'Assunta, Ventimiglia

❷❽ Ventimiglia

Imperia. **Road Map** A5. 🚉 26,000.
🚊 🚌 *i* Via Cavour 61, 0184 351
183. 🎭 Corteo Storico, historical
procession (1st or 2nd Sun in Aug,
odd years); Battaglia di Fiori (summer).
🌐 rivieradeifiori.org and
🌐 ventimiglia.it

Ventimiglia is the last major
town on the Riviera di Ponente
before the French border. It
is a perfect synthesis of the
characteristics of towns along
this part of the coast, and, more
generally, of all coastal towns in
the region: a place where past
and present seem to co-exist
quite happily, where Roman
ruins rub shoulders with the
latest tourist facilities.

A frontier town par excellence
(its history is studded with
numerous disputes with nearby
France over the national border
lines), Ventimiglia straddles the
Roia and the Nervia valleys,
among the most beautiful in
the Ligurian Alps. Nearby are
marvels of nature such as the
Grotte dei Balzi Rossi and

the Hanbury Botanical Gardens
(see pp174–5).

The River Roia divides
Ventimiglia into two: the
medieval part on a hill to the
west, and the modern town
on the coastal plain to the east.
Traces of the era of Roman
domination, which followed
rule by the Liguri Intemelii
people, can be seen at
Albintimilium, on the eastern
periphery of the new town.
Clearly visible from the flyover
on the Via Aurelia, the ruins
consist of a stretch of the
decumanus maximus (or main
street), a few houses and the
great baths (the source of the
lovely Mosaico di Arione, now
in front of the hospital). More
important than any of these,
however, is the small **Theatre**,
the most significant Roman
monument in Liguria. Dating
from the early 3rd century BC,
the theatre could seat more
than 5,000 spectators. Ten levels
of steps in the lower section,
made from Turbia stone, are
still well preserved, while the
western entrance gate is
practically intact. Various finds
discovered at the site are on
display in the nearby **Museo
Archeologico Gerolamo Rossi**,
in the Forte dell'Annunziata
in town.

Via Garibaldi (also known
as "la piazza") is the main street
through the cobbled and
charming *centro storico*. There
are some fine palazzi here, some
with hanging gardens to the
back opening onto the upper
floors, in the 16th-century
tradition. Among the most
important buildings are the
Palazzo Pubblico, the Loggia

Marble cover of a funerary urn,
1st century AD

del Magistrato dell'Abbondanza,
and the Neo-Classical former
Teatro Civico. This houses the
Civica Biblioteca Aprosiana,
the oldest public library in
Liguria (founded in 1648) with
a fine collection of rare books
and manuscripts.

At the heart of Via Garibaldi
is the imposing bulk of the
Cattedrale dell'Assunta. This
was built in place of an 8th-
century Carolingian chuch in
the 11th and 12th centuries,
and has been modified at
intervals since: the façade is
Romanesque, for example,
while the portico, added in
1222, is Gothic. The bell tower,
constructed on a 12th-century
base, was rebuilt in the Baroque
era and remodelled once again
in the 19th century. Inside,
there is not much to see,
though in the crypt you can
see parts of the old medieval
church, as well as some pre-
Roman sculptures.

Adjoining the Assunta is
the octagonal **Baptistry**
(11th century); this contains
a wonderful font dating from
the 12th–13th centuries.

Continuing along Via
Garibaldi, past another couple
of churches, you eventually
reach Porta Nizza. From here,
following Via della Torre and Via
Appio, you reach Piazza Colletta
and the lovely Romanesque
church of **San Michele**. The
unimpressive façade is 19th-
century, but the main body of
the church, of which only the
central nave survives, dates
from the 11th century; the bell
tower, apse and vault are from
the 12th century. Inside is an
interesting 11th-century crypt,

The Roman theatre in Ventimiglia, dating from the 3rd century AD

For hotels and restaurants in this region see pp182–3 and pp194–7

Overlooking the town of Ventimiglia

incorporating various Roman materials, including columns used in the high altar.

From Porta Nizza, you can also climb up west of the old city to the ruins of three medieval forts, a reminder of the battles once fought over Ventimiglia. One of these, the **Castel d'Appio**, built by the Genoese in the 13th century, occupies the site not only of a Roman military camp (castrum) but also of an early Ligurian defence post. There are marvellous views of the Riviera from here.

The modern, eastern part of Ventimiglia, complete with seaside promenades, is a shopping mecca and is very popular with the French. The streets are busy at weekends and on Fridays, when people from the surrounding area flood in for the weekly market.

🏛 Albintimilium
Corso Genova. **Tel** 0184 252 320.
Open 3–6pm Sat, Sun.

🏛 Museo Archeologico Gerolamo Rossi
Via Verdi 41. **Tel** 0184 351 181.
Open 9am–12:30pm, 3–5pm Tue–Sat; 10am–12:30pm Sun. 🖼 📷

㉙ Balzi Rossi

Grimaldi di Ventimiglia (Imperia).
Road Map A5.

This prehistoric site, one of the most famous in the western Mediterranean, lies about 10 km (6 miles) west of Ventimiglia, below the village of Grimaldi and just a stone's throw from the Italy-France frontier. It

consists of nine caves, which have been explored at various times since the 19th century. The name of Balzi Rossi (meaning "red rocks") derives from the reddish colour of the precipitous limestone cliffs.

This atmospheric place has yielded fascinating evidence of human settlement in this part of Liguria, going back as far as the Paleolithic age. The area was probably chosen because of the favourable natural conditions, including the warm climate and the proximity of the sea. There is a walkway connecting some of the caves, some of which you are also allowed to enter.

Numerous stone and bone instruments, fossil remains of animals, and various

Necklace found in the Triple Tomb

ornamental and artistic objects have been discovered in the caves, in particular in the Grotta del Principe, slightly removed from the other caves and also the largest.

Of greatest interest are the many tombs, which provide a few tangible snippets of information about the people who lived here some 240,000 years ago. They were undoubtedly among the most sophisticated of any people then living in Europe.

The most famous of these tombs, known as the **Triple Tomb**, was discovered in Barma Grande cave in 1892. Today, it is on display in the **Museo Preistorico dei Balzi Rossi**, founded by the Englishman Sir Thomas Hanbury (see p174) in 1898. To the sides are two male individuals, a boy on the left and a man over 2 m (6 ft) tall on the right. At the centre is a girl of around 16 years old. Funerary objects, such as sea shells, pendants of worked bone, deer teeth and necklaces fashioned out of fish vertebrae traditionally accompanied the deceased.

The museum also has on display a reproduction of the only figure engraved in a naturalistic style to be discovered at Balzi Rossi. Found in the Grotta del Caviglione, it is the profile of a shortish, stocky horse, 40 cm (16 in) long and 20 cm (8 in) high. It is known as the **Przewalskii Horse**; a few rare examples of the breed survive in Mongolia. Also on display are stone instruments, animal skeletons and small statues.

🏛 Grotte e Museo Preistorico dei Balzi Rossi
Ponte San Ludovico, Via Balzi Rossi 9. **Tel** 0184 381 13.
Open Museum: 8:30am–7:30pm Tue–Sun; Grotte: 8:30am–1 hour before sunset. 📷 hourly. 🖼

One of the nine Balzi Rossi caves

㉚ Hanbury Botanical Gardens

This splendid botanical garden was founded in 1867 by Sir Thomas Hanbury, a rich English businessman, and his brother Daniel, a botanist, with the help of the eminent German botanist Ludovico Winter. Sir Thomas was passionate about Liguria, and saw the opportunity that its warm climate provided: the exotic plants that he brought back from his travels, particularly those from hot, dry areas such as Southern Africa and Mexico, he was able to acclimatize to co-exist with the local flora. By 1898, the garden included more than 7,000 plant species. The gardens were left to decay during much of the 20th century but are now being coaxed back to their former glory by the University of Genoa.

Agave
Aloes and agaves, particular favourites of Sir Thomas, are planted among the rocks to re-create the desert habitat they come from.

★ Dragon Fountain
Encircled by papyruses, warm-climate plants which have acclimatized well here, this fountain has an ancient and rather mysterious air. Sitting on the rim is a dragon, an echo of Sir Thomas's beloved Far East.

Temple of the Four Seasons
This is one of many temples that Sir Thomas had built around the gardens, in line with late 19th-century taste. Its classical style is evocative of an Italian Renaissance garden.

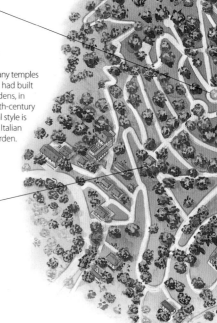

KEY

① **The Viale dei Cipressi**
(avenue of cypresses) is one of the most charming parts of the garden, with its lines of tall trees, a familiar sight in the Italian countryside.

0 metres		50
0 yards		50

The Terraces
In this part of the garden the plants are grouped so as to form "themed gardens". There are wonderful views from the Pavilion.

VISITORS' CHECKLIST

Practical Information
Corso Montecarlo 43, La Mortola Inferiore (Imperia).
Road Map A5.
Tel 0184 229 507. **W** **parks.it**
and **W** **giardinihanbury.com**
Open Mar–mid-Jun & mid-Sep–mid-Oct: 9:30am–5pm daily; mid-Jun–mid-Sep: 9:30am–6pm daily; mid-Oct–28 Feb: 9:30am–4pm.

Transport
FS Ventimiglia.

★ The Villa
The original palazzo was built in the 14th century and extended in the 17th. In the 1930s, Mussolini held a notorious meeting with General Franco here. The villa now houses offices and is not open to the public, but you can enjoy the lovely views over the gardens and down to the sea from the villa's loggia.

TRAVELLERS' NEEDS

WHERE TO STAY

Liguria has long been popular with holiday-makers and therefore has a long tradition of providing a wide range of accommodation, particularly on the coast. Along both the Riviera di Levante and the Riviera di Ponente, with their collection of renowned resorts, visitors will find an almost uninterrupted string of sumptuous hotels and family-run *pensioni*, which are open virtually all year round. Genoa, sandwiched between the two rivieras, has accommodation to suit all tastes and budgets, both in the Centro Storico and in the immediate vicinity. In general, visitors tend to stay on the coast and make day trips inland. If you want to try out the increasingly popular option of *agriturismo*, which means staying on a farm, then head into the Ligurian hinterland. Camping is another option, which you can explore either inland or along the coast.

Hotel Categories and Prices

In Liguria, hotels are classified according to the Italian national system. The categories go from one up to five stars, that is, from budget accommodation to luxury hotels. In general, you can expect services to be of a good standard, but the best value for money is generally found in the three-star category. Note that hotels in the lower categories may not accept credit cards.

Prices vary according to the season, rising in the (admittedly long) high season or during major festivals and cultural events. Guests should expect to be charged a tourist tax of €1 (one- to three-star hotels), €2 (four-star hotels) and €3 (five-star hotels) per night; this is not applicable to children under 14.

Booking

Liguria is a very popular region, especially in summer, when the long coastline and beaches attract big crowds. Visitors are advised to book accommodation well in advance, confirming the booking through e-mail.

Hotels

A region that depends to a large extent on tourism, Liguria has a well-developed network of hotels, with generally good facilites. The one exception on the coast is the Cinque Terre, where accommodation tends to be fairly simple. Most coastal resorts offer hotels in all five cate-gories. A list of hotels, including family-run *pensioni*, with prices, can be obtained from the regional tourist (IAT) offices (*see opposite*) or from local offices in the larger resorts (*see p207*).

Agriturismo and Bed & Breakfast

Particularly among people who love the outdoors or who want

Holidaymakers relaxing on the beach at Monterosso

to choose from activites such as fishing or horse riding, *agri-turismo* (or farm holidays) have become a popular alternative form of accommodation. The *agriturismo* formula is simple: working farms offer rooms (including self-catering options), and home-made food based on local products, in many cases grown or made by the owners themselves, as well as other facilities ranging from children's play areas to swimming pools.

Bed & breakfast accommoda-tion, also available in Liguria, is generally comfortable and inexpensive. This type of lodging is found mainly in larger cities and in principal coastal resorts, rarely in the interior.

Camping

Camping in Italy does not have as big a following as in some other European countries. Many camp sites are situated close to

Comfortable public rooms at the Royal Hotel *(see p183)* in San Remo

◀ Bicycle parked near a market stall in La Spezia

The seafront at Bordighera, lined with hotels

DIRECTORY

**Agenzia Regionale
per la Promozione Turistica
"In Liguria"**

Piazza de Ferrari 1,
Genova.
Tel 010 548 51.
Fax 010 548 87 42.
🆆 turismoinligura.it

APT Genova

Palazzo delle Torrette
Via Garibaldi 12r, Genova.
Tel 010 557 29 03.
Fax 010 557 24 14.
🆆 apt.genova.it

IAT Riviera dei Fiori

Largo Nuvoloni 1,
San Remo.
Tel 0184 590 59.
Fax 0184 507 649.
🆆 rivieradeifiori.org

IAT Tigullio

Via XXV Aprile 4,
Santa Margherita Ligure.
Tel 0185 287 485.
Fax 0185 283 034.
🆆 provincia.genova.it

**Provincia La Spezia
Sezione Turismo**

Viale Mazzini 45,
La Spezia.
Tel 0187 770 900.
Fax 0187 770 908.

**UIT Riviera Ligure
delle Palme**

Via Sormano 12,
Alassio.
Tel 019 831 33 26.
Fax 019 831 32 69.
🆆 turismo.provincia.savona.it

the sea, while some have private beaches reserved for camp residents. These sites are usually clean, well-cared for and in reasonably natural surroundings. Coastal sites are often particularly busy in August, so book in advance. And, since camping is not necessarily a cheap option in Italy, always check the rates.

Note that there are strict regulations as to where camper vans can be parked. A list of camp sites can be found at any regional tourist (IAT) office.

Tourist signs

Self-Catering

Besides self-catering on an agriturismo farm or camp site, there are also self-catering apartments available for rent. These can be found mainly in the largest seaside resorts along the riviera, and may suit

Bedroom at Grand Hotel Savoia *(see p180)*

families with young children better than a hotel. Again, the accommodation listings provided by tourist offices (IAT) should provide the names, addresses and numbers of various agencies which deal with short-term rentals. In addition, the tourist literature will also include the details of private individuals who offer apartments for rent.

Recommended Hotels

The hotels in the listings that follow have been divided into the following categories: B&B, Family-Run, Modern, Historic and Charming.

Bed-and-breakfasts guarantee inexpensive, comfortable rooms with, of course, the promise of a great breakfast. What distinguishes a family-run hotel is the friendly staff, a homely ambience, and a great atmosphere of warm hospitality. Modern hotels offer good service in hassle-free rooms, with facilities such as gyms, spas, swimming pools and tennis courts. There are many historic hotels across Liguria, like much of Italy, with beautiful period furnishings. The charming category features enchanting residences and villas, sometimes overlooking the sea, or located in small picturesque villages. These guarantee a relaxing holiday in elegantly furnished rooms.

The DK Choice hotels are extra special. These hotels may have above average standards, or a breathtaking location, or they may simply have an appeal that sets them apart.

Where to Stay

Genoa

Il Centro Storico

Il Bel Soggiorno　€
B&B　**Map** 3 A3
Via XX Settembre 19, 16121
Tel *010 542 880*
Ⓦ belsoggiornohotel.com
Clean, simple rooms at this B&B
in an Art Nouveau building.
Buffet breakfast. Pets allowed.

Il Borgo di Genova　€
Charming　**Map** 3 C2
Via Borgo degli Incrociati 7, 16137
Tel *347 602 55 78*
Ⓦ ilborgodigenova.com
Lovely B&B run by a young couple,
close to main tourist sites. All
rooms with en suite bathrooms.

Veronese　€
B&B　**Map** 5 B2
Vico Cicala 3, 16124
Tel *010 251 0771*
Ⓦ hotelveronese.com
Set in a historic palace, near
Genoa's main attractions. Quiet,
clean and well serviced rooms.
Parking at extra cost.

NH Marina　€€
Modern　**Map** 2 E5
Molo Ponte Calvi 5, 16124
Tel *010 25 391*
Ⓦ nh-hotels.it
Elegantly contemporary, with a
bar, two summer terraces and
meeting rooms.

DK Choice

Palazzo Cicala　€€
Historic　**Map** 5 C3
Piazza san Lorenzo 16, 16123
Tel *010 251 8824*
Ⓦ palazzocicala.it
A chic hotel on the first floor
of the superbly restored 16th-
century Palazzo Cicala. It features contemporary decor, with
a few pieces of antique furniture
adding to the charm. Rooms are
spacious and bright, with high
vaulted ceilings. The hotel also
offers apartments in some of
the most beautiful historic
palazzi of the city.

Bristol Palace　€€€
Historic　**Map** 6 E4
Via XX Settembre 35, 16123
Tel *010 592 541*
Ⓦ hotelbristolpalace.it
Modern rooms, some of them
have baths with whirlpools. Enjoy
breakfast in a magnificent room
with frescoes. Close to attractions.

Le Strade Nuove

Agnello d'Oro　€
Family-run　**Map** 2 D2
Vico delle Monachette 6, 16126
Tel *010 246 2084*
Ⓦ hotelagnellodoro.it
In a former convent, with bright
rooms and modern facilities.

Astoria　€
Historic　**Map** 2 E2
Piazza Brignole 4, 16122
Tel *010 873 316*
Ⓦ hotelastoriagenova.it
Rooms with frescoed ceilings, and
antiques set in a centrally located
19th-century aristocratic palazzo.

Balbi　€
B&B　**Map** 2 D2
Via Balbi 21, 16126
Tel *010 275 9288*
Ⓦ hotelbalbigenova.it
Housed in a historic palace with
frescoes and parquet floors. Large
rooms; breakfast room has a bar.

Best Western City　€
Modern　**Map** 3 A2
Via S. Sebastiano 6, 16123
Tel *010 584 707*
Ⓦ bwcityhotel-ge.it
Wide range of rooms: from singles
to suites with facilities for tour
groups and business clients.

Best Western Metropoli　€
Pension　**Map** 6 D2
Piazza Fontane Marose, 16123
Tel *010 24 68 88 8*
Ⓦ bestwestern.it/metropoli_ge
Modern, comfortable, in a pretty
piazza, near museums and opera.

Cairoli　€
Modern　**Map** 2 F3
Via Cairoli 14/4, 16124
Tel *010 246 1454*
Ⓦ hotelcairoligenova.com

Imposing façade of the five-star Grand
Hotel Savoia

A 16th-century palazzo with
modern art interiors, family
rooms, suites and a sun terrace.

Vittoria & Orlandini　€
Family-run　**Map** 2 E2
Via Balbi 33, 16126
Tel *010 261 923*
Ⓦ vittoriaorlandini.com
Well-appointed rooms, good ser-
vice. Easy access to train station.

Cit Hotels Britannia　€€
Modern　**Map** 2 E2
Via Balbi 38, 16123
Tel *010 247 0800*
Ⓦ cithotels-britannia-genoa.
h-rez.com
Centrally located, near main train
station. Spacious and clean rooms.

Grand Hotel Savoia　€€
Historic　**Map** 2 D2
Via Arsenale di Terra 5, 16126
Tel *010 261 641*
Ⓦ hotelsavoiagenova.it
A 19th-century palazzo, with a
spa, gym and solarium.

Further Afield

AC Hotel　€
Modern　**Map** D3
Corso Europa 1075, 16146
Tel *010 307 1180*
Ⓦ it.ac-hotels.com
This hotel offers plenty of comfort
and style. There's a sun terrace,
fitness centre and Turkish bath.

Bellevue　€
B&B　**Map** 2 D1
Salita della Provvidenza 1, 16134
Tel *010 246 2400*
Ⓦ hotelbellevuegenova.it
Centrally located, Bellevue has
basic rooms, and a sun terrace.

Columbus Sea Hotel　€
Modern　**Map** 1 B3
Via Milano 63, 16125
Tel *010 265 051*
Ⓦ columbussea.com
Half the rooms overlook the port.
Rooms have mini-bars and wireless
Internet access. Dogs allowed.

La Capannina　€
Family-run　**Map** D3
Via Tito Speri 7, 16146
Tel *010 317 131*
Ⓦ lacapanninagenova.it

Outside Genoa, with easy access. Upper rooms have great sea views, some have balconies. Free parking.

Méditerranée €
Charming **Map** D3
Lungomare di Pegli 69, 16155
Tel *010 697 3850*
w hotel-mediterraneegenoa.it
Well-equipped family-run hotel with spacious, bright and tastefully furnished rooms.

Moderno Verdi €
Historic **Map** 3 C3
Piazza Giuseppe Verdi 5, 16121
Tel *010 553 2104*
w modernoverdi.it
In an Art Nouveau building, with attention to detail and comfort.

Serafino €
Family-run **Map** D3
Via Verona 8, 16152
Tel *010 650 7261*
w hotelserafino.it
A simple establishment, well connected, with good service.

Sheraton €
Modern **Map** D3
Via Pionieri e Aviatori d'Italia 44, 16154
Tel *010 65 491*
w sheratongenova.com
Geared towards business clients. Modern and close to the airport, with a free shuttle bus to the city.

Starhotel President €
Modern **Map** 3 C3
Via Corte Lambruschini 4, 16129
Tel *010 5727*
w starhotels.it
Glass skyscraper with magnificent views, fitness centre and gourmet restaurant. Near the Aquarium and Christopher Columbus' house.

Hermitage €€
Modern **Map** 4 E5
Via Alberto Liri 29, 16145
Tel *010 311 605*
w hermitagehotel.ge.it
Clean and modern with attractive decor. Sea or mountain views.

Novotel Genova City €€
Modern **Map** 1 A3
Via Antonio Cantore, 8, 16126
Tel *010 648 41*
w novotel.com
Near harbour and city centre. Contemporary design and facilities. Bar and private garage.

DK Choice

Torre Cambiaso €€
Historic **Map** D3
Via Scarpanto 49, 16157
Tel *010 698 0636*
w torre-cambiaso.com

Housed in an aristocratic 14th-century villa, this hotel stands on a promontory between Pegli and Prà with an orchard and lush gardens. Rooms are individually furnished and extremely comfortable. The terrace has panoramic views, and there is also a heated outdoor pool.

Villa Pagoda €€
Historic **Map** D3
Via Capolungo 15, 16167
Tel *010 372 6161*
w villapagoda.it
Former 18th-century villa hotel in picturesque Nervi. Oriental decor; no two rooms are alike.

Riviera di Levante

AMEGLIA:
Locanda dell'Angelo €€
Family-run **Map** F5
Viale XXV Aprile 60, 19031
Tel *0187 643 91*
w paracucchilocanda.it
In the countryside, close to the Roman ruins of Luni. Suites have lovely views. Facilities include swimming, tennis, golf and riding.

BONASSOLA: Villa Belvedere €
Modern **Map** E4
Via Ammiraglio Serra 33, 19011
Tel *0187 813 622*
w bonassolahotelvillabelvedere.com
This charming place, with olive and lemon trees around it, has some suites with superb sea views. Pet-friendly.

CAMOGLI:
Cenobio Dei Dogi €€
Historic **Map** D4
Via Nicolò Cuneo 34, 16032
Tel *0185 72 41*
w cenobio.it
Vast 17th-century luxury villa with gorgeous sun terraces and a private beach. Comfortable rooms decorated in sea-blue tones.

DK Choice

CAMOGLI: Locanda I Tre Merli €€
B&B **Map** D4
Via Scalo, 5 6032
Tel *0185 77 67 52*
w locandaitremerli.com
In the enchanting fishing port of Camogli, this hotel has great sea views and personalized service. Rooms have flat screen TVs and clock radios. There's a small spa. Parking (request when booking) is available.

Tasteful decor and contemporary interior of the Villa Rosmarino, Camogli

CAMOGLI:
Villa Rosmarino €€
Boutique **Map** D4
Via Figari 38, 16032
Tel *0185 77 15 80*
w villarosmarino.com
At the foot of Monte di Portofino, Villa Rosmarino offers stunning views and an outdoor pool.

CHIAVARI: Santa Maria €
Modern **Map** E4
Viale Tito Groppo 29, 16043
Tel *0185 363 321*
w santamaria-hotel.com
A short walk from the town centre, Santa Maria is tastefully furnished, with a bar, garden and restaurant, and offers bikes to guests on rent.

DK Choice

FIASCHERINO: Il Nido €€
B&B **Map** F5
Via Fiascherino 75, 19030
Tel *0187 967 286*
w hotelnido.com
Elegant and modern furnishings grace the interiors of this remodelled hotel. Some rooms have balconies overlooking the Golfo dei Poeti – expect great views. Breakfast is served on a panoramic terrace. A staircase leads to a peaceful private beach, with a snack bar serving fresh salads and *focaccia*. The hotel is located close to many restaurants and is just a short distance away from Lerici by public bus.

ISOLA PALMARIA:
Locanda Lorena €€
Rooms with a view **Map** F5
Via Cavour 4, 19025
Tel *0187 79 23 70*
w locandalorena.com
A small bright beach hotel, famous for its seafood.

For more information on types of hotels see p179

LA SPEZIA: Corallo €
Family-run **Map** F4
Via Crispi 32, 19124
Tel *0187 731 366*
W hotelcorallospezia.com
Classic Italian decor, bright
rooms. A good base for boat
trips along the coast.

LA SPEZIA:
Firenze e Continentale €
Historic **Map** F4
Via Paleocapa 7, 19122
Tel *0187 713 210*
W hotelfirenzecontinentale.it
Marble floors and mahogany
woodwork at this classic hotel.
Close to the central train station.

LERICI: Florida €€
Charming **Map** F5
Lungomare Biaggini 35, 19032
Tel *0187 967 332*
W hotelflorida.it
Family-run hotel on the seafront
with bright and airy rooms, and a
panoramic roof terrace.

LEVANTO: Hotel Stella Maris €€
Boutique **Map** E4
Via Marconi 4, 19015
Tel *0187 80 82 58*
W hotelstellamaris.it
Close to the beach, decorated
with frescoes and antiques. Free
Internet access is provided, as
well as bikes and beach towels.

MANAROLA: Ca' D'andrean €
Family-run **Map** F4
Via Discovolo 101, 19017
Tel *0187 92 00 40*
W cadandrean.it
Breakfast is served under lemon
trees in this former olive press.
Bright rooms, some with a terrace.

MONTEROSSO AL MARE:
Porto Roca €€
B&B **Map** E4
Via Corone 1, 19016
Tel *0187 817 502*
W portoroca.it
A stunning cliffside location,
a private beach and a lovely
garden terrace draw visitors here.

PORTOVENERE:
Hotel Della Baia €€
Rooms with a view **Map** F5
Via Lungomare 111, 19025
Tel *0187 79 07 97*
W baiahotel.com
A good base for trips to Cinque
Terre, this hotel has rooms with
balconies overlooking the bay, a
pool and restaurant.

PORTOFINO: Nazionale €€
Family-run **Map** D4
Vico Dritto 3, 16034
Tel *0185 269 575*
W nazionaleportofino.com

Small and charming, set in the
main square. Most rooms have a
sitting room and extra bed.

PORTOFINO: Splendido €€€
Luxury **Map** D4
Salita Baratta 16, 16034
Tel *0185 26 78 01*
W hotelsplendido.com
Housed in a former monastery,
Splendido overlooks the resort
of Portofino and is a magnificent
place to stay.

RAPALLO: Rosa Bianca €
Modern **Map** E4
Lungomare V. Veneto 42, 16035
Tel *0185 50 390*
W hotelrosabianca.it
Large, pleasant and comfortable
sea-front hotel with bright rooms,
some with a small balcony.

RAPALLO: Hotel Italia E Lido €€
Rooms with a view **Map** E4
Lungomare Castello 1, 16035
Tel *0185 50 49 4*
W italiaelido.com
Set between Portofino and Cinque
Terre, the hotel overlooks the
promenade and medieval castle
of Rapallo, and has a private beach

SANTA MARGHERITA LIGURE:
Hotel Jolanda €€
Modern **Map** E4
Via Luisito Costa 6, 16035
Tel *0185 287 512*
W hoteljolanda.it
Comfortable and spacious rooms
with modern amenities including
a well-equipped gym and a
Turkish bath.

SANTA MARGHERITA LIGURE:
Hotel Santa
Margherita Palace
Design **Map** E4
Via Roma 9, 16038
Tel *0185 28 71 39*

Stylish, minimalist decor at Villa Agnese,
Sestri Levant

W santamargheritapalace.com
Centrally located hotel close to
the beach and harbour; a good
base from which to visit the area.

SESTRI LEVANTE:
Villa Agnese €€
Historic **Map** E4
Via alla Fattoria Pallavicini 1A, 16039
Tel *0185 457 583*
W hotelvillaagnese.com
A charming B&B in an idyllic
setting. Offers an organic buffet
breakfast along with many facil-
ities for outdoor activities. Pets
are welcome.

VENTIMIGLIA: La Riserva Di
Castel D'appio €€
Rooms with a view **Map** A5
Via Redaigo 71, 18039
Tel *0184 22 95 33*
W lariserva.it
Panoramic views of the Italian
Riviera and Cote D'Azur at this
hotel with a restaurant, fitness
centre and pool.

Riviera di Ponente

ALASSIO: Beau Rivage €€
Family-run **Map** B4
Via Roma 82, 17021
Tel *0182 640 585*
W hotelbeaurivage.it
Just across the road from a lovely
beach. Rooms are simple and
pleasant, some with frescoes and
vaulted ceilings. Good restaurant.

ALBENGA: Marisa €
Modern **Map** B4
Via Pisa 28, 17031
Tel *0182 50 241*
W marisahotel.com
Period decor and modern
facilities at this clean, spacious
hotel. Close to the seafront and
town centre. Private parking.

ALBISSOLA MARINA:
Hotel Garden €€
Modern **Map** C4
Viale Faraggiana 6, 17012
Tel *019 485 253*
W hotelgardenalbissola.com
Airy rooms with sea views;
Jacuzzi in bathroom, gym,
outdoor pool and bar. There
are also apartments to let.

APRICALE: Locanda dei Carugi €
Charming **Map** A4
Via Roma 12, 18030
Tel *327 886 89 65*
W locandadeicarugi.it
This is a charming B&B in the
centre of the medieval village
of Apricale. Rooms are small but
well equipped and furnished
with restored antiques.

DK Choice
BORDIGHERA: Grand Hotel del Mare
Modern €€ Map A5
Via Portico della Punta 34, 18012
Tel *0184 262 201*
W grandhoteldelmare.it
Situated in a park leading to the sea, this classy hotel boasts an outdoor seawater pool and an indoor spa with a Turkish bath and sauna. All rooms and suites have sea views and balconies. Breakfast is an elaborate affair.

BORDIGHERA: Villa Elisa €€
Charming Map A5
Via Romana 70, 18012
Tel *0184 261 313*
W villaelisa.com
An Art Nouveau style villa set amidst citrus trees, with a pool, play area, restaurant and also a mini-apartment.

BORGIO VEREZZI:
Villa delle Rose €
Family-run Map C4
Via Nazario Sauro 1, 17022
Tel *019 610 461*
W villarose.it
Set in a sleepy village away from the coast, the hotel features rooms with sea or mountain views.

FINALE LIGURE: Punta Est €€
Rooms with a view Map C4
Via Aurelia 1, 17024
Tel *019 60 06 11*
W puntaest.com
Views over the Ligurian bay, and a lovely pool at this historic villa with paths leading to the sea.

GARLENDA: La Meridiana €€
Resort Map B4
Via ai Castelli, 17033
Tel *0182 58 02 71*
W lameridianaresort.com
Set in a Golf Club, close to the beach, this country house-style hotel is great for outdoor activities.

IMPERIA: Hotel Kristina €
Modern Map B5
Spianata Borgo Peri 8, 18100
Tel *0183 297 434*
W hotelkristina.com
On the waterfront with its own private beach. Most rooms have large balconies.

IMPERIA: Grand Hotel Diana Majestic
Modern €€ Map B5
Via degli Oleandri 15, 180/3
Tel *0182 642 701*
W dianamajestic.com
Elegant rooms with Carrara marble bathrooms. The hotel has a private beach and free parking.

LAIGUEGLIA:
Hotel Ambassador €
Historic Map B4
Via dei Pini 5, 17053
Tel *0182 690 011*
W kinghotelambassador.com
Relaxing atmosphere, sea-view rooms, large terrace, snack bar, reading room and private parking.

LOANO: Grand Hotel Garden Lido €€
Modern Map B4
Lungomare Nazario Sauro 9, 17025
Tel *019 669 666*
W gardenlido.com
Modern hotel with a private beach, pool and spa. Offers facilities for the disabled. Good service.

NOLI: Miramare €
Historic Map C4
Corso Italia 2, 17026
Tel *019 748 926*
W hotelmiramarenoli.it
Miramare has varied room sizes with garden or sea views, a bar and a restaurant-pizzeria.

PIETRA LIGURE:
Hotel Ca' Ligure €
Charming Map B4
Via Concezione 10, 17027
Tel *019 625181*
W caligure.it
Hillside hotel with pool. Rooms have a private bathroom and balcony.

SAN REMO: Nyala Suite €
Modern Map A5
Via Solaro 134, 18038
Tel *0184 667 668*
W nyalahotel.com
This quiet hotel has a botanical garden and solarium. Dogs and cats are welcome too.

SAN REMO: Paradiso €€
Family-run Map A5
Via Roccasterone 12, 18038
Tel *0184 571 211*
W paradisohotel.it
In a quiet area with comfortable and clean rooms. Lovely verandah restaurant and pool.

SAN REMO: ROYAL HOTEL €€€
Luxury Map A5
Corso Imperatrice 80, 18038
Tel *0184 53 91*
W royalhotelsanremo.com
Famous for its gardens and three restaurants, this "grande dame" hotel has tennis courts, pool, sunbeds and more.

SAVONA: NH Savona Darsena €
Modern Map C4
Via Agostino Chiodo 9, 17100
Tel *019 803 211*
W nh-hotels.it
Set in the old port. Rooms feature LCD TVs and a mini-bar.

Picturesque setting of Punta Est in the town of Finale Ligure

SPOTORNO:
Best Western Acqua Novella €
Modern Map C4
Via Acqua Novella 1, 17028
Tel *019 741 665*
W acquanovella.it
There's a variety of rooms, a fitness centre, pool and solarium here. Lift access to a private beach.

VARAZZE:
Best Western El Chico €€
Historic Map C3
Strada Romana 63, 17019
Tel *019 931 388*
W elchico.eu
A villa-type complex that offers its guests bright, airy rooms with balconies. Pool and olive trees. Impeccable service.

DK Choice
VARIGOTTI: Hotel Albatros €€
Charming Map C4
Via Aurelia 58, 17024
Tel *019 698 039*
W hotelalbatrosvarigotti.it
Set in a charming village of Saracen origin on the beautiful beach of Varigotti, Albatros is just minutes from the pedestrian zone. The rooms are bright and elegant, some overlooking the beach. The terrace offers stunning sea views. There is a classic Mediterranean buffet breakfast with home-made cakes and freshly baked *focaccia*. Pets are welcome.

VENTIMIGLIA:
Kaly Residence Hotel €
B&B Map A5
Lungomare Trento e Trieste 67, 18039
Tel *0184 295 218*
W hotelkaly.it
An excellent base to explore the area. Modern apartments are on weekly rentals; suites have kitchen facilities.

For more information on types of hotels *see p179*

WHERE TO EAT AND DRINK

Meat does feature on menus in the region of Liguria, but anyone who does not eat fish is likely to feel that they are missing out. Ligurian cooking revolves around seafood, particularly on the coast. Liguria has some excellent upmarket restaurants, but more pleasure can often be derived from a family-run *trattoria* in the historic district of a resort or in one of the hilltowns of the interior. A good opportunity to try the local specialities is during the many gastronomic festivals that take place in every season. *Agriturismo*, or farm holidays, also give visitors the chance to taste home cooking. The restaurants listed on pages 188–97 have been selected from the best on offer, across all price ranges. They are organized by region and price. The phrasebook on page 224 will help you order a meal although most restaurants will have English menus.

Opening Hours and Prices

Lunch is usually served from midday to 2:30 or 3pm, while dinner is served from 7pm until late in the evening, the later hours being kept in the big resorts with an active nightlife. Closing days depend both on the season and on the type of establishment; in general, restaurants and *trattorias* stay open most of the year, particularly in the towns along the coast. In many restaurants the bill can easily exceed €50 per head, excluding wine, especially if the meal includes fresh fish; in a more everyday *trattoria*, the bill is likely to come to around €25–30. In terms of tipping, it is usual to leave around 5 per cent of the total bill in a *trattoria*, and 10 per cent in a restaurant.

Local Produce

Ligurian cooking is inspired by an ancient tradition born out of the superb fruits of the land and the sea. The variety of seafood on local menus is huge: bream *(orata)*, red mullet *(triglia)* and sea bass *(branzino)* are all popular, alongside staple shellfish such as prawns and mussels. Many restaurants offer fish soups and stews, a choice of grilled or roasted fish, or a mix of fried fish. Fancier fish dishes include *cappon magro*, a salad of fish, greens and hard-boiled eggs in garlic sauce. Dried cod *(stoccafisso)* is also popular. Along with being combined with fish or meat, vegetables are also the focus of many dishes. Stuffed *(ripieni* or *farciti)* vegetables are very popular.

The olives that are the source of the region's rightly sought-after olive oil are also used in cooking. Olives known as *taggiasca*, which means from

Summer tables at a Ligurian restaurant, placed in the characteristic *carruggi*

the area around Taggia, are particularly renowned.

Basil, thyme, rosemary and marjoram, all of which are grown in the mountain valleys, are the classic Ligurian herbs. Supreme among these is basil *(basilico)*, the basis for the region's world-famous pesto. This is served with the region's fantastic array of local pastas, with intriguing names such as *fidelini, fazzoletti* and *stracci*. The best-known pastas are *trofie* (twists from Genoa) and *trenette* (flat cousins of spaghetti), while the most popular stuffed pastas are *pansôti (see p186)* and ravioli.

Ligurian *Trattorias*

Typical Ligurian *trattorias* may provide more modest decor and simpler menus than the average restaurant, but they often cook excellent meals. Unfortunately, tourist development along the coast has brought with it a proliferation of fast food joints and pizza

Fresh fish, abundant in the seas along the Riviera

parlours, which means that it can be hard to find a good *trattoria* there. Your best chance of finding one is in the hinterland by asking the local residents. An alternative, if you want to eat genuine local food, is to visit an *agriturismo* farm, one that offers rooms and home-cooked meals to visitors *(see p178)*.

Bars and Cafés

A typical day in Liguria starts with a visit to a café or bar for breakfast while reading the newspaper or just to watch the world go by. The best cafés offer cakes and pastries, often along with delicious home-made ice creams. Note that in Liguria's most historic cafés and those in the fashionable resorts, prices can be high.

See pages 202–3 for more details on some of the region's grandest cafés.

Food Festivals

Food and village festivals in Liguria provide great opportunities for visitors to try the local food. Among the main food festivals that take place in this region, some of the highlights include: the Sagra delle Focaccette (focaccia

Relaxing at one of Liguria's many seaside bars

Vegetable tart and *focaccia*, typical produce

festival) at Recco, at the end of April; the Festa dell'Olio (olive oil festival) in Baiardo, near San Remo, and the Festa del Basilico (basil festival) in Diano Marina, both in May; and the famous Sagra del Pesce (fish festival) in Camogli, in mid-May. During the Festa del Limone (lemon festival), which is held in Monterosso al Mare, one of the towns on the pretty Cinque Terre, at the end of May, the heaviest lemon wins a prize. On the last Sunday in June, the Sagra dell'Acciuga (anchovy festival) takes place in Lavagna, while between 4 and 8 July, Sestri Levante hosts the Sagra del Totano (squid festival). At Riva Trigoso, the popular Sagra del Bagnun (a local dish made with anchovies) is held on 15 July; on the same day, in Diano Borganzo, everyone turns out for the Sagra delle Trenette al Pesto (*trenette* is a traditional Ligurian pasta). Finally, around the middle of September at Badalucco, around 500 kg (1,100 lb) of stockfish (dried cod) is cooked and distributed each year at the Sagra del Stoccafisso.

A traditional *trattoria* offering authentic Ligurian cuisine

Disabled Access

Restaurants in Liguria are now improving facilities for the disabled. In spite of this, in the more old-fashioned restaurants, the disabled may still have difficulty moving around.

Smoking

It has been illegal to smoke in any bar, café or restaurant since 2005. However, some establishments do have proper ventilated rooms for smokers, and the no-smoking restrictions do not apply to outdoor tables.

Recommended Restaurants

The restaurant listings that follow offer Ligurian recipes, with an emphasis on local produce and the flavours of Mediterranean herbs. Since Liguria is located close to the sea, plenty of seafood restaurants are found here, most of them are mainly located in the little squares of fishing villages, with outdoor seating allowing for a fantastic culinary experience that is paired with breathtaking sea views. The listings cover a variety of eateries, from the traditional *trattoria* to the simple *pizzeria* and the *enoteche* or wine bar, which offer a fine selection of wines. There are also restaurants, which serve Middle Eastern and Argentinian cuisine.

The DK Choice restaurants are regarded as extra special. They may have historical charm, especially high standards or be in an above average location.

The Flavours of the Italian Riviera

The quintessentially Mediterranean cuisine of the Italian Riviera can be sampled in sophisticated upmarket restaurants, but it is best enjoyed in simple local *trattorias* using age-old recipes. The hallmark flavours are the exceptionally delicate local olive oil and herbs like marjoram, oregano, rosemary and sage that grow wild, perfuming the inland hills. Symbolic of Liguria is the bright green aromatic basil that is pounded in a mortar with garlic, olive oil, pine nuts and pecorino cheese to produce pesto, a local speciality. Fish, either fresh, dried or preserved in oil, is another of the region's many culinary assets.

Fresh basil

Delicious *foccacia* bread made with Ligurian olive oil

Food from the Land

Liguria's narrow belt of steeply terraced land, sandwiched between the sea and the mountains, has always been a challenge to farmers. This is not cattle-grazing country; lamb and goat are much better suited to this terrain. Menus feature lamb, kid, hare and rabbit either stewed or roasted, and cheeses are made from ewe's and goat's milk. Poultry is also raised for meat and eggs.

Olive and citrus trees, and even vines, manage to thrive on almost vertical terraces carved centuries ago into the hillsides. The mild winter climate and year-round sunshine are the perfect growing conditions for the commercial production of fresh produce in the green-houses that flank the coastline. More than meat, or even fish, Ligurian cooking is dependent on a wide range of fresh vegetables, including artichokes, pumpkins (squash) and courgettes (zucchini). Wild mushrooms and herbs are picked and dried to provide distinctive flavours through the year, while local almonds, walnuts, chestnuts and

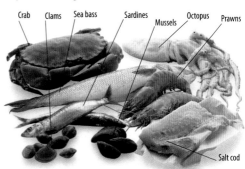

Crab Clams Sea bass Sardines Mussels Octopus Prawns Salt cod

Some of the seafood to be found in a Ligurian fish market

Ligurian Dishes and Specialities

Olives and olive oil

Pansoti is a type of ravioli, stuffed with spinach, ricotta or offal and often served with a creamy walnut sauce *(salsa di noci)*. Meat and fish courses include chicken or rabbit *alla cacciatore* (with olives, wine and herbs) and red mullet is braised with olives too. Vegetables are given the grand treatment in *torta pasqualina* (Easter pie) filled with layers of different vegetables and sometimes egg or cheese. Many foods are cooked in local olive oil: *gattafin* is fried vegetable-filled ravioli. *Friggitorie* (from *friggere*, to fry) sell flaky pastry pies stuffed with cheese and vegetables. *Farinata* is a pancake made from chickpea (garbanzo) flour, crispy outside and moist inside. Cooked in a wood-fired oven and topped with onions, cheese and herbs, it is eaten by the slice as a snack.

Cuippin, from Sestri Levante, is a puréed soup made from fish and shellfish, tomatoes, parsley, wine and garlic.

Boxes of fresh fish are unloaded onto a Ligurian quayside

hazelnuts are used in pasta sauces, casseroles, and in cake-making.

Food from the Sea

Fish and seafood from the Mediterranean have always been part of the local diet. Recently it has become more common for restaurants to import some of the fish they use, however mullet (cèfalo), bream (dorata) and sea bass (spigola) are usually local. Many traditional dishes rely on the "poor" fish that are so plentiful – such as sardines (sarde), octopus (polpo), squid (calamari), cuttlefish (seppia), mussels (cozze) and clams (vongole). Cooked with olive oil, vegetables and herbs, they are made into soups, stews and sauces for pasta. Anchovies (acchiughe) are a staple, used fresh or preserved in salt or oil. The Ligurian passion for dried salt cod (baccalà) dates back to the Viking traders. It is often served gently braised.

Genoese Food

As a major port, Genoa has always been a gateway for delicacies from around the world. The dish corzetti, which means "little crosses", was created for Genoese crusaders; the coin-sized discs of pasta were stamped with the shape

Fresh artichokes on a market stall on the Italian Riviera

of a cross. Aristocrats and merchants would later modify the design to include their family crests, using wooden stamps made in nearby Chiavari. Sailors returning from long voyages at sea would crave the taste of fresh food. The flavourful vegetable soup minestrone alla genovese, was a particular favourite, with its all-important dollop of pesto, which was reputedly invented to help sailors avoid scurvy. The city has also given its name to fagiolini alla genovese (green beans with anchovies and herbs) and focaccia alla genovese, the famous flat bread made with olive oil.

WHAT TO DRINK

Liguria's steep terrain is not ideal for vines, but eight DOC wines are produced. Among the most highly regarded are:

Pigato A light, perfumed white wine that goes well with seafood or farinata.

Cinque Terra Light, dry white wines from the terraces of the region of the same name.

Sciacchetrà A delicious sweet variety of Cinque Terra wine with an intense, flowery scent.

Rossese A light but full-flavoured red wine, often known as Dolceacqua.

Ormeasco di Pornassio A rich red with a red berry perfume.

Trenette con pesto, a Genoese speciality, is flat noodles with a sauce of basil, garlic, pine nuts and olive oil.

La Cima is poached veal stuffed with meat, cheese, egg and vegetables, usually eaten cold in thin slices.

Pandolce is a cross between cake and bread, with raisins, candied fruit, fennel seeds, pine nuts and orange water.

Where to Eat and Drink

Genoa

Il Centro Storico

Briciole   €
Pizzeria   **Map** 3 B3
Via Brigata Liguria 67r, 16121
Tel *010 58 16 54*   **Closed** *Sun*
Typical fresh home-made *focaccia*, pies and desserts, all accompanied by a good selection of beers. Products of Ligurian cuisine can be purchased here.

Cafè Klainguti   €
Bar   **Map** 5 C3
Piazza Soziglia 98, 16123
Tel *010 860 26 28*   **Closed** *Sun*
Set in an 18th-century Baroque hall in the Old Town. Don't forget to try the Zena, a *zabaglione*-filled pastry.

DK Choice

Caffè degli Specchi   €
Bar   **Map** 5 C4
Salita Pollaioli 43r, 16123
Tel *010 246 81 93*   **Closed** *Sun*
This traditional bar and café, located downtown in the narrow streets of Genoa, serves delicious snacks and excellent coffee. It attracts a young crowd, particularly during the *aperitivo* hour, and offers good value for money. There is a lovely Art Nouveau room upstairs and an elegant ground floor dining room.

Da Genio   €
Seafood   **Map** 6 E5
Salita San Leonardo 61r, 16128
Tel *010 58 84 63*   **Closed** *Sun:
open for groups only by reservation*
Enjoy Ligurian cuisine with all its specialities: *trenette al pesto* (pasta with pesto sauce), dried cod, and *pansoti* (a type of ravioli) cooked with fresh and top quality ingredients.

Il Genovese   €
Local   **Map** 3 B2
Via Galata 35r, 16121
Tel *010 869 29 37*   **Closed** *Sun*
Il Genovese revisits traditional Genoese cuisine. *Mesciua* (soup with chickpeas, cannellini beans and farro), fried fish and *gnocchi* with pesto are some of the dishes that feature on the menu. Ligurian and international wines on offer.

In Vino Veritas   €
Mediterranean   **Map** 5 A4
Vico delle Vele 27r, 16128
Tel *010 247 22 93*
Refined but informal atmosphere.

The star of the menu is the risotto followed by a meat dish. More than 70 Italian wines for guests to choose from.

Nabil   €
Middle Eastern   **Map** 5 C3
Vico Falamonica 21r, 16123
Tel *010 247 61 14*   **Closed** *Sat
lunch, Sun & Mon*
Explore tastes from Palestine and Jordan. Try the *mansaf* – the Jordanian national lamb dish, with pine nuts, toasted almonds, rice and yogurt.

Ombre Rosse   €
Seafood   **Map** 2 F4
Vico Indoratori 22, 16100
Tel *010 275 76 08*   **Closed** *Sun
lunch*
Great for *aperitivo*, dinner and Sunday brunch. Food is simple, local and made with fresh, high quality ingredients. Extensive range of wines.

Onde Quadre   €
Wine Bar   **Map** 2 F4
Via di Santa Croce 2, 16128
Tel *010 860 60 76*   **Closed** *Mon
lunch*
Every dish is accompanied by wine selected by the owners. Try meat dishes such as tartare of beef, plus vegetable flans, fresh fish, as well as the *testaroli al pesto* (flat-squared Ligurian pasta). Quick snacks and fixed menu at lunch.

Ristorante Yuan   €
Chinese   **Map** 6 D4
Via Ettore Vernazza 8, 16123
Tel *010 570 23 27*   **Closed** *Mon*
Sample sushi, prawn ravioli, tempura and chicken with chestnut, all in a refined, elegant atmosphere at good value prices.

Sa' Pesta   €
Trattoria   **Map** 5 C4
Via dei Giustiniani 16r, 16123
Tel *010 246 83 36*   **Closed** *Sun*
Simple *trattoria* with decor typical of old Genoese palaces. Taste the special *farinata*, pancake made from chickpea flour. Best to book on weekends.

Tristano & Isotta   €
Pizzeria   **Map** 5 C3
Vico del Fieno 33r, 16123
Tel *010 247 43 01*   **Closed** *Mon*
This is a pleasant pizzeria offering vegetarian and non-vegetarian menus, gluten-free, fresh pasta and home-made desserts. Try wood-oven pizzas with charming names like "Tristano e Isotta" or "Centro Storico".

Vegia Zena   €
Local   **Map** 5 B2
Vico del Serriglio 15r, 16124
Tel *010 251 33 32*   **Closed** *Mon*
Situated near the old port, Vegia Zena ("old Genoa") is a historic restaurant best known for its friendly atmosphere. It offers fresh fish such as gallinelle, codfish and stockfish. Try seafood ravioli or *trenette* with pesto sauce.

Cantine Squarciafico   €€
Local   **Map** 5 C3
Piazza Invrea 3r, 16123
Tel *010 247 08 23* **Closed** *Two weeks
in Aug & one week in Jan*
This Ligurian wine bar just behind

Outdoor tables at Caffè degli Specchi, a perfect spot for people-watching

Dining room at Zeffirino, a favourite among celebrities

the cathedral serves up local specialities, including *stracci* (a kind of lasagna).

Da Rina €€
Seafood **Map** 2 F5
Mura delle Grazie 3r, 16128
Tel *010 246 64 75* **Closed** *Mon*
Traditional Genoese cuisine as well as the chef's new creations based on local produce. A house speciality is fish with anchovies, mushrooms and vegetables.

Da Toto €€
Seafood **Map** 5 A2
Molo Ponte Morosini Sud 19–20, 16121
Tel *010 254 38 79* **Closed** *Sun only by reservation*
Freshly caught fish cooked with Ligurian recipes. Starters include original fish pie, and home-made *bricchetti* (short thick pasta) served with a courgette sauce.

Il Brigantino €€
Seafood **Map** 5 A2
Molo Ponte Morosini 16 , 16100
Tel *010 26 78 17* **Closed** *Tue & Wed dinner*
Ligurian and Italian cuisine with fish of the day and seasonal pro-ducts. Enjoy coffee or an *aperitivo* in the tranquillity of the pier.

Maxelâ €€
Trattoria **Map** 5 C2
Vico Inferiore del Ferro 9r, 16123
Tel *010 247 42 09* **Closed** *Sun*
Partly a butcher's, partly a casual *trattoria* in a former stable dating back to 1790. Meat is served raw, grilled, pan-fried and fried. Good value fixed menu at lunch. Valid Italian wine labels.

Panson €€
Seafood **Map** 5 C4
Piazza delle Erbe 5r, 16123
Tel *010 246 89 03* **Closed** *Sun dinner*
Typical local cuisine combining

fresh Ligurian fish and herbs. Try the basil *gnocchi* in prawn sauce, or the *pansoti* (ravioli-style pasta) in nut sauce.

Soho Restaurant and Fish Work €€
Seafood **Map** 2 F4
Via al Ponte Calvi 20r, 16123
Tel *010 869 25 48*
Choose your fish from the daily catch on display. The tasting and the champagne menu are fixed. Wide range of quick snacks.

Sul Fronte del Porto €€
Brasserie **Map** 5 B3
Calata Cattaneo, Palazzina Millo, 16123
Tel *010 251 83 84*
A bar, restaurant and sushi bar in a very pleasant location that allows you to dine while looking out over the Old Harbour.

Zeffirino €€€
Innovative **Map** 6 F4
Via XX Settembre 20, 16121
Tel *010 570 59 39*
Three types of fixed menus are offered: a welcoming, a tasting and an à la carte menu. Try the *pansoti* with pesto, and the fresh fish courses based on the daily catch. There is also a bar for *aperitivo* or after dinner drinks.

Le Strade Nuove

Da Maria €
Trattoria **Map** 6 D3
Vico Testadoro 14, 16100
Tel *010 58 10 80* **Closed** *Sun*
Simple family-run *trattoria*, with *focaccias*, soups and pasta dishes on the menu. Go for the *trenette* (flat noodles) with pesto and the excellent stuffed anchovies.

Le Mamme del Clan €
Local **Map** 6 D3
Salita Pallavicini 16r, 16123
Tel *010 25 28 82* **Closed** *Sun*

Sophisticated decor with arched vaulted ceilings and soft lighting. Le Mamme offers simple cooking focused on Ligurian cuisine. Catch the Thursday evening cabaret and DJ set on Saturdays.

Le Rune €
Seafood **Map** 6 D3
Vico Domoculta 14r, 16123
Tel *010 59 49 51* **Closed** *Sat & Sun lunch*
A great variety of traditional fish dishes, good wines and desserts based on Ligurian recipes with Italian influences. Various fixed menus available at lunch, dinner and on weekends.

Antica Cantina I Tre Merli €€
Winery **Map** 5 C2
Vico dietro il Coro della Maddalena 26r, 16124
Tel *010 247 40 95* **Closed** *Mon & Sun dinner*
Housed in a former stable, this restaurant offers a selection of more than 300 fine wines. There is a regional tasting menu. Gluten-free courses available.

Europa €€
Local **Map** 6 D3
Galleria G. Mazzini 53r, 16123
Tel *010 58 12 59* **Closed** *Sun*
Set in a colonnaded arcade in the city centre. Items on the menu include home-made ravioli, pesto and fresh fish dishes, served with olive oil. Fixed lunch menu.

Saint Cyr €€
Local **Map** 3 A1
Via Assarotti 36, 16122
Tel *010 88 68 97* **Closed** *Sat lunch & Sun lunch*
Refined restaurant with elegant furnishings, beautiful lighting effects, and a great deal of atten-tion to detail. Dishes are based on the Ligurian and Piedmontese traditions. Great meat and delicious first courses.

For more information on types of restaurants *see page 185*

Simple decor at Edilio, known for its Piedmontese cuisine

DK Choice

Il Genovino €€
Local **Map** 3 C1
3 Via alla Stazione per Casale
Tel 010 831 1362 Closed Sat
lunch and Sun dinner
Il Genovino offers great value
for money, serving excellent
Genovese cuisine in a warm
atmosphere. Dishes are reasonably priced, and the restaurant
has a good selection of wines.

Further Afield

Da ù Braxèa €
Pizzeria **Map** D3
Via Degola 2b, 16151
Tel 010 469 49 23 Closed Mon
A brasserie, pizzeria, bar and
restaurant. Sample Scottish and
Argentinian meat and Ligurian
and Italian cuisine. Over 50 types
of pizza, farinata (chickpea-flour
pancake) and cheese focaccia to
choose from.

Osteria Da O Colla €
Local **Map** D3
Via alla Chiesa di Murta 10, 16162
Localita' Balzaneto
Tel 010 740 85 7 9 Closed Mon
& Sun dinner
Excellent home-cooked Ligurian
cuisine, 8 miles (12.8 km) from
the city centre, but well worth
the taxi fare.

Osteria dell'Acqua Santa €
Local **Map** D3
Via Acquasanta 281,16100
Tel 010 63 80 35 Closed Mon
Try the specials, which include
carciofi in umido ripieni (stuffed
artichokes), tagliolini con funghi
(pasta in mushroom sauce) as
well as pesto lasagna. Reasonably
priced, with good selections of
cheese and wine.

Piuma €
Focacceria **Map** D3
Via Tabarca, 16147
Tel 010 999 03 37 Closed Mon
& lunch
This focacceria also serves a wide
variety of first and second courses,
with a limited but good wine list.

Ristorante Chiara €
Pizzeria **Map** D3
Via Padre Garre' 14, 16010
Tel 010 967 70 40 Closed Mon
& Tue dinner during winter
Grilled meat, pizza and Ligurian
cuisine, served on a garden
terrace. Fish menu available if
you book in advance.

Sapori di Sori €
Focacceria **Map** D3
Via Pionieri e Aviatori
d'Italia 109, 16154
Tel 010 651 93 79 Closed Mon
in winter
Authentic cheese focaccia and
Ligurian cuisine, and a panoramic
view of the port. Good value for
money in a friendly atmosphere.

A Due Passi dal Mare €€
Traditional **Map** 4 D4
Via Casaregis 52r, 16129
Tel 010 58 85 43 Closed Mon
Specials include tuna tartare with
julienne artichokes, ravioli stuffed
with ricotta and artichokes with
prawn sauce. Don't miss the
Bavarian coffee dessert. Excellent
wine list.

Bruxaboschi €€
Local **Map** D3
Via F. Mignone 8, 16133 San Desiderio
Tel 010 345 03 02 Closed Mon
& Sun dinner
Sit outside or in the relaxed dining
room at this family-run restaurant
and enjoy Ligurian specialities.
Home-made pasta with mush-
rooms are among the favourites.

Da Giacomo €€
Seafood **Map** D3
Corso Italia 1r, 16129
Tel 010 31 10 41
Excellent quality restaurant with
affordable prices. The fish and
seafood dishes are highly recommended, as are the wines. Ample
parking available.

Edilio €€
Piedmontese **Map** D3
Corso A. De Stefanis 104r, 16139
Tel 010 81 12 60
Enjoy a mix of Ligurian and
Piedmontese cuisine. The restau-
rant's specialities include funghi
e tartufi (mushrooms and truffles),
stuffed anchovies and green
gnocchi in velvety lobster sauce.

Enoteca Sola €€
Winery **Map** 3 C4
Via Carlo Barabino 120r, 16129
Tel 010 59 45 13 Closed Sun
A varied Ligurian menu of meat
and fish, served with a wide
selection of local and Italian
wines. Best to book ahead.

Gran Gotto €€
Local **Map** 3 C4
Viale Brigata Bisagno 69r, 16129
Tel 010 56 43 44 Closed Sat lunch
& Sun
Traditional Genoese dishes with
tasting menus at lunch and dinner.
The menu changes often to adapt
to the fresh fish or meat available.

La Pineta €€
Mediterranean **Map** D3
Via Gualco 82, 16165 Struppa
Tel 010 80 27 72 Closed Mon
& Sun dinner
Located at the edge of a pine
forest, La Pineta specializes in
grilled meat and game. Home-
made pastas and desserts are
excellent. Ample parking.

L'Angolo della Lucania €€
Mediterranean **Map** 3 C4
Via della Libertà 112r, 16129
Tel 392 981 57 87 Closed Mon
dinner & Tue
Small family-run restaurant that
offers cuisine from the Basilicata
region. Good fish courses and a
delicious cold/hot dessert with
ice-cream and hot chocolate.

Le Cicale in Città €€
Local **Map** 3 B4
Via Macaggi 53r, 16100
Tel 010 59 25 81 Closed Sat
lunch & Sun
Centrally located restaurant
offering interesting choices,
including sea bass with potatoes, lemon sauce, peanuts
and laurel, or a small pork fillet
in lettuce sauce.

Osvaldo Antica Trattoria €€
Seafood **Map** D3
Via della Casa 2r, 16100 Boccadasse,
Tel *010 377 18 81* **Closed** *Mon (except mid-Sep–mid-Jun at lunch)*
A small, family-run restaurant located on a small square. The seafood and pasta dishes here are simple, but flavourful. Be sure to try the *frittura mista* (plate of fried fish).

Pintori €€
Sardinian **Map** D3
Via San Bernardo 68r, 16123
Tel *010 275 75 07* **Closed** *Sun & Mon*
A local favourite, Pintori offers innovative Sardinian and Ligurian flavours. Specials include vegetarian dishes such as *torta di verdura* (vegetable flan), as well as *maialino sardo* (Sardinian pork).

Toe Drue €€
Innovative
Mediterranean **Map** D3
Via C. Corsi 44r, 16154 Sestri Ponente
Tel *010 650 01 00* **Closed** *Sat lunch & Sun*
Cuisine based on fresh seafood with dishes like *cappon magro* (fish and vegetables), pesto and a good choice of Piedmontese meat.

Antica Osteria del Bai €€€
Seafood **Map** D3
Via Quarto 12, 16148 Quarto dei Mille
Tel *010 38 74 78* **Closed** *Mon*
An ancient *osteria*, in a lovely romantic location close to the sea. Serves fresh fish and seafood in traditional Ligurian style.

Astor €€€
Local **Map** D3
Via delle Palme 16-18, 16167 Nervi
Tel *010 32 90 11*
Fine Ligurian cuisine and good wines served in a simple, elegant setting. The house special is the *pansotti al sugo di noci* (fresh pasta filled with ricotta cheese, herbs and lemon zest).

DK Choice

Baldin €€€
Innovative **Map** D3
Piazza Tazzoli 20r, 16154 Sestri Ponente
Tel *010 653 14 00* **Closed** *Mon & Sun*
Contemporary decor and 17th-century vaulted ceilings mingle with ease at this innovative restaurant. The chef proposes some creative cuisine but also revisits some of the Genoese classics. Excellent dishes that incorporate fish, wild mushrooms as well as

truffles have earned the eatery a Michelin star. Superb chocolate desserts to tempt chocolate lovers. Best to book in advance.

Le Perlage €€€
Innovative **Map** 3 C5
Via Mascherpa 4r, 16129
Tel *010 58 85 51* **Closed** *Sun*
An elegant but welcoming restaurant, offering innovative dishes blended with traditional Ligurian cuisine. A good wine list.

Santa Chiara €€€
Local **Map** D3
Via al capo di Santa Chiara 69, 16146 Boccadasse
Tel *010 307 51 55* **Closed** *Mon*
Set in an amazing location, with a sea-cliff terrace overlooking the ancient fishing village. Serves Ligurian specialities like *trofiette* (flat spaghetti) *al pesto* and dried cod *alla Ligure*. Don't miss the Bavarian cream with passion fruit dessert. Great selection of wines.

Riviera di Levante

AMEGLIA: Locanda dei Poeti €
Pizzeria **Map** F5
Piazza della Libertà 4, 19030
Tel *0187 60 80 68* **Closed** *Tue & lunch in Oct–Feb*
A café, wine bar and pizzeria, which also hosts art exhibitions. Everything from appetizers to dessert is entirely home-made.

AMEGLIA: Da Mauro Ricciardi alla Locanda dell'Angelo €€€
Mediterranean **Map** F5
Viale XXV Aprile 60, 19031
Tel *0187 643 91*
Closed *Mon & Tue*

Charming outdoor seating at Osvaldo Antica Trattoria

Creative Mediterranean dishes based on selected ingredients of the area and beyond. Enjoy a meal in the beautiful garden. Staff are friendly and service is good.

AMEGLIA: Locanda delle Tamerici €€€
Innovative **Map** F5
Via Litoranea 106,19031 Fiumaretta di Ameglia
Tel *0187 642 62* **Closed** *Mon & Tue*
A refined restaurant, located a few metres from the sea. It offers fish specialities and local cuisine in original combinations. Specials include scallops with eggplant, and *gnocchi* (potato dumplings) with lobster and asparagus.

BOGLIASCO: Agriturismo le Pale €
Agritourism **Map** D4
Via Pale 5, 16031
Tel *010 347 03 88* **Closed** *Mon–Thu*
A fixed menu with appetizers, vegetables, dessert, coffee, water and liqueurs. Everything is home-made. Half price for children up to age 10.

BOGLIASCO: Il Tipico €€
Seafood **Map** D4
Via Poggia Favoro 20, 16032 San Bernardo
Tel *010 347 07 54* **Closed** *Mon*
Housed in an old maritime fortress that overlooks the Golfo Paradiso, Il Tipico serves Ligurian fish and seafood specialities. Sample fresh raw fish for appetizers, the superb risotto, mixed-fish grill and delicious desserts. Two fixed menus, a tasting menu and a tourist menu, are on offer.

CAMOGLI: La Cucina di Nonna Nina €
Local **Map** D4
Via Molfino 126, 16032
Tel *0185 77 38 35* **Closed** *Wed, Nov & 10 days in Jan*
This homely restaurant is located on a picturesque hill. Sit inside in the clean, airy dining room or outside on the terrace. All products used are locally sourced. The *focaccia*, cakes and Ligurian pasta are home-made.

CAMOGLI: Rosa €€
Seafood **Map** D4
Via Ruffini 13, 16032
Tel *0185 77 34 11* **Closed** *Tue & Wed lunch*
Explore seafood and pasta specialities in this Art Nouveau style villa restaurant, while enjoying stunning views of Camogli bay. Gluten-free and vegetarian dishes available.

For more information on types of restaurants *see page 185*

Sophisticated and tasteful interiors at La Brinca

CASTELNUOVO DI MAGRA:
Da Armanda   €€
Local   Map F5
Piazza Garibaldi 6, 19030
Tel *0187 67 44 10*   **Closed** *Tue eve*
& Wed
Fish and traditional dishes all
accompanied by good wine labels
of the area. Great *focaccia* and
local ham. Simple decor and
panoramic views.

CHIAVARI: Lord Nelson   €€€
Innovative   Map E4
Corso Valparaiso 27, 16043
Tel *0185 30 25 95*   **Closed** *Wed*
A pub and inn with five rooms,
traditional decor, a well-stocked
wine cellar and a summer terrace.
Fresh fish and light pasta dishes
feature on the menu, along with
à la carte dishes.

CORNIGLIA: Ristorante Cecio €€
Traditional   Map E4
Via Serra 58, 19010
Tel *0187 81 20 43*   **Closed** *Wed*
Housed in a former stone-built
winery with a terrace overlooking
the sea. Dishes are made with
traditional Ligurian recipes.

DEIVA MARINA: La Lampara   €
Seafood   Map E4
Lungomare Colombo 17, 19013
Tel *0187 81 58 71*
Set on the seafront, La Lampara
offers fresh seafood. It also serves
grilled meats and quick menus for
those wishing to return to the sea.

LA SPEZIA: La Pia   €
Pizzeria   Map F4
Via Magenta 12, 19124
Tel *0187 73 99 99*   **Closed** *Sun*
Excellent *farinata*, *focaccia* and
pizza, which you can choose to
eat in the restaurant or have
wrapped to take away.

LA SPEZIA: Antica Trattoria
Sevieri   €€
Trattoria   Map F4
Via delle Canonica 13, 19121
Tel *0187 75 17 76*   **Closed** *Sun*
Antica offers a varied menu, which
includes marinated anchovies
with lemon sauce or home-made
gnocchi with *scampi* and tomato
sauce. Extensive list of Italian and
international wines also on offer.

DK Choice

LAVAGNA: La Brinca   €€
Innovative   Map E4
58 Località Campo di Ne,16040
Ne in Val Graveglia
Tel *0185 33 74 80*   **Closed** *Mon*
& lunch from Tue–Fri
Tucked away in the small village
of Campo di Ne, La Brinca is
surrounded by olive groves and
vineyards. It offers country fare
based on local and seasonal
products. A specialty is *noix*
de veal served with a pine-nut
sauce. This is a family-run
restaurant with its own oil
press. Tasting and vegetarian
menus are available.

LAVAGNA: Raieü   €€
Seafood   Map E4
Via Milite Ignoto 25, 16033
Tel *0185 39 01 45*   **Closed** *Mon*
The fresh fish that is served here
is caught by the owners. On the
menu are hand-made ravioli (*raieü*
in Genoese dialect) as well as fish
gnocchi, pansoti, mussels and
seafood soup. Parking available.

LERICI: Il Frantoio   €€
Traditional Fine Cuisine Map F5
Via Cavour 19, 19032
Tel *0187 96 41 74*
Il Frantoio is housed in a 200-year

old former olive oil factory
(*frantoio*) with stone walls. The
restaurant serves fine cuisine,
with abundant seafood appetizers,
including *carpaccio* of swordfish
as well as marinated anchovies.

LERICI: Le Bontà Nascoste €€
Traditional   Map F5
Via Cavour 52, 19032
Tel *0187 96 55 00*   **Closed** *Tue*
& Wed at lunch
This restaurant offers some of the
best pizza and *farinata* in the area.
Other specials to look out for are
pasta with *scampi* and beef fillet
in pepper sauce.

LERICI: L'Orto di Ameste   €€
Mediterranean   Map F5
Casamento 18, La Serra , 19032
Tel *0187 96 46 28*   **Closed** *Mon*
except from Jul–Sep
The decor here is simple but
elegant. Fresh fish, home-made
pasta, fantastic desserts and large
portions are on the menu. The
house wine is also excellent.

LEVANTO: Cavour   €€
Trattoria   Map E4
Piazza Cavour 1, 19015
Tel *0187 80 77 86*   **Closed** *Mon*
& Dec–Jan
A typical *trattoria* specializing
in local fish dishes. The original
restaurant dates back to 1800.
Dishes on the menu include
gattafin (large fried ravioli with
herbs, eggs, onion and cheese).

LEVANTO: Tumelin   €€€
Seafood   Map E4
Via Grillo 32, 19015
Tel *0187 80 83 79* **Closed** *Thu except*
from mid-Jun–mid-Sep
Begin the meal with a fish hors
d'oeuvre. Follow this up with
pasta and shrimps or Tumelin's

tagliolini, or seafood risotto. Guests can hand-pick their own fish for the main course.

MANARELA: La Scogliera €€
Local Map F4
Via Birolli 103, 19017
Tel *0187 92 07 47* **Closed** *Thu*
A pretty family-run restaurant that offers Ligurian cuisine. La Scogliera is renowned for its seafood specialities.

MANAROLA: Marina Piccola €€
Seafood Map F4
Via Lo Scalo 16, 19010
Tel *0187 92 09 23* **Closed** *Tue*
Enjoy great views of the village and the sea, while savouring fish soup made from the local catch. Regional seafood dishes, various antipasti and mixed grilled fish are on offer.

MONEGLIA: Le Palme €€
Seafood Map E4
Via Longhi 4, 16030
Tel *0185 493 83*
This family-run restaurant is one of the oldest in this small village, and offers delicious fish-based Ligurian cuisine. In summer, be sure to dine in the verandah on the square.

MONEGLIA: La Ruota €€€
Mediterranean
Innovative Map E4
Via per Lemeglio 6, 16030
Tel *0185 495 65* **Closed** *Wed*
La Ruota offers a set menu that includes seafood, pasta, vegetables and starters like squid with mushrooms. Try the special *piatto mediterraneo* (baby squid, tomatoes, potatoes, parsley and olive oil) and crêpes suzettes.

Framed cartoon drawings adorn the walls of U Giancu, Rapallo

MONTEROSSO AL MARE:
Miky €€
Seafood Map E4
Via Fegina 104, 16030
Tel *0187 81 76 08* **Closed** *Tue*
A characteristic seafront bistro. Try the linguine with lobster or the grilled calamari. Ask to be seated in the garden among the jasmine and wisteria.

PORTOFINO: Da Puny €€
Local Map D4
Piazza Martiri dell'Olivetta 5, 16034
Tel *0185 26 90 37* **Closed** *Thu*
Set In the harbour square. Specials such as the pasta in *pesto corto* (basil, cheese, pine nuts and tomato) and the house antipasti are excellent.

PORTOFINO: Da u Batti €€
Seafood Map D4
Vico Nuovo 18, 16034
Tel *0185 26 93 79* **Closed** *Mon*
& Nov~mid-Jan
A chic and intimate restaurant offering exceptional fish dishes, and located in one of Liguria's most elegant towns.

PORTOFINO: El Portico €€
Pizzeria Map D4
Via Roma 21, 16034
Tel *0185 26 92 39* **Closed** *Tue*
An informal, pleasant and affordable pizzeria that offers excellent views across Portofino harbour. Pizzas are baked in the traditional manner in old tins. Pesto accompanies most dishes.

PORTOFINO: Chuflay,
Splendido Mare €€€
Local Map D4
Via Roma 2, 16034
Tel *0185 26 78 02*
This restaurant offers local dishes of suberb quality such as fresh clam soup with pine nuts, black olives and marjoram. Excellent selection of wines.

PORTOVENERE: Da Iseo €€
Trattoria Map F5
Calata Doria 9, 19025
Tel *0187 79 06 10* **Closed** *Wed*
& 20 days in Nov
On the waterfront with panoramic views, this *trattoria* serves typical fish dishes.

PORTOVENERE: La Chiglia €€
Local Map F5
Via Olivo 317, 19025
Tel *0187 79 21 79* **Closed** *Wed*
A popular restaurant, located under vast umbrella pines with stunning views of the island of Palmaria. The menu consists of reinvented Ligurian dishes, primarily seafood. There's also a good wine list.

Pretty terrace with a lovely view of the Piazzetta at Chuflay, Portofino

PORTOVENERE: Le Bocche €€
Local Map F5
Calata Doria 102, 19025
Tel *0187 79 06 22* **Closed** *Tue*
from Sep~Apr & Jan
Located right on the seafront. Savour delicately prepared Ligurian fish dishes served on shaded outdoor tables, overlooking the town of Portovenere.

RAPALLO: Hostaria Vecchia
Rapallo €
Seafood Map E4
Via Cairoli 10, 16035
Tel *0185 500 53* **Closed** *Mon;*
beginning of Dec to first week of Feb
This old tavern has been transformed into an elegant restaurant that offers creative seafood dishes, accompanied by a good selection of wines.

RAPALLO: U Giancu €
Local Map E4
Via San Massimo 78, 16035 Localita'
San Massimo
Tel *0185 26 05 05* **Closed** *Thu,*
lunch & last two weeks of Dec
Decorated with framed cartoon drawings and comic strips on the walls, this simple restaurant serves up typical Ligurian specialities, and complements these with fresh vegetables from the garden.

RAPALLO: Elite €€
Traditional Map E4
Via Milite Ignoto 19, 16035
Tel *0185 505 51* **Closed** *Wed*
Family-run restaurant with a small hotel above. Simple dishes such as *pansoti*, black ravioli filled with fish, rocket and large prawns are on the menu.

For more information on types of restaurants *see page 185*

RAPALLO: La Nave €€
Seafood Map E4
Via Pomaro 15, 16035
San Michele di Pagana
Tel *0185 66 95 02* **Closed** *Wed*
On the beach near Rapallo. Try
the tasty *frittura di pesce* (fried
fish) and home-made pesto sauce.

RAPALLO: Luca €€
Seafood Map E4
Via Langano 32, Porto Turistico
Carlo Riva, 16035
Tel *0185 603 23* **Closed** *Tue*
This is a good place to sample
seafood specialities such as pep-
pered mussels, lemon anchovies,
black dumplings with shrimp and
scampi with lemon.

RAPALLO: Trattoria Ö Bansin €€
Mediterrenean Map E4
Via Venezia 105, 16035
Tel *0185 23 11 19* **Closed** *Mon*
dinner & Sun lunch in summer
Traditional Ligurian dishes such
as *trenette al pesto*, fried anchovies and dried cod are available at
this *trattoria*. An economical fixed
menu is also available through
the week during lunch hours.

RECCO: Manuelina €€
Innovative Map D4
Via Roma 296, 16036
Tel *0185 741 28* **Closed** *Wed*
The restaurant is renowned for its
cheese *focaccia*. Look out for the
marinated anchovies with vegetables, as well as the black rice
with coconut cream dessert in
the tasting menu.

RIOMAGGIORE: Dau Cila €
Winery Map F5
Via San Giacomo 65, 19017
Tel *0187 76 00 32* **Closed** *Mon*
Home-made pasta and local
dishes are served with an excep-
tional selection of Italian wines.

Try the Cinque Terre wines and the
Sciacchetrà dessert wine. Good
service, and friendly atmosphere.

RIOMAGGIORE: Cappun
Magru €€€
Traditional Map F5
Via Volastra 19, 19017 Località Groppo
Tel *0187 92 05 63* **Closed** *Mon & Tue*
The menu changes each day
according to the fish and produce
available in the local market. The
Sea Tasting Menu offers good
value. Book in advance.

SANTA MARGHERITA LIGURE:
Cinzia e Mario €
Seafood Map E4
Via Palestro 6, 16038
Tel *0185 28 75 05* **Closed** *Thu*
Four different tasting menus,
together with à la carte dishes
and a variety of pizzas.

SANTA MARGHERITA LIGURE:
L'Insolita Zuppa €
Traditional Map E4
Via Romana 7, 16038
Tel *0185 28 95 94* **Closed** *Wed,*
lunch, two weeks in Nov & two
weeks in Feb
Savour simple meat and fish dishes
grounded in local tradition but with
a modern twist at this restaurant.

SANTA MARGHERITA LIGURE:
Oca Bianca €€
Meat Map E4
Via XXV Aprile 21, 16038
Tel *0185 28 84 11* **Closed** *Mon*
A great selection of various types
of meat, as well as excellent veg-
etable and cheese dishes.

SANTA MARGHERITA LIGURE:
Trattoria dei Pescatori €€
Trattoria Map E4
Via Bottaro 43-45, 16038
Tel *0185 28 67 47* **Closed** *Tue*
except Jul & Aug

This is a good place to sample
the local *pansoti* (stuffed pasta in
nut sauce) or the fish from the
local fisheries. Home-made pasta
and desserts.

SARZANA: Taverna
Napoleone €€
Traditional Map F5
Via Bonaparte 16, 19068
Tel *0187 62 79 74* **Closed** *Mon*
Exotic seasonal regional dishes,
such as artichoke pie with saffron
sauce and stuffed truffles ravioli
with pistacchio sauce. Excellent
choice of wines.

SESTRI LEVANTE:
Portobello €€
Innovative Seafood Map E4
Via Portobello 16, 16039
Tel *0185 415 66* **Closed** *Wed*
Overlooks the magnificent
beach of the Baia del Silenzio.
The cuisine, mainly seafood,
combines the lovely flavours
of Ligurian tradition with
Mediterranean tastes.

SESTRI LEVANTE: Polpo
Mario €€€
Seafood Map E4
Via XXV Aprile 163, 16039
Tel *0185 48 02 03* **Closed** *Mon*
Set in a former papal summer
residence dating from the 16th
century. The proprietors' boat
brings in the daily catch. Smart
and chic, with a summer terrace
and a good wine list.

TELLARO: Locanda Miranda €€
Seafood Map F5
Via Fiascherino 92, 19030
Tel *0187 96 81 30* **Closed** *Mon*
The creative menu consists of
seafood specialities and delicious fish dishes. It also has a
seven-room B&B with plenty
of rustic charm.

VERNAZZA: Gambero Rosso €€
Innovative Map E4
Piazza Marconi 7, 19018
Tel *0187 81 22 65* **Closed** *Thu*
This place is well known for its
imaginative and creative cuisine,
which primarily consists of seafood dishes based in the Ligurian
tradition. The fish ravioli and
lemon risotto are delicious.

Riviera di Ponente

ALASSIO: Palma €€€
Innovative Map B4
Via Cavour 5, 17021
Tel *0182 64 03 14* **Closed** *Wed &*
Nov–Mar from Mon–Fri
Housed in an 18th-century
palazzo, this Michelin-star

Polpo Mario, famous for its traditional Genoese recipes, Sestri Levante

Key to Price Guide *see page 188*

restaurant offers specials that include seared tuna with goat's cheese, or buffalo mozzarella flan with orange, tomato and red pepper sauce.

ALBENGA: Lo Scoglio €€
Seafood   Map B4
Viale Che Guevara 40, 17031
Tel *0182 54 18 93*   **Closed** *Mon*
Unpretentious restaurant built on a small pier. No written menu available – simply walk in and ask for the daily specials. The fish is excellent, especially the sword-fish and the cod tartare. Enjoy the bar on the beach in the summer.

ALBENGA: Babette €€€
Local   Map B4
Via Michelangelo 17, 17031
Tel *0182 54 45 56*   **Closed** *Tue*
Perfect for a lunch break or a gourmet dinner, with tasting and children's menus at lunch. Make sure you try the Mediterranean fish fantasy, drizzled with olive oil and marjoram.

ALBENGA: Il Pernambucco €€€
Local   Map B4
Viale Italia 35, 17031
Tel *0182 534 58*   **Closed** *Wed*
Good choice of refined fish and meat dishes, accompanied by international wines, with more than 400 labels on offer, includ-ing their own.

ALBISSOLA MARINA:
La Caravella €€
Seafood   Map C4
Piazza dei Leuti 5, 17012
Tel *019 48 13 38*   **Closed** *Thu*
Simple restaurant where visitors can enjoy fresh seafood and generous portions. The specials include seafood risotto and fish ravioli. Good selection of desserts. Best to book in advance.

ALBISSOLA MARINA: T21.9 €€€
Mediterranean   Map C3
Corso Bigliati 70, 17012
Tel *019 400 45 43*   **Closed** *Thu & Fri lunch*
Three tasting menus on offer as well as a low-cost menu. Some of the interesting dishes include fish in champagne sauce, home-made *focaccia* and bread.

ALBISSOLA SUPERIORE:
U Fundegu €€
Traditional   Map C3
Via Spotorno 87, 17013
Tel *019 528 22 86*   **Closed** *Wed from Sep–Apr; May–Oct at lunch except Sat & Sun*
Located in the ancient vaulted outbuilding of a castle, with an elegant and refined atmosphere. Typical Ligurian specialities that

Smart, subtle decor at U Fundegu, Albissola Superiore

range from fish to vegetables and delicious desserts feature on the menu.

ALTARE: Quintilio €
Piedmontese/Local   Map C3
Via Gramsci 23, 17041
Tel *019 580 00*   **Closed** *Mon & Sun dinner*
Recipes of the Ligurian and the Piedmontese traditions reinter-preted using fresh ingredients. Mushrooms and truffles available in season. Try stuffed peppers, artichoke tart and *pansoti* (stuffed pasta). Extensive wine list.

ANDORA: Casa del Priore €
Brasserie   Map B4
Via Castello 34, 17051
Tel *0182 873 30*   **Closed** *Mon*
Former medieval Benedictine hilltop monastery, which enjoys stunning views. There is a res-taurant, brasserie and piano bar. Fish dishes, shellfish, and foie gras are creatively combined with seasonal ingredients. Wine list includes over 400 labels.

ARENZANO: Il Portichetto €€
Pizzeria   Map C4
Piazza del Centro 12, 16011
Tel *010 913 53 09*   **Closed** *Tue & Wed*
Il Portichetto is well known among pizza lovers, but also offers an ample choice of fresh, home-made pasta dishes, most accompanied by fish sauces. Try appetizers such as tuna tartare, or classic dishes such as octopus with potatoes and *farinata*.

ARENZANO: L'Agueta
du Sciria €€
Traditional   Map C4
Via Pecorara 18, 16011
Tel *010 911 07 62*   **Closed** *Mon*
The menu is set according to a specific theme, ranging from

grilled fish to game dishes. For children, there is a fixed menu at half price.

ARMA DI TAGGIA:
La Conchiglia €€€
Innovative   Map A5
Via Lungomare 33, 18011
Tel *0184 431 69*   **Closed** *Wed & Thu lunch*
Here you can explore cuisine based on local and seasonal products. Try the San Remo speciality of prawns on a bed of beans, or the artichoke-filled *tortelli* with fish sauce.

BAIARDO: Armonia dei Sapori €
Local   Map A4
Via Roma 124 18031
Tel *0184 67 32 40*   **Closed** *Wed*
This restaurant offers Ligurian and Sardinian specialities, along with pizza. Enjoy the view of the Alps from either the dining room or the verandah. The delicious fruit tart is prepared with fresh seasonal fruits.

BERGEGGI: Claudio €€€
Seafood   Map C4
Via XXV Aprile 37, 17028
Tel *019 85 97 50*   **Closed** *Mon*
An elegant fish and shellfish restaurant in a 25-room hotel with spectacular sea views. Try the bouquet of shellfish with citrus fruits and Mediterranean herbs.

BORDIGHERA: Magiargé Vino e
Cucina €
Local   Map A5
Piazza Padre Giacomo Viale 1, 18012
Tel *0184 26 29 46*   **Closed** *Mon except in Aug*
Dishes and specials include roasted local lamb, salted cod, artichokes from Albenga and pesto lasagna. Tables in the square in summer. Booking recommended.

For more information on types of restaurants *see page 185*

BORDIGHERA: La Réserve €€
Modern **Map** A5
Via Arziglia 20, 18012
Tel *0184 26 13 22* **Closed** *Wed*
Typical dishes include sea bass ravioli, *gnocchi* in a coral-coloured sauce and fresh grilled fish. The limoncello liqueur is worth trying.

BORDIGHERA: Osteria dei Bagordi €€
Alehouse **Map** A5
Via Lunga 2, 18012
Tel *0184 189 26 16* **Closed** *Thu & lunch*
Mainly an alehouse with artisanal beers made using local ingredients. The cuisine is simple and accompanied by good wines. Open at *aperitivo* time.

BORGIO: Verezzi Doc €€€
Refined Regional **Map** C4
Via Vittorio Veneto 1, 17022
Tel *019 61 14 77* **Closed** *Mon, also Tue in winter*
Set in a flower-filled villa. Try specialities such as *fantasia di mare* (assorted fish with basil), artichoke soufflé or *gnocchi* with beetroot and mullet.

CERVO: San Giorgio €€€
Winery **Map** B5
Via Volta 19, 18010
Tel *0183 40 01 75* **Closed** *Mon & Tue dinner*
Simple and creative cuisine based on a combination of fish, crustaceans, shellfish and vegetables according to the season. Booking is recommended.

COGOLETO: A Begûdda €
Seafood **Map** C3
Lungomare Santa Maria 69, 16016
Tel *010 918 90 71* **Closed** *Sun dinner*
Try the lobster *taglierini* pasta, or the risotto with peppers and *scampi* sauce, or the sushi. The restaurant has a contemporary ambience. Excellent tiramisu and mint *pannacotta* desserts.

COLDIROLI: Gabry €
Mediterranean **Map** A5
Via Monte Ortigara 43, 18038
Tel *0184 67 00 38* **Closed** *Mon*
Gabry offers panoramic views from its hilltop location and classic traditional Italian cuisine served with its own wines.

DK Choice

DOLCEACQUA/APRICALE: Apricale Da Delio €€
Local **Map** A4
Piazza Vittorio Veneto 9 , 18030
Tel *0184 20 80 08* **Closed** *Mon & Tue except from Jun–Aug*
This restaurant is in a small and charming village, and offers regional cuisine made with fresh local products. Enjoy your meal on a terrace with a great view. Try home-made pasta and meat dishes such as rabbit ravioli, goat stews with white beans or stuffed vegetables. Don't miss the delicate *zabaglione*.

DOLCEDO: Casa della Rocca €€
Mediterranean **Map** B4
Via Ripalta 3, 18100
Tel *0183 28 0138* **Closed** *Mon, also Tue in winter*
A culinary delight. Only a tasting menu is offered (two appetizers, one first course, two main dishes and dessert), all with fine wines.

FINALE LIGURE: Ai Cuattru Canti €
Local **Map** C4
Via Torcelli 22, 17024
Tel *019 68 05 40* **Closed** *Sun & Mon*
A small restaurant with a very welcoming atmosphere. Try the *farinata*, *tagliolini* with squid ink, octopus or rabbit Ligurian style.

FINALE LIGURE: Ai Torchi €€€
Sicilian/Neapolitan **Map** C4
Via dell'Annunziata 12, 17024
Tel *019 69 05 31* **Closed** *Tue*
Housed in an old olive-oil factory, Ai Torchi offers a taste of southern Italian cuisine. Don't forget to try the *maccheroncini al sugo di polpo e zucchini* (courgette and octopus pasta).

IMPERIA: Osteria Didu €
Innovative
Mediterranean **Map** B5
Viale Matteotti 76, Oneglia 18100
Tel *0183 27 36 36* **Closed** *Mon & Tue*

Casual seating at the marina-styled Lanterna Blu in Imperia

The chef changes the menu every day according to the ingredients available. Dishes here are simple and at affordable prices, made with vegetables from the restaurant's own garden. Try inventive dishes such as stuffed squid or *buridda* (fish soup) with octopus and red wine. Excellent wines available.

IMPERIA: Trattoria dalla Etta €
Trattoria **Map** B5
Via Roma 33, Lucinasco 18100
Tel *0183 523 67* **Closed** *Mon*
Simple dishes and home-made extra virgin olive oil (also for sale). In winter, dine in an intimate dining room and in summer under the *pergola* overlooking the valley.

IMPERIA: Lanterna Blu €€€
Mediterranean **Map** B5
Via Scarincio 32, 18100
Tel *0183 638 59* **Closed** *Mon–Wed; Sun dinner & lunch from Thu–Sat*
Overlooking the port, this restaurant offers excellent Ligurian cuisine with a touch of the Neapolitan tradition. Dishes here are made using high quality products and Mediterranean herbs.

LAIGUEGLIA: U Gussu €
Mediterranean **Map** B4
Via Dante 41, 17053
Tel *0182 49 92 78* **Closed** *Tue*
Tasty Mediterranean recipes based mainly on fish dishes, with generous portions. Try the spaghetti with mussels. Good selection of cheese and desserts on offer.

LAIGUEGLIA: Baia del Sole €€
Seafood **Map** B4
Piazza Cavour 8, 17053
Tel *0182 69 00 19*
Set in a 17th-century seaside palace with a dining terrace directly on the beach. The restaurant offers inventive Mediterranean cuisine along with Ligurian traditional dishes.

NOLI: Lilliput €€€
Seafood **Map** C4
Via Zuglieno 49, Vioze, 17027
Tel *019 74 80 09* **Closed** *Mon*
Fresh ingredients and simple cuisine, in a hilltop location with breathtaking views. For starters, try the platter of shellfish, vegetables and fish in lemon cream.

PIETRA LIGURE: Osteria Ciassa Nova €
Traditional **Map** B4
Via Matteotti 21, 17027
Tel *019 62 50 56* **Closed** *Tue eve & Wed*
A family-run restaurant that offers

Ligurian cuisine cooked with seasonal ingredients. In summer, sit outside on the square.

SAN REMO: Buena Vista €€
Argentinian **Map** A5
Corso degli Ingleasi 15, 18038
Tel 0184 50 90 60
Near the Casinò, this Argentinian restaurant welcomes visitors with a glass of sangria and offers a varied menu of Latin American and Italian dishes, including Argentinian beef.

SAN REMO: Da Paolo e Barbara €€
Seafood **Map** A5
Via Roma 47, 18038 San Remo
Tel 0184 53 16 53 **Closed** Wed; Thu; lunch except Sat and Sun; 17–28 Dec, one weekend in Jan & two weeks in mid-Jun
Small family-run restaurant that serves local fresh fish and vegetables from its own farm, homemade breads and focaccia. Main courses include local seafood products, or veal cutlets made with meat from the Langhe region. 'Saturday shopping' menu on offer for those who want a break from San Remo's boutiques.

SAN REMO: Da Vittorio €€
Seafood **Map** A5
Piazza Bresca 16, 18038 San Remo
Tel 0184 50 19 24 **Closed** Two weeks in Nov
A traditional favourite specializing in fish and fish soup. Located a short distance from the shore.

SAN REMO: La Pignese €€
Traditional **Map** A5
Piazza Sardi 7, 18038
Tel 0184 50 19 29 **Closed** Mon
One of the oldest restaurants in Liguria, with an outdoor terrace overlooking the fishermen's port. Excellent shellfish and fresh fish of the day.

SAVONA: Conca Verde €
Game **Map** C4
Via Strà 27, 17100
Tel 019 26 33 31 **Closed** Mon
Friendly restaurant, with a lovely terrace and gardens, great views and ample parking. Wide range of specialities: fish, game as well as grilled meat. Good wines and seasonal desserts.

SPOTORNO: Pinna Rossa €
Traditional **Map** C4
Via Aurelia 39, 17028
Tel 019 74 51 61
A bright little restaurant with tables outside for alfresco dining. Offers traditional Ligurian cuisine, such as scaloppino di ombrina (finely sliced fillets of sea perch).

Spacious terrace with wonderful sea views, Balzi Rossi, Ventimiglia

TAGGIA: Osteria Germinal €€
Mediterranean **Map** A5
Via Gastaldi 15b, 18018
Tel 0184 411 53 **Closed** Mon–Wed
Simple, welcoming trattoria, well known for its traditional dishes and 'Slow Food' approach. Be sure to try the lean meat and thyme ravioli.

TOIRANO: Al Ravanello Incoronato €
Local **Map** B4
Via Parodi 27/A, 17100
Tel 0182 92 19 91 **Closed** Tue
Set in the medieval village of Toirano, this elegant restaurant offers both local and regional dishes enhanced by seasonal flavours. Enjoy fresh pasta and a good selection of Piedmontese meat, along with vegetables and herbs from the garden. Alfresco dining option in the summer. Parking available nearby.

VARAZZE: Bri €
Local **Map** C3
Piazza Nello Bovani 12, 17019
Tel 019 93 56 05 **Closed** Wed except Jul–Aug
Enjoy traditional cuisine at this centrally located restaurant, with outdoor tables set on the small square. Try specials such as stoccafisso in buridda (dried cod with tomato, pine nuts, artichokes, peppers and potatoes).

VARAZZE: Pesce Pazzo €€
Seafood **Map** C3
Via Maestri d'Ascia 1, 17019
Tel 019 93 00 32 **Closed** Mon in winter
Savour fresh fish and Ligurian cuisine right at the entrance to the port of Varazze. The restaurant also lets you go on fishing excursions where you can catch your own dinner!

VARIGOTTI: Aqua €€
Local **Map** C4
Via Aurelia 46, 17024
Tel 019 74 87 54 **Closed** Tue lunch & Wed dinner
Located right on the seafront of Varigotti, Aqua offers easy and direct access to the beach. Don't miss the excellent fritto misto (mixed fried fish), which is made with the daily catch. It also hosts a jazz festival in summer.

VARIGOTTI: Al Saraceno €€€
Traditional **Map** C4
Via Al Capo 2, 17024
Tel 019 698 81 82 **Closed** Lunch by reservation from Mon–Fri
With a terrace overlooking the sea, this is a romantic spot to enjoy a traditional meal with a modern twist – meat and fish dishes with Mediterranean flavours and high quality ingredients.

VARIGOTTI: Muraglia-Conchiglia d'Oro €€€
Seafood **Map** C4
Via Aurelia 133, 17029
Tel 019 69 80 15 **Closed** Wed, also Tue in winter
Excellent fresh fish and seafood dishes on offer. Choose your own fish from the daily catch as it is presented in large wicker baskets, and then watch as it is grilled in front of you.

VENTIMIGLIA: Balzi Rossi €€€
Seafood **Map** A5
Piazzale A De Gasperi 2 18039
Tel 0184 381 32 **Closed** Mon & Tue lunch except Jul–Sep
Located near the French border, the restaurant offers panoramic views of the sea from the terrace. Dishes are prepared using fresh ingredients such as tuna, artichokes and courgettes, cod and locally made olive oil.

For more information on types of restaurants see page 185

SHOPPING

Shopping is an enjoyable experience in Liguria, as it is in the whole of Italy. If it's choice or designer clothes you're after, Genoa and San Remo are the places to go, though the big resorts have lots of boutiques, too. In terms of crafts, Liguria is a good place for buying ceramics, an ancient craft associated with Albisola and Savona. You can also find good-quality glass (Altare), lace (Rapallo and Portofino), macramé and woodcarving (Chiavari). As in other regions

of Italy, you can find some great markets. Most towns have a market every week, while larger places such as Genoa, Ventimiglia and Rapallo, have one every day. Most visitors may not consider taking any of Liguria's famous fresh flowers home, but San Remo's flower market, the largest in Europe, is well worth a visit.

Wherever you go there are shops selling local olive oil and wine, as well as Liguria's other gastronomic delights.

Throwing a pot, a tradition with a long history in Liguria

Ceramics

This is one of the oldest handicrafts practised in Liguria. Evidence of ceramic production dates back to at least the 15th century.

The twin-city of Albisola, the main ceramics centre in Liguria, has been a town of potters since the Renaissance. Here you can find all sorts of objects made from the local clay and typically coloured blue and white, from decorative tiles to old pharmacy jars.

In nearby Savona, pots are also traditionally painted blue and white, though you can find more modern designs and other colours, as well as figures from nativity scenes *(presepi)*.

You can buy ceramics either in specialist shops and art galleries or, sometimes, from the potters' own workshops.

Antiques

Before you start shopping for antiques (or modern art, in fact), you should be aware that if you want to take any such object out of the country you will need to apply to the Italian Department of Exports for an export licence (for which you will have to pay). Any reputable antiques dealer will be able to give you the details.

Antique shops proliferate in Liguria, above all in the large towns, and some are of an excellent standard. Items for sale range from objets d'art to books and prints, furniture, statues, jewellery and antique posters. Model ships and other seafaring memorabilia, such as shipboard furniture, instruments and even figureheads, are particularly sought after.

Several important antiques fairs are held in the region, including "Antiqua" and "Tuttantico" in Genoa, and the annual fair held in August in Sarzana. There is also a monthly antiques market in Genoa's Palazzo Ducale.

Wherever you shop, always ask for evidence of the authenticity of your purchase.

Plants and Flowers

Thanks to its mild climate, Liguria is one of Italy's foremost

regions in the field of horticulture: nurseries and glasshouses housing everything from camellias, to citrus trees under one roof seem to dominate the landscape in some areas, and flower shops abound.

Bonsai trees (including even miniature olive trees) are popular buys, as are cacti and orchids. All kinds of tropical plants are available, too.

Plants and flowers, the pride of Liguria

Olive Oil

A natural product that is of great importance to the region's economy is the olive, and also the oil made from it. No one knows who first planted olives along this coast but, in the Middle Ages, the monasteries played an important role in developing the art of olive-pressing. Olives are cultivated all along

Shop selling locally made handicrafts

Dried beans sold by the sackful in a Ligurian market

the coast, but the best grow along the Riviera di Ponente, none more so than the small black olives of Taggia, which yield a golden olive oil with green tints and an almondy, lightly fruity aroma. In the area between Taggia and Albenga you can buy olive oil direct from the producers: look for signs saying *frantoio*, which means presshouse.

Most Ligurian olive oil carries the quality mark of Denominazione d'Origine Protetta (DOP), which guarantees the provenance of the olives and the cold-pressing methods used in the manufacture.

Note that the price of a good-quality olive oil (ideally extra virgin) bought from a press-house is higher than everyday oil from a supermarket or grocer's shop, but will definitely be worth taking home.

Wine

Liguria is not a major wine producer but still has some respected wines, both whites and reds *(see p187)*. It is fun to buy wine direct from the producers. Sometimes you have

to pay to taste the wine, which may be accompanied by cheese and salami, and you usually need to book ahead.

Gastronomy

The main problem with buying food in Liguria is that it's hard to know where to start, and stop. Much of what you see is best eaten on the spot. This applies to the wonderful snacks that the Ligurians love so much. Baked or fried snacks come in all shapes and sizes: from the famous *focaccia (see p186)* to *cuculli* (fritters) and *torta sardenaira*, a sort of pizza topped with tomatoes and anchovies (popular in San Remo).

Bakeries and *pasticcerie* (pastry shops) sell all manner of wonderful cakes and biscuits, too.

In terms of foods to take home, you'd do better to concentrate on the local cured meats and preserved vegetables, such as sundried tomatoes, local artichoke paste and dried porcini mushrooms. Ancho-vies in olive oil are another good buy.

Olio Carli, a fine olive oil from Imperia

DIRECTORY

Antiques

Antiqua & Tuttantico
Genoa
Fiera Internazionale.
Tel 010 539 11.
Ⓦ fiera.ge.it

Ceramics

Ceramiche Fenice
Albissola Marina
Via Repetio 22.
Tel 019 481 668.

Studio d'Arte Esedra
Dolceacqua
Via Castello 11.
Tel 0184 200 969.

Studio Ernan Desion
Albisola Superiore
Corso Mazzini 7.
Tel 019 489 916.

Glass and Lace

Soffieria Bormioli (glass)
Altare
Via Paleologo 16.
Tel 019 58 254.

E. Gandolfi (lace)
Rapallo
Piazza Cavour 1.
Tel 0185 50 234.

Plants

Stern & Dellerba (cacti & succulents)
San Remo
Via Privata delle Rose 7.
Tel 0184 661 290.

Vivai Olcese (plants)
Genova
Via Borghero 6.
Tel 010 380 290.

Local Produce

Antico Frantoio Sommariva (oil)
Albenga
Via Mameli 7.
Tel 0182 559 222.

Bottega del Formaggio (cheese & salami)
Chiavari
Via Martiri della Liberazione 208.
Tel 0185 314 225.

Bruciamonti (deli)
Genoa
Via Roma 81.
Tel 010 562 515.

Bottega della Strega (deli)
Triora
Corso Italia 48.
Tel 0184 94 278.

Cascina dei Peri (wine and oil)
Castelnuovo Magra
Via Montefrancio 71.
Tel 0187 674 085.

Enoteca Sciacchetrà (wine)
Vernazza Via Roma 50.
Tel 0187 821 210.

Panificio Canale (bakery)
Portofino
Via Roma 30.
Tel 0185 269 248.

A'Pestun'à (bakery)
Genoa
Via Boccadasse 9.
Tel 010 377 75 75.

Revello Dolce e Salato (bakery)
Camogli
Via Garibaldi 183.
Tel 0185 770 777.

OUTDOOR ACTIVITIES

More than 300 km (186 miles) of coastline provide a wonderful playground for anyone who loves sports associated with the sea, from windsurfing and diving to sailing (Liguria has more than 60 sailing clubs). Swimming is popular too, of course, though many beaches are pebbly. There is plenty to do away from the coast, too. In the hills of the interior there are numerous trails that are used by hikers, horse riders and mountain bikers, though the terrain makes any of these activities a relatively energetic option. The region's parks and nature reserves all have hiking trails, while the peaks of the Ligurian Alps and of the Apennines provide some scope for skiing and other winter sports. For those who take a more leisurely approach, there is always golf: there are courses in San Remo, Rapallo, Lerici, Garlenda (near Albenga) and Arenzano (near Genoa).

The breezy coastline, a boon for enthusiastic windsurfers

Information

For those intending to do some serious sport, the best source of information is CONI, the Ligurian sports committee. The Club Alpino Italiano (CAI) is a good source for anyone venturing into the mountains, whether it's to hike, ski or rock-climb.

Sailing

Liguria has a most beautiful coastline and is a great place to go sailing. From La Spezia to Ventimiglia, the coast has countless beaches and inlets, some accessible only by boat. While it is not difficult to navigate along this coast, it is important not to underestimate the dangers of a changing sea, even in the summer. The to-and-fro of sea bathers can be problematic in high season.

If you do not have a boat, there are many brokerage agencies which have plenty of yachts and motor-driven boats for hire.

A good source of general information are the Pagine Azzurre (published annually in English), which includes official charts and plans of every harbour.

Canoeing

Canoes are a common sight along the coast. Inland, there are some opportunities for downhill canoeing during the winter and the spring thaw, when water is abundant in the local rivers.

Windsurfing

Waves and year-round winds combine to make certain stretches of the Riviera di Ponente popular with wind-surfers, though not everyone finds the relatively sheltered conditions exciting. Arma di Taggia, around Porto Maurizio, Capo Mimosa (near Andora) and Levanto are among the best places to windsurf. You can hire boards in most of the big resorts along the coast, however.

Diving

A few areas along the coast of Liguria provide some great opportunities for diving. The most popular spots include the headland of Portofino, Ventimiglia, Alassio and the Cinque Terre marine park (with diving centres in Riomaggiore and Monterosso). The latter, created only in 1997, has some rare white and black corals, and is also home to many of the species of dolphin and whale that inhabit the Ligurian Sea. Note that diving numbers are strictly controlled here, so it is worth booking ahead.

There are around 60 dive centres in Liguria: their addresses are given on the regional tourist board websites (see Directory).

Rock Climbing

Stony cliffs facing the sea enable rock climbers to enjoy the sport all year round. The most popular

Exploring the fascinating sea beds along the coast

Players on one of Liguria's three 18-hole golf courses

sites are found in the area of Le Manie near Finale Ligure *(see p148)*, and nearby at Capo di Noli. Other popular sites include the cliffs at Muzzerone, near Portovenere, and Castelbianco (Albenga).

Mountain Biking

The area around Finale Ligure is one of the most popular areas for mountain biking, with paths penetrating the Mediteranean maquis. Capo di Noli is an excellent place for exploring, for cyclists of all abilities.

Hiking

The longest signposted route in the region is the Alta Via dei Monti Liguri, which travels the full length of the Ligurian hinterland, from outside Ventimiglia to north of La Spezia. At 440 km (275 miles), it is Italy's longest continuous walk. The terrain is not difficult and the route never isolated, passing through many villages.

The Cinque Terre is another walker's paradise and has several trails. Most famous of these is the Sentiero Azzurro (Blue Path), a relatively easy route which gets very busy in summer, when it can be hard to find a room for the night without booking ahead. A quieter option is the Sentiero Crinale, which runs along the clifftop. There are also spectacular but steep trails leading to the sanctuaries scattered around this area.

Another good area to walk in is in the French part of the Val Roja, north of Ventimiglia: particularly in the Vallée des Merveilles and on the slopes of Monte Bego.

Horse Riding

Horse riding is popular in Liguria, and there are plenty of stables offering treks lasting a day or more. You can do some great day treks in the Cinque Terre. *Agriturismo* farms may also offer trekking opportunities.

Skiing

The Alps and the Apennines provide some opportunities for skiing, though most resorts are small. Monte Saccarello (near Móneri di Triora) and Colizzano (north of Toirano) are both good for downhill skiing. Cross-country skiing is possible from Santo Stefano Aveto, in the Apennines.

A varied and challenging landscape for mountain bikers

DIRECTORY

Information

Club Alpino Italiano (CAI)
W cai.it

CONI
W coni.it

Sailing

Italian Sailing Federation (FIV)
Genoa
Tel 010 513 975.
W federvela.it

Italian Yacht Club (YCI)
W yachtclubitalia.it

Pagine Azzurre
W pagineazzurre.com

Weather and shipping reports
W eurometeo.com

Diving

5 Terre Diving
Riomaggiore
Tel 0187 920 011.

Punta Mesco
Levanto
W divingcenter.net
W puntamesco diving. com

San Fruttuoso Diving Center
Santa Margherita Ligure
Tel 0185 280 862.

Rock Climbing

Information
W thecrag.com

Rock Store
Finalborgo
Tel 019 690 208.

Bike Hire

Blu Bike
Finale Ligure
Tel 019 680 564.

Hiking

Information
W parks.it

Alta Via
W altaviadeimonti liguri.it

Horse Riding

Centro Turismo Equestre 5 Terre
Campiglia
Tel 0187 758 114.

Monte Beigua Riding
Alpicella (Varazze)
Tel 010 553 1878.

Skiing

Information
W liguriasci.it
W fisiliguria.org

Golf

Information
W federgolf.it

ENTERTAINMENT

Alittle bit of everything summarizes the variety of entertainment available in Liguria. There are cinemas and theatres (the Teatro Carlo Felice in Genoa is one of Italy's most famous historic theatres), casinos, discos, nightclubs, wine bars and all sorts of venues hosting live music. The vast majority of such entertainment is, inevitably, focused along the coast, and the choice is greatest during the summer. Be warned that clubs and bars in the resorts tend to be very expensive. For a cheaper night out, simply find the best bar on the seafront and watch the world go by.

Attending one of the region's numerous festivals can sometimes provide the highlight of a trip to Liguria. In addition to the many regattas and food festivals, there are various events focused around music, both modern and classical. The Festival della Canzone Italiana, held in San Remo in February *(see p35)*, is one of the most important dates in the Italian pop music calendar.

The casino in San Remo, one of Liguria's best-known nightspots

Theatres

Every town of any size in Liguria has its own theatre, and some of the cities have several. Classical concerts, operas and ballet tend to be held in their own dedicated theatre, though San Remo's famous **Casino** hosts a whole range of entertainment, from touring ballet concerts to live music.

The main theatrical and classical music seasons tend to run in the winter, but Liguria is not a cultural desert during the summer. Outdoor performances are particularly common at this time of year.

In Genoa, for example, films are shown in various parks around the city, and the ballet festival in the parks in nearby Nervi is hugely popular. The summer theatre season held in the pretty town square at Borgio Verezzi is also another permanent fixture.

Discos and Clubs

There is a trend nowadays for discos and clubs to offer far more than just a chance to dance and have a drink.

Some of Liguria's major dance venues have been turned into multi-functional venues where, in addition to dance floors and bars, there are restaurants, shops, five-a-side football pitches and perhaps even a private beach. Such a description would fit **Estoril Moonlight**, one of the top clubs in Genoa.

San Remo has some of the best nightlife along the coast, and Santa Margherita is buzzing, too (it's just a short drive for revellers from Genoa): here, the **Carillon** is a gorgeous but trendy restaurant-cum-disco, which can be very hard to get into unless you book a table.

Bars and Cafés

Italians spend half their lives in bars and cafés, and Ligurians are no exception. The beauty of these places is that many are open in the evening, sometimes even late into the night in the resorts, and serve snacks as well as coffee and alcohol.

Typical of the riviera are the fabulous historic cafés, in business since the region's heyday in the 19th century. These usually have wonderful decor and a great atmosphere.

Caffè Klainguti is a fine example in Genoa. Founded in 1828, it was beloved of the composer Giuseppe Verdi and serves delicious coffee and pastries. In Santa Margherita Ligure, the Art Nouveau decor is one of the big attractions of the **Caffè Colombo**. In Chiavari, **Defilla** is well worth seeking out. The latter, with mirrors, paintings and stucco galore, becomes a piano bar at night. In San Remo, try the **Bar delle Rose** at the Royal Hotel, and in Alassio the **Giacomel**, which serves fantastic ice cream.

Increasingly, Italians are in the habit of meeting up with friends at a wine bar, whether it's before dinner or after the theatre. Wine bars offer a good choice

The Teatro Chiabrera at Savona

of wines, as well light snacks. In Genoa, one name that emerges above the rest is **I Tre Merli**, attractively located in the Palazzina Millo in the Porto Antico. Also in Genoa are **Monumento**, with a bar and terrace overlooking the sea at Quarto, and **La Lepre**, a popular place in which to chill out and enjoy a drink or two; both of these open late.

Other famous names are **Winterose** in Portofino, a celebrity haunt, and **La Mandragola**, housed in an old mill in Santa Margherita.

Live Music

There are all sorts of venues to which to go to hear live music, from the roof garden of San Remo's casino (in the summer) to the so-called disco-pubs, where you can have a drink, listen to some music, and maybe even have...

In...
conv...

The Genoa Derby

Local football fans love to attend matches played by the two city teams, Genova and Sampdoria, a lively meeting known as the "Derby della Lanterna". Genova, set up by a group of Englishmen in 1893, is the oldest football team in Italy, while Sampdoria was formed in 1946. The two teams share grounds at the Luigi Ferrari stadium, so on Derby Day neither team has the home turf advantage.

Sampdoria emblem

Genova emblem

the Lanterna, has live music in addition to some of the hottest international DJs. For something rather different, try the **Louisiana Jazz Club**, a relaxed venue with a bar and both local and international musicians. In summer, there is usually a programme of jazz concerts all along the coast.

Sabot in Santa Margherita Ligure stages all manner of live bands that attract a predominantly young crowd. It also holds popular live music ...gs outside during the ...r. In Savona, the best

bands appear at **Ju Bamboo**, a club decked out in tropical fashion, complete with palms.

Water Parks

Aimed of course at children, but also great fun for adults is the water park of **Le Caravelle** in Ceriale, a small resort just north of Albenga. This, the only aquapark in Liguria, has swimming pools with artificial waves, water slides, chutes, waterfalls, whirlpools and all sorts of seriously wet entertainment, as well as animated figures and shows.

DIRECTORY

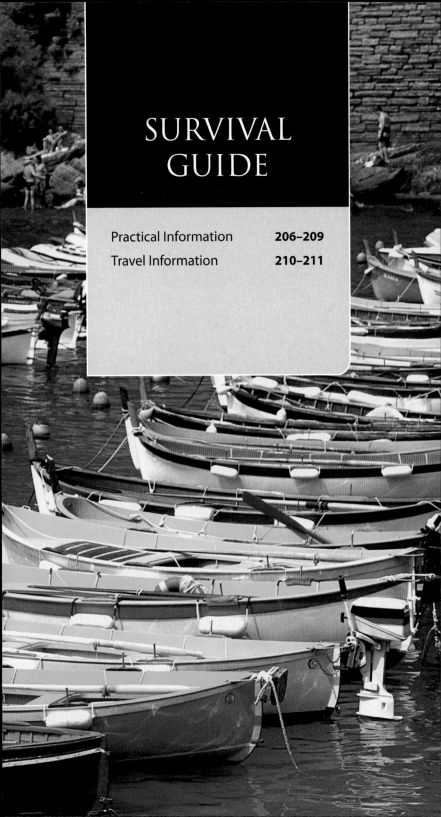

SURVIVAL
GUIDE

PRACTICAL INFORMATION

On the whole, you will find that Liguria has a good standard of services and infrastructure. It is easy to travel around, particularly along the coast; the people are friendly; and, in a region that has such a long and well-established tourist season, there are good sources of information, whether you go to a local tourist office or surf the Internet – many of the tourist-oriented websites have text in English as well as Italian.

Healthcare in its all its usual forms is available throughout the region, though the best facilities are inevitably found along the coast, where you are also much more likely to find English-speaking medical staff.

In general, Ligurian museums are modern and well laid-out. Many are also accessible to people with disabilities, who are well catered for in Liguria, with good sources of information as well as other services.

The crowded beach at Camogli in the summer

When to Visit

Of all the Italian regions, Liguria is the one with the most temperate climate. Even in winter, its climate is generally warmer than in much of Italy, with the exception of Sicily. As a result, there is only a relatively short period when tourists don't visit. Furthermore, such are the cultural attractions of the region, that there is plenty to do even when the climate isn't hot enough for long stints by the seaside.

But while Liguria is virtually a year-round attraction, there is still an identifiable high season, which extends from May to the end of September. Tourists from Britain, France, Germany and Holland, as well as Italy, pour into the region during this period, when the entire coast can become extremely crowded.

Visitors more interested in cultural pursuits should

Sign for a local tourist office

consider visiting in March and April or September and October, when the weather is cooler and the hotels quieter.

Tourist Information

There are four Ligurian provinces – Genoa, Imperia, La Spezia and Savona – but five tourist boards or Informazione e Accoglienza Turistica (IAT): Riviera dei Fiori for Imperia; Riviera delle Palme for Savona; Genoa for the city and its environs; Tigullio, with responsibility for the rest of the province of Genoa; and lastly Cinque Terre e Golfo dei Poeti, which covers the La Spezia area. In every good-sized town you will find a tourist office (or, in the smaller towns, a "Pro loco" office), which will have information about the local sights as well as the hotels and restaurants. Local tourist offices usually open from

8am–12:30pm and 3–7pm Monday to Friday, with some larger offices opening for longer during the summer. Some offices open on Saturday mornings.

Keep in mind that the tourist information kiosks found at major transport terminals are generally fairly basic.

Communications

Post offices are found in all Ligurian towns and there is often more than one branch. They are usually open in the morning only, from 8:30am to 1:30pm (noon on Saturdays and the last day of the month), although in the large towns there are usually post offices that stay open until 5pm. You can also buy stamps (for

Sailing along the coast, a very popular sport in Liguria

◀ Rows of colourful boats in Vernazza, Cinque Terre

postcards and normal letters) from any tobacconist shop, called a *tabaccaio*.

Public telephones are not as common as they once were, owing to the growth in use of mobile phones. Those that remain are almost all operated by phone card, which you can buy from tobacconists, certain kiosks and in post offices.

There are plenty of Internet cafés along the coast for

Entrance to a pharmacy in the old centre of Albenga

surfing the Internet or sending e-mails, and more are opening up all the time.

Hospitals and Pharmacies

Pharmacies observe the hours of 9am–1pm and 4–8pm, closing on Saturday afternoons and all day Sunday. These hours may be extended in the larger tourist resorts on the coast, where some pharmacies stay open continuously until 8pm and sometimes later. Every city in Liguria has a hospital. EU citizens with form E111 are entitled to emergency medical assistance free of charge, but you may have to pay for other treatments. It is therefore vital

that you take out proper travel insurance.

Liguria on the Internet

Although websites can vary considerably in terms of the information provided – in particular whether this is precise and up-to-date – the range of information available on the Internet about Liguria is of a much better standard than that provided in most other Italian regions.

All the five regional tourist offices, as well as each local tourist office, have their own specific website, which can provide information about local events, among other things. Many museums and other attractions have their own websites, too.

For a greater overview, particularly if you haven't decided where in Liguria you wish to go, you should visit the Ligurian regional website *(see Directory)*, which is a hugely useful resource and includes links to many other local websites.

DIRECTORY

Tourist Information

APT Genova
Tel 010 557 28 78.

IAT Riviera dei Fiori
Tel 0184 590 59.

IAT Tigullio
Tel 0185 287 485.

Provincia La Spezia Servizio Turismo
Tel 0187 770 900.

Provincia Savona Servizio Turismo
Tel 019 831 33 26.

Local Tourist Offices

Alassio
Tel 0182 647 027.

Albenga
Tel 0182 558 444.

Albisola Superiore
Tel 019 400 25 25.

Andora
Tel 0182 681 004.

Arma di Taggia
Tel 0184 437 33.

Bordighera
Tel 0184 262 322.

Borgio Verezzi
Tel 019 610 412.

Camogli
Tel 0185 771 066.

Castelnuovo Magra
Tel 0187 693 306.

Chiavari
Tel 0185 325 198.

Dolceacqua
Tel 0184 206 666.

Finale Ligure
Tel 019 681 019.

Imperia
Tel 0183 660 140.

La Spezia
Tel 0187 770 900.

Lavagna
Tel 0185 395 070.

Lerici
Tel 0187 967 346.

Levanto
Tel 0187 808 125.

Loano
Tel 019 676 007.

Moneglia
Tel 0185 490 576.

Pietra Ligure
Tel 019 629 003.

Portofino
Tel 0185 269 024.

Portovenere
Tel 0187 790 691.

Rapallo
Tel 0185 230 346.

Sarzana
Tel 0187 620 419.

Santa Margherita Ligure
Tel 0185 287 485.

Sestri Levante
Tel 0185 457 011.

San Remo
Tel 0184 590 59.

Spotorno
Tel 019 741 50 08.

Varazze
Tel 019 935 043.

Internet

Liguria Region
Ⓦ turismoinliguria.it
and Ⓦ regione.liguria.it

IAT Cinque Terre e Golfo dei Poeti
Ⓦ provinciasp.it

Genoa
Ⓦ apt.genova.it

Riviera delle Palme
Ⓦ inforiviera.it

Riviera dei Fiori
Ⓦ rivieradeifiori.org

Other Useful Information

In common with the other regions of Italy, Liguria does not present any particular problems as far as crime is concerned, even in the most popular tourist resorts. You should, however, always observe the usual rules of common sense when travelling around. Every town possesses, besides a traffic police station, a police *(carabinieri)* station, which is open 24 hours a day and to which visitors should turn in an emergency. All towns have banks with cash machines where visitors can withdraw euros.

A team of *carabinieri* in their distinctive uniform

Law and Order

In Italy the forces of law and order are organized into two divisions: the *carabinieri* and the *polizia*. The former are responsible for public order, with communal, provincial or regional jurisdiction, and are commonly seen on patrol in the streets. The duties of the *polizia* are more wide-ranging, being generally more concerned with criminal investigations. At local level, you also find the municipal police, including the traffic police *(vigili urbani)*, who can deal with minor or emergency situations that do not involve traffic.

In the event of a theft, you should report the crime at the nearest police station in order to validate any insurance claim.

Firefighters

In Liguria, forest fires, often encouraged by the constant wind that blows throughout the year, are suprisingly frequent. Therefore, if you are exploring the countryside it is essential to observe all the standard countryside code practices, especially with regard to not lighting a fire outside designated areas and making sure that cigarettes are completely extinguished.

The region is well equipped with fire stations, even in rural areas, and fire engines respond rapidly to alarm calls. Firefighters also attend other kinds of emergency.

Personal Safety

Use common sense when it comes to personal safety. Do not carry large sums of cash with you when you are out, and leave any valuables, at your hotel, in a safe if possible.

You may wish to keep a separate photocopy of personal documents, so that you can request duplicates in the event of theft. Of course, you should never leave home without taking out full insurance cover.

Places where you are most likely to encounter pickpockets include railway stations and ferry terminals, or any crowded place, such as a bus, market or a street festival. If you are travelling by car, make sure that you always leave the vehicle locked, and don't leave any items in full view.

Municipal Policeman

Genoa is a large bustling port city with, inevitably, some districts that it is best to steer clear of. (On arrival at your hotel, it is a good idea to ask the reception staff about areas that are best avoided.) In the countryside, however, and in the resorts, you need have few concerns about your personal safety, though it pays to be alert if you are out late at night.

If you wish to hire a taxi, make sure that you choose an official one. Your hotel should be able to recommend a reputable taxi firm. Make sure that the meter is switched on or that the fee is agreed in advance.

Disabled Visitors

Liguria provides relatively good information for people with disabilities. Genoa has a helpful service called Terre di Mare (www.terredimare), which is designed specifically for tourists. The national hotel site (www.italiapertutti) is also a useful resource.

It is always wise to phone a hotel or attraction in advance to check their facilities.

A firefighting plane in action during a summer fire in the hinterland

Entrance to one of the larger banks in Liguria

Banks and Exchange

Currency can be changed in various ways. You will find bureaux de change in the larger airports and towns, and it is also possible to change money in hotels and travel agencies. As a general rule, however, the banks offer the best exchange rates. Banks in Italy normally open from 8:30am to 1:30pm, and from 3pm to 4pm, Monday to Friday; note that the banks often close early the day before a public holiday. Opening hours of bureaux de change are more variable. Every town in Liguria

has cashpoint/ATM machines (known as bancomat), where it is possible to withdraw money using a debit or credit card. These can normally be used 24 hours a day.

Despite these options, you are still advised to arrive in Liguria with at least a few euros for immediate use, particularly if you are due to arrive late in the day or at a weekend. Remember that for all kinds of transaction you will need to show some form of identification.

Credit cards are widely accepted for purchases and

can also be used to withdraw cash (though the latter transaction is not normally good value for money). VISA, American Express, MasterCard and Diners Club are the most commonly used cards.

The Euro

Since January 2002 the euro has been the sole official currency in all participating states of the European Union. This means that euro notes and coins are valid throughout the so-called "eurozone", including Italy.

DIRECTORY

General Emergencies
Tel 113.

Carabinieri (Police)
Tel 112.

Fire Service
Tel 115.

Breakdown Service
Tel 116.

Ambulance
Tel 118.

Coastguard
Tel 15 30.

Banknotes and Coins

Banknotes come in seven denominations. The 5-euro note is grey, the 10-euro is pink, the 20 is blue, the 50 orange, the 100 green, the 200 yellow and the 500 purple. There are eight different coins. The 1- and 2-euro coins are silver and gold; those worth 50, 20 and 10 cents are gold, while those worth 5, 2 and 1 cent are bronze.

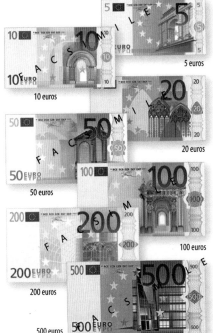

5 euros

10 euros

20 euros

50 euros

100 euros

200 euros

500 euros

2 euros

1 euro

50 cents

20 cents

10 cents

5 cents

2 cents

1 cent

TRAVEL INFORMATION

Liguria is a narrow and relatively small region, so moving from place to place is usually easy. This is particularly true of the coast, which has good train and bus services as well as a decent road network (though traffic can be a problem in high season). While there are buses to the main inland towns, you need a car to explore inland areas properly. A car can be a hindrance on the coast in summer, however, when parking is virtually impossible in some places, including the Cinque Terre, to which you are advised to travel by foot, train

or boat. In terms of reaching Liguria, Genoa has one of Italy's major airports. There are also long-distance train and coach services, with good links from France and from other parts of Italy. There are various ferry services, too, though most of these operate from within Italy. Of more use to visitors are the ferries which ply between the main Ligurian resorts in summer. For those with a private yacht, there are plenty of marinas; most of these can offer good facilities and moorings for all sizes of craft.

Arriving by Air

The main airport in Liguria is the Cristoforo Colombo at Genova-Sestri, west of the city. Ryanair and BA flights arrive here direct from the United Kingdom. Alternative entry points are Nice (with easyjet, British Midland and BA), an easy train ride from the Riviera di Ponente, and Pisa (with Ryanair and BA), just 85 km (53 miles) from La Spezia. The closest airports receiving flights from North America are Milan and Rome.

A stretch of the motorway linking Liguria's main towns

Regular buses link Cristoforo Colombo airport with the ferry terminal and Principe and Brignole train stations in Genoa, running from 5:30am to 11:45pm.

There is also a small airport at Villanova d'Albenga, on the Riviera di Ponente, but at present this receives only domestic flights.

Travelling by Car

Since driving to Liguria from the UK (either via the Swiss Alps or the French riviera) takes

the best part of 24 hours, you would do better to fly and hire a car on arrival. The main rental companies have desks in the airport, but car hire in Italy can be expensive; you'll often get a better rate if you arrange the car before leaving home.

A motorway (autostrada) – the A10 and its continuation the A12 – provides fast access along the Ligurian coast, though this route can get busy in holiday season and at weekends. Heading inland,

motorways link the coast with Parma, Milan and Turin. The other principal route is state road no. 1 (SS1), the so-called Via Aurelia, first laid by the Romans. It runs the length of the coast, sometimes offering glimpses of the sea. Inland roads tend to be narrow and winding but are in good condition and pass through often stunning scenery.

If you plan to drive, note that parking in the resorts can be difficult (and stressful) in high season, and also that petrol stations are scarce in the hinterland once you head away from the main towns, with few opening on Sundays or in the evening.

Travelling by Train

It is much simpler to reach Liguria by train than it used to be, though it is a more expensive option than flying. From the UK, you can take the

Genoa's port and airport, both busy traffic hubs

Eurostar to Paris, and then the TGV right down to Nice (a journey of around 12 hours), from where the coastal line runs east into Liguria.

Both fast and slow trains serve the towns along the Ligurian coast. In general, trains from the north or west arrive at Genoa's Stazione Principe, while those from the south and east arrive at Stazione Brignole. Both stations have good bus connections.

The historic Genoa–Casella line, which runs inland to the Apennines, is a rare example of a narrow-gauge railway (see p92).

Logo of Riviera Trasporti

Travelling by Coach

Eurolines runs coaches to Liguria from elsewhere in Europe, but travelling by train or air doesn't cost much more.

Within Liguria, coach travel (often more expensive than train travel) is most useful for journeys into the mountains: in many inland areas coaches are the only sole of transport. Coach services from Genoa (run by different companies) leave from Piazza Acquaverde and Piazza della Vittoria, close to Stazione Principe and Stazione Brignole respectively.

City Transport

Buses in Genoa, run by the Azienda Mobilità e Trasporti (AMT), are easy to use since they charge a flat rate for trips within the city limits

and nearby suburbs. Tourist tickets valid for 24 or 48 hours are also available. Tickets, sold by newspaper kiosks and tobacconists, must be bought in advance and validated in the machine once on board.

Genoa also has a nascent metro, and two funiculars, which link Piazza del Portello and Largo della Zecca with Genoa's upper districts. From Piazza del Portello you can also take the lift up to the belvedere at Castelletto.

Ferries and Marinas

It is possible to travel to Liguria by sea, though most services are from within Italy. Genoa's splendid Stazione Marittima is the main hub for ferries, with connections to Cagliari and other ports in Sardinia, and Palermo in Sicily. Overseas links are with Corsica, Tunis and Barcelona. Ferries from Corsica also arrive at Vado, near Savona. Several companies operate these services, including Tirrenia and Grimaldi.

In summer, local ferry services run along the Ligurian coast, primarily in the Golfo del Tigullio, the Golfo dei Poeti and along the coast of the Cinque Terre.

For those with their own boat, there are more than 60 landing points and marinas along the coast, including the famous tiny harbour at Portofino. The marinas are generally well equipped and can accommodate a total of around 16,000 boats.

San Remo Train Station

General Index

Acknowledgments

Dorling Kindersley would like to thank the following people and institutions whose contributions and assistance have made the preparation of this book possible.

Special Thanks

Agenzia Regionale per la Promozione Turistica "In Liguria"; APT Cinque Terre e Golfo dei Poeti; APT di Genova; APT Riviera Ligure delle Palme; APT Riviera dei Fiori; APT Tigullio; Banca Carige, Genoa; Emma Brown; Giardini Botanici Hanbury, Ventimiglia; Grotte di Toirano, Toirano; Soprintendenza per i Beni Archeologici della Liguria, Genoa; the restaurant *Il Sommergibile* in San Remo.

Design and Editorial

Publishing Managers Fay Franklin, Kate Poole
Senior Art Editor Marisa Renzullo
Revisions Designer Collette Sadler
Revisions and Relaunch Team Asad Ali, Subhashree Bharti, Stuti Tiwari Bhatia, Madhura Birdi, Anna Freiberger, Beverley Ager, Claire Baranowski, Uma Bhattacharya, Sally Ann Bloomfield, Susi Cheshire, Rebecca Ford, Vinod Harish, Amy Harrison, Mohammad Hassan, Jasneet Kaur, Sumita Khatwani, Vincent Kurien, Megan McCaffrey, Deepak Mittal, Sonal Modha, Rada Radojicic, Ellen Root, Beverly Smart, Sands Publishing Solutions, Azeem Siddiqui, Conrad Van Dyk.

Photography Permissions

Thanks are due to those bodies and societies who authorized the reproduction of images, in particular:
Accademia Ligustica di Belle Arti, Genoa; Acquario di Genova; Banca Carige (coin collection and photographic archive, Genoa); Galleria di Palazzo Rosso (photographic archive of Genoa town council); Genoa Cricket and Football Club, Genoa; Museo Amedeo Lia, La Spezia; Museo Archeologico dei Balzi Rossi, Ventimiglia; Regione Liguria; Palazzo Ducale, Genoa; Società Editrice Buonaparte, Sarzana; UC Sampdoria, Genoa.

While every effort has been made to contact the copyright holders, we apologize for any omissions and will be happy to include them in future editions of the guide.

Owen Franken 39br; John Heseltine 171bl; Hulton-Deutsch Collection 8-9; Massimo Listri 84; Gianni Dagli Orti 38bl; Gustavo Tomisch 39tr; Ron Watts 204-5.
Hotel Punta Est: 183tr. **Hotel Villa Agnese:** 182bc.

Il Dagherrotipo: Giorgio Oddi 153bc; **DK Images:** 186cr; John Heseltine 208c **DK Images:** Ian O'Leary all 186-187 except 187tl, 187c.
Dreamstime.com: 2circles 14br; Btvphoto 52; Danbreckwoldt 14tl; Paoloairenti 13cl; Unknown1861 13tr.

Mary Evans Picture Library: 45ca.

Farabolafoto, Milan: 14, 20cr, 21cr, 23tl, 23tr, 23bl, 23br, 27tr, 32cla, 38tr, 46c, 47t, 47bc, 47br, 65bc, 69tr, 69cl, 110br, 114cl, 115crb, 131tl, 178cr, 184cr, 185c, 200cl, 206ctl. **Fotolia:** Miroslawa Drozdowski 2-3; Freesurf 11br; LiliGraphie 116-7.

Getty Images: Kevin T. Levesque/Lonely Planet Images Filippo Monteforte/AFP 32bc; 47cr; Andrea Pucci 126-7; Murat Taner 48-9; Taxi/Maremagnum 11tr. **Grand Hotel Savoia:** 179bl, 180bc.

Marka, Milan: Danilo Donadoni 132bl.

Peter Noble: 208tr.
Osvaldo Antica Trattoria: 191bc.

Lino Pastorelli, Sanremo: 34cla. **Andrea Pistolesi:** 72cl. **Polpo Mario:** 194bl.
Francine Reculez: 172cla. **Restaurant Lanterna Blu:** 196bc. **Ristorante Zeffirino:** 189t; Daniele Robotti, Alessandria: 81tl, 92bl, 123cr, 123br. **Roger-Viollet,** Archivi Alinari, Firenze: 41tc. **Ghigo Roli,** Modena: 23cra, 23crb, 24cla, 25cra, 174bl.

Photo Scala, Florence: Museo Navale di Pegli 42bl; Musei di Strada Nuova - Sant'Agostino, Genoa 54bl. **Superstock:** Marco Brivio/age fotostock 18; Glow Images 176-7; Marka 108; José Antonio Moreno/age fotostock 166-7; Francesco Tomasinelli/Tips Images 87br.

U Fundegu: 195tr. **U Giancu:** 193bl.

Villa Rosmarino: 181tr.

Front endpapers: Alamy Images: imagebroker Lcla; Stefano Ravera Rtc. **Corbis:** Massimo Listri Rtr. **Dreamstime:** Btvphoto Rtl. **Superstock:** Marka Rbl.

Map Cover: Superstock: age fotostock main

Jacket: Front and Spine – **Superstock:** age fotostock main

All the other photos are from **Archivio Fabio Ratti, Archivio Mondadori, Archivio Arnoldo Mondadori Editore,** Milan.

Special Editions of DK Travel Guides

Phrase Book

In Emergency

Help!	Aiuto!	eye-**yoo**-toh
Stop!	Fermate!	fair-**mah**-teh
Call a doctor.	Chiama un medico	kee-**ah**-mah oon **meh**-dee-koh
Call an ambulance.	Chiama un' ambulanza	kee-**ah**-mah oon am-boo-**lan**-tsa
Call the police.	Chiama la polizia	kee-**ah**-mah lah pol-ee-**tsee**-ah
Call the fire brigade.	Chiama i pompieri	kee-**ah**-mah ee pom-pee-**air**-ee
Where is the telephone?	Dov'è il telefono?	dov-**eh** eel teh-**leh**-foh-noh?
The nearest hospital?	L'ospedale più vicino?	loss-peh-**dah**-leh pee-oo vee-**chee**-noh?

Communication Essentials

Yes/No	Sì/No	see/noh
Please	Per favore	pair fah-**vor**-eh
Thank you	Grazie	**grah**-tsee-eh
Excuse me	Mi scusi	mee **skoo**-zee
Hello	Buon giorno	bwon jor-noh
Goodbye	Arrivederci	ah-ree-veh-**dair**-chee
Good evening	Buona sera	**bwon**-ah **sair**-ah
morning	la mattina	lah mah-**tee**-nah
afternoon	il pomeriggio	eel poh-mah-**ree**-joh
evening	la sera	lah **sair**-ah
yesterday	ieri	ee-**air**-ee
today	oggi	**oh**-jee
tomorrow	domani	doh-**mah**-nee
here	qui	kwee
there	la	lah
What?	Quale?	**kwah**-leh?
When?	Quando?	**kwan**-doh?
Why?	Perchè?	pair-**keh**?
Where?	Dove?	**doh**-veh?

Useful Phrases

How are you?	Come sta?	**koh**-meh stah?
Very well, thank you.	Molto bene, grazie.	**moll**-toh beh-neh **grah**-tsee-eh
Pleased to meet you.	Piacere di conoscerla.	pee-ah-**chair**-eh dee coh-noh-**shair**-lah
See you later.	A più tardi.	ah pee-oo **tar**-dee
That's fine.	Va bene.	va **beh**-neh
Where is/are …?	Dov'è/Dove sono …?	dov-**eh**/doveh **soh**-noh?
How long does it take to get to …?	Quanto tempo ci vuole per andare a …?	**kwan**-toh **tem**-poh chee voo-**oh**-leh pair an-**dar**-eh ah …?
How do I get to …?	Come faccio per arrivare a …?	**koh**-meh **fah**-choh pair arri-**var**-eh ah…?
Do you speak English?	Parla inglese?	par-lah een-**gleh**-zeh?
I don't understand.	Non capisco.	non ka-**pee**-skoh
Could you speak more slowly, please?	Può parlare più lentamente, per favore?	pwoh par-**lah**-reh pee-**oo** len-ta-**men**-teh pair fah-**vor**-eh?
I'm sorry.	Mi dispiace.	mee dee-spee-**ah**-cheh

Useful Words

big	grande	**gran**-deh
small	piccolo	**pee**-koh-loh
hot	caldo	**kal**-doh
cold	freddo	**fred**-doh
good	buono	**bwoh**-noh
bad	cattivo	kat-**tee**-voh
enough	basta	**bas**-tah
well	bene	**beh**-neh
open	aperto	ah-**pair**-toh
closed	chiuso	kee-**oo**-zoh
left	a sinistra	ah see-**nee**-strah
right	a destra	ah **dess**-trah
straight on	sempre dritto	**sem**-preh **dree**-toh
near	vicino	vee-**chee**-noh
far	lontano	lon-**tah**-noh
up	su	soo
down	giù	joo
early	presto	**press**-toh
late	tardi	**tar**-dee
entrance	entrata	en-**trah**-tah
exit	uscita	oo-**shee**-ta
toilet	il gabinetto	eel gah-bee-**net**-toh
free, unoccupied	libero	**lee**-bair-oh
free, no charge	gratuito	grah-**too**-ee-toh

Making a Telephone Call

I'd like to place a long-distance call.	Vorrei fare una interurbana.	vor-**ray far**-eh oona in-tair-oor-**bah**-nah
I'd like to make a reverse-charge call.	Vorrei fare una telefonata a carico del destinatario.	vor-**ray far**-eh oona teh-leh-fon-**ah**-tah ah **kar**-ee-koh dell dess-tee-nah-**tar**-ree-oh
I'll try again later.	Ritelefono più tardi.	ree-teh-**leh**-foh-noh pee-oo **tar**-dee
Can I leave a message?	Posso lasciare un messaggio?	**poss**-oh lash-**ah**-reh oon mess-**sah**-joh?
Hold on.	Un attimo, per favore	oon **ah**-tee-moh, pair fah-**vor**-eh
Could you speak up a little please?	Può parlare più forte, per favore?	pwoh par-**lah**-reh pee-**oo for**-teh, pair fah-**vor**-eh
local call	telefonata locale	te-leh-fon-**ah**-tah loh-cah-leh

Shopping

How much does this cost?	Quant'è, per favore?	kwan-**teh** pair fah-**vor**-eh?
I would like …	Vorrei …	vor-**ray**
Do you have …?	Avete …?	ah-**veh**-teh…?
I'm just looking.	Sto soltanto guardando.	stoh sol-**tan**-toh gwar-**dan**-doh
Do you take credit cards?	Accettate carte di credito?	ah-chet-**tah**-teh **kar**-teh dee **creh**-dee-toh?
What time do you open/close?	A che ora apre/chiude?	ah keh or-ah **ah**-preh/kee-**oo**-deh?
this one	questo	**kweh**-stoh
that one	quello	**kwell**-oh
expensive	caro	**kar**-oh
cheap	a buon prezzo	ah bwon **pret**-soh
size, clothes	la taglia	lah **tah**-lee-ah
size, shoes	il numero	eel **noo**-mair-oh
white	bianco	bee-**ang**-koh
black	nero	**neh**-roh
red	rosso	**ross**-oh
yellow	giallo	**jal**-loh
green	verde	**vair**-deh
blue	blu	bloo

Types of Shop

antique dealer	l'antiquario	lan-tee-**kwah**-ree-oh
bakery	il forno /il panificio	eel forn-oh /eel pan-ee-**fee**-choh
bank	la banca	lah **bang**-kah
bookshop	la libreria	lah lee-breh-**ree**-ah
butcher	la macelleria	lah mah-chell-eh-**ree**-ah
cake shop	la pasticceria	lah pas-tee-chair-**ree**-ah
chemist	la farmacia	lah far-mah-**chee**-ah
delicatessen	la salumeria	lah sah-loo-meh-**ree**-ah
department store	il grande magazzino	eel **gran**-deh mag-gad-**zee**-noh
fishmonger	il pescivendolo	eel pesh-ee-**ven**-doh-loh
florist	il fioraio	eel fee-or-**eye**-oh
greengrocer	il fruttivendolo	eel froo-tee-**ven**-doh-loh
grocery	alimentari	ah-lee-men-**tah**-ree
hairdresser	il parrucchiere	eel par-oo-kee-**air**-eh
ice cream parlour	la gelateria	lah jel-lah-tair-**ree**-ah
market	il mercato	eel mair-**kah**-toh
newsstand	l'edicola	leh-**dee**-koh-lah
post office	l'ufficio postale	loo-**fee**-choh pos-**tah**-leh
shoe shop	il negozio di scarpe	eel neh-**goh**-tsioh dee **skar**-peh
supermarket	il supermercato	eel su-pair-mair-**kah**-toh
tobacconist	il tabaccaio	eel tab-bak-**eye**-oh
travel agency	l'agenzia di viaggi	lah-jen-**tsee**-ah dee vee-**ad**-jee

Sightseeing

art gallery	la pinacoteca	lah peena-koh-**teh**-kah
bus stop	la fermata dell'autobus	lah fair-**mah**-tah dell ow-toh-booss
church	la chiesa	lah kee-**eh**-zah
	la basilica	lah bah-**seel**-i-kah
closed for holidays	chiuso per le ferie	kee-**oo**-zoh pair leh **fair**-ee-eh
garden	il giardino	eel jar-**dee**-no
library	la biblioteca	lah beeb-lee-oh-**teh**-kah
museum	il museo	eel moo-**zeh**-oh
railway station	la stazione	lah stah-tsee-**oh**-neh
tourist information	l'ufficio di turismo	loo-**fee**-choh dee too-**ree**-smoh

alternatives for a female speaker are shown in brackets

Staying in a Hotel

Do you have any vacant rooms?	**Avete camere libere?**	ah-**veh**-teh kah-mair-eh **lee**-bair-eh?
double room	**una camera doppia**	oona kah-mair-ah **doh**-pee-ah
with double bed	**con letto matrimoniale**	kon **let**-toh mah-tree-moh-nee-**ah**-leh
twin room	**una camera con due letti**	oona kah-mair-ah kon **doo**-eh let-tee
single room	**una camera singola**	oona kah-mair-ah **sing**-goh-lah
room with a bath, shower	**una camera con bagno, con doccia**	oona kah-mair-ah kon ban-yoh, kon dot-chah
porter	**il facchino**	eel fah-**kee**-noh
key	**la chiave**	lah kee-**ah**-veh
I have a reservation.	**Ho fatto una prenotazione.**	oh **fat**-toh oona preh-noh-tah-tsee-**oh**-neh

Eating Out

Have you got a table for …?	**Avete una tavola per … ?**	ah-**veh**-teh oona **tah**-voh-lah pair …?
I'd like to reserve a table.	**Vorrei riservare una tavola.**	vor-**ray** ree-sair-**vah**-reh oona **tah**-voh-lah
breakfast	**colazione**	koh-lah-tsee-**oh**-neh
lunch	**pranzo**	**pran**-tsoh
dinner	**cena**	**cheh**-nah
The bill, please.	**Il conto, per favore.**	eel **kon**-toh pair fah-**vor**-eh
I am a vegetarian.	**Sono vegetariano/a.**	soh-noh veh-jeh-tar-ee-**ah**-noh/nah
waitress	**cameriera**	kah-mair-ee-**air**-ah
waiter	**cameriere**	kah-mair-ee-**air**-eh
fixed price menu	**il menù a prezzo fisso**	eel meh-**noo** ah pret-soh **fee**-soh
dish of the day	**piatto del giorno**	pee-**ah**-toh dell **jor**-no
starter	**antipasto**	an-tee-**pass**-toh
first course	**il primo**	eel **pree**-moh
main course	**il secondo**	eel seh-**kon**-doh
vegetables	**il contorno**	eel kon-**tor**-noh
dessert	**il dolce**	eel **doll**-cheh
cover charge	**il coperto**	eel koh-**pair**-toh
wine list	**la lista dei vini**	lah **lee**-stah day **vee**-nee
rare	**al sangue**	al **sang**-gweh
medium	**al puntino**	al poon-**tee**-noh
well done	**ben cotto**	ben **kot**-toh
glass	**il bicchiere**	eel bee-kee-**air**-eh
bottle	**la bottiglia**	lah bot-**teel**-yah
knife	**il coltello**	eel kol-**tell**-oh
fork	**la forchetta**	lah for-**ket**-tah
spoon	**il cucchiaio**	eel koo-kee-**eye**-oh

Menu Decoder

l'acqua minerale gassata/naturale	**lah**-kwah mee-nair-**ah**-leh gah-**zah**-tah/nah-too-rah-leh	mineral water fizzy/still
agnello	ah-**niell**-oh	lamb
aceto	ah-**cheh**-toh	vinegar
aglio	**al**-ee-oh	garlic
al forno	al **for**-noh	baked
alla griglia	ah-lah **greel**-yah	grilled
l'aragosta	lah-rah-**goss**-tah	lobster
arrosto	ar-**ross**-toh	roast
la birra	lah **beer**-rah	beer
la bistecca	lah bee-**stek**-kah	steak
il brodo	eel **broh**-doh	broth
il burro	eel **boor**-oh	butter
il caffè	eel kah-**feh**	coffee
i calamari	ee kah-lah-**mah**-ree	squid
i carciofi	ee kar-**choff**-ee	artichokes
la carne	la **kar**-neh	meat
carne di maiale	**kar**-neh dee mah-**yah**-leh	pork
la cipolla	la chip-**oh**-lah	onion
i contorni	ee kon-**tor**-nee	vegetables
i fagioli	ee fah-**joh**-lee	beans
il fegato	eel **fay**-gah-toh	liver
il finocchio	eel fee-**nok**-ee-oh	fennel
il formaggio	eel for-**mad**-joh	cheese
le fragole	leh **frah**-goh-leh	strawberries
il fritto misto	eel free-toh **mees**-toh	mixed fried dish
la frutta	la **froot**-tah	fruit
frutti di mare	**froo**-tee dee mah-reh	seafood
i funghi	ee **foon**-ghee	mushrooms
i gamberi	ee **gam**-bair-ee	prawns
il gelato	eel jel-**lah**-toh	ice cream
l'insalata	leen-sah-lah-tah	salad
il latte	eel **laht**-teh	milk

lesso	**less**-oh	boiled
il manzo	eel **man**-tsoh	beef
la melanzana	lah meh-lan-**tsah**-nah	aubergine
la minestra	lah mee-**ness**-trah	soup
l'olio	loh-lee-oh	oil
il pane	eel **pah**-neh	bread
le patate	leh pah-**tah**-teh	potatoes
le patatine fritte	leh pah-tah-**teen**-eh **free**-teh	chips
il pepe	eel **peh**-peh	pepper
la pesca	lah **pess**-kah	peach
il pesce	eel **pesh**-eh	fish
il pollo	eel **poll**-oh	chicken
il pomodoro	eel poh-moh-**dor**-oh	tomato
il prosciutto cotto/crudo	eel pro-**shoo**-toh **kot**-toh/**kroo**-doh	ham cooked/cured
il riso	eel **ree**-zoh	rice
il sale	eel **sah**-leh	salt
la salsiccia	lah sal-**see**-chah	sausage
le seppie	leh **sep**-pee-eh	cuttlefish
secco	**sek**-koh	dry
la sogliola	lah **soll**-yoh-lah	sole
i spinaci	ee spee-**nah**-chee	spinach
succo d'arancia/ di limone	**soo**-koh dah-**ran**-chah/ dee lee-**moh**-neh	orange/lemon juice
il tè	eel **teh**	tea
la tisana	lah tee-**zah**-nah	herbal tea
il tonno	eel **ton**-noh	tuna
la torta	lah **tor**-tah	cake/tart
l'uovo	loo-**oh**-voh	egg
vino bianco	**vee**-noh bee-**ang**-koh	white wine
vino rosso	**vee**-noh **ross**-oh	red wine
il vitello	eel vee-**tell**-oh	veal
le vongole	leh **von**-goh-leh	clams
lo zucchero	loh **zoo**-kair-oh	sugar
gli zucchini	lyee dzu-**kee**-nee	courgettes
la zuppa	lah **tsoo**-pah	soup

Numbers

1	**uno**	**oo**-noh
2	**due**	**doo**-eh
3	**tre**	treh
4	**quattro**	**kwat**-roh
5	**cinque**	**ching**-kweh
6	**sei**	**say**-ee
7	**sette**	**set**-teh
8	**otto**	**ot**-toh
9	**nove**	**noh**-veh
10	**dieci**	dee-**eh**-chee
11	**undici**	**oon**-dee-chee
12	**dodici**	**doh**-dee-chee
13	**tredici**	**tray**-dee-chee
14	**quattordici**	kwat-**tor**-dee-chee
15	**quindici**	**kwin**-dee-chee
16	**sedici**	**say**-dee-chee
17	**diciassette**	dee-chah-**set**-teh
18	**diciotto**	dee-**chot**-toh
19	**diciannove**	dee-chah-**noh**-veh
20	**venti**	**ven**-tee
30	**trenta**	**tren**-tah
40	**quaranta**	kwah-**ran**-tah
50	**cinquanta**	ching-**kwan**-tah
60	**sessanta**	sess-**an**-tah
70	**settanta**	set-**tan**-tah
80	**ottanta**	ot-**tan**-tah
90	**novanta**	noh-**van**-tah
100	**cento**	**chen**-toh
1,000	**mille**	**mee**-leh
2,000	**duemila**	**doo**-eh mee-lah
5,000	**cinquemila**	**ching**-kweh mee-lah
1,000,000	**un milione**	oon meel-**yoh**-neh

Time

one minute	**un minuto**	oon mee-**noo**-toh
one hour	**un'ora**	oon **or**-ah
half an hour	**mezz'ora**	medz-**or**-ah
a day	**un giorno**	oon **jor**-noh
a week	**una settimana**	oona set-tee-**mah**-nah
Monday	**lunedì**	loo-neh-**dee**
Tuesday	**martedì**	mar-teh-**dee**
Wednesday	**mercoledì**	mair-koh-leh-**dee**
Thursday	**giovedì**	joh-veh-**dee**
Friday	**venerdì**	ven-air-**dee**
Saturday	**sabato**	**sah**-bah-toh
Sunday	**domenica**	doh-**meh**-nee-kah

alternatives for a female speaker are shown in brackets

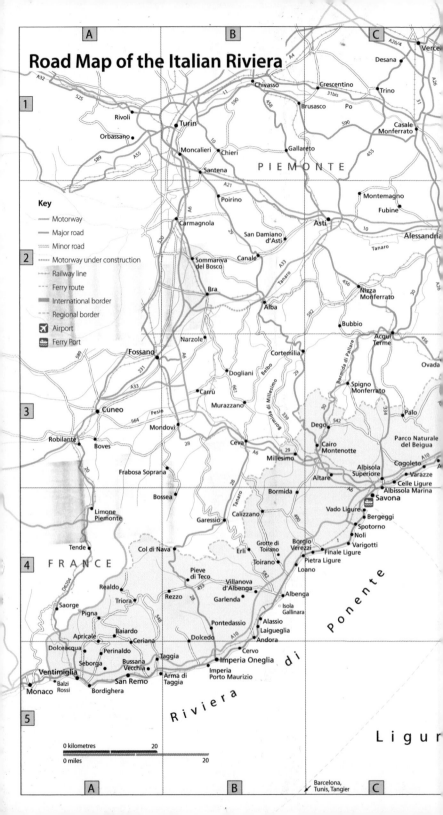